Lexcel Assessment Guide

Lexcel Assessment Guide

The Law Society

The Law Society

All rights reserved. No part of this publication may be reproduced in any material form, whether by photocopying, scanning, downloading onto computer or otherwise without the written permission of the Law Society except in accordance with the provisions of the Copyright, Designs and Patents Act 1988. Any unauthorised or restricted act in relation to this publication may result in civil proceedings and/or criminal prosecution.

© The Law Society 2004

First edition published in 1997 as *The Assessment Guide*
Second edition published in 2001 as the *Lexcel Assessment Guide*

This third edition published in 2004 by the Law Society
113 Chancery Lane, London WC2A 1PL

ISBN 1–85328–921–3

Typeset by Columns Design Ltd., Reading

Printed by TJ International, Padstow, Cornwall

Contents

Preface vii

I. The Lexcel scheme 1

Introduction to the scheme 1
Revisions to Lexcel 2
The philosophy of assessment 2
Joint assessments to ISO9000 or Investors in People 2
Lexcel and the Community Legal Service Quality Mark 3
Who may apply for accreditation? 3
Charges 4

II. Applying for accreditation 5

The application process 5
Preparing for the application 5
The commitment scheme 5
Pre-application assessment 5
Choosing an assessment body 6
Applying for assessment 6

III. The assessment process 7

The assessment 7
The assessment criteria 7
Planning the assessment 7
What happens during the assessment 8
Obtaining a cost quotation for the assessment 9
Duration of assessment 9
Interview sample sizes 10
Case file samples 11
Inspection of documentation 12
Assessment interviews 12
Case management audits 12
Client confidentiality and the contents of files 13
Non-compliances 15
Accreditation 15
Annual maintenance visits 16
Mergers and de-mergers 17
Fraud/dishonesty discovered during an assessment 17
Withdrawal or suspension of certification 18
Appeals and complaints 18

IV. The Lexcel standard 2004 — **19**
Introduction — 19
The standard — 20

V. Assessment criteria — **29**
Section 1 Structures and policies — 29
Section 2 Strategy, the provision of services and marketing — 38
Section 3 Financial management — 43
Section 4 Facilities and IT — 46
Section 5 People management — 52
Section 6 Supervision and operational risk management — 59
Section 7 Client care — 68
Section 8 File and case management — 74

Appendix: Summary of substantive changes in Lexcel 2004 version — **88**

Index — 95

Preface

This publication sets out the information that will be required by practitioners, assessors and consultants on the 2004 version of the Lexcel standard. The aim has been to replace the former *Lexcel Assessment Guide*, which formed part of the previous edition of the *Lexcel Practice Excellence Kit*, and the *Guidelines for Assessors* which formed part of the Lexcel training materials. Both former publications are now consolidated into this work.

The *Lexcel Assessment Guide* should be read in conjunction with the *Lexcel Office Procedures Manual*, which has also been revised to take into account the 2004 version of the Lexcel standard.

The process of reviewing Lexcel was undertaken throughout 2003 by a revisions committee under the chairmanship of John Pickup, Council member and then chair of the Lexcel Assessment Panel. The other members of the panel were Alex Bannister (vice-chair of the Lexcel Assessment Panel), Simon Young (Council member), Brian Capstick (private practice representative), Sue Carter (Sole Practitioners Group), Stephen Rickitt (local government representative), Mark Spash (private practice representative) and James Sandbach (NACAB). In addition, two consultants were part of the committee – Matthew Moore (principal trainer in the Lexcel scheme) and Vicky Ling. Rupert Kendrick was consulted on computer use issues. The Law Society officers involved were Victor Olowe, Tracey Stanley and Iona Milton-Jones.

This publication has been the responsibility of the Lexcel Office who would wish to acknowledge the role of Matthew Moore and Vicky Ling in writing most of the contents.

February 2004

1 The Lexcel scheme

Introduction to the scheme

The Practice Management Standards (PMS) are a set of requirements designed specifically with the needs of solicitors in mind.

The Lexcel scheme allows practices to undergo assessment by an independent assessor who can certify that the practice has complied with the core requirements of the PMS. The Lexcel certificate is awarded for three years, subject to satisfactory interim annual maintenance visits. The Law Society awards the certificate, and is the 'certificating body' for the scheme.

Assessments are carried out by specially trained assessors who are already qualified assessors of ISO9000 or Investors in People working with one of the established ISO9000 certification bodies or Regional Quality Centres. This has the added advantage of enabling practices, if they wish, to be assessed to one of these other standards at the same time as Lexcel, so saving time and resources.

By using experienced and qualified assessors from these bodies, we can ensure that assessments are conducted independently, fairly and uniformly and that the award of the Lexcel certificate is a mark of quality respected by clients. It should be noted that these organisations are themselves subject to rigorous quality control.

An organisation that has carried out advisory work for a practice will *not* be eligible to conduct any of its assessments. This applies to both employees and associates of the organisation in question.

Practices and all relevant personnel will be asked for consent for a search to be made of their indemnity insurance and disciplinary records prior to certification being awarded. If fraud or serious professional misconduct is revealed, the Law Society reserves the right to suspend, withdraw, withhold or defer certification, and/or to consider whether an assessment should be allowed to proceed.

The Law Society has a confidentiality agreement with the assessment bodies requiring staff members to keep all information confidential. Practices may also consider obtaining an independent agreement from their assessment body.

Details of the assessment bodies taking part in the scheme and information on how to apply for certification are available from the Lexcel Office, telephone: 020 7320 5749; address: The Law Society, 113 Chancery Lane, London WC2A 1PL or DX 56 London/Chancery Ln.

The Lexcel website address is **www.lexcel.lawsociety.org.uk**

Revisions to Lexcel

Since the launch of Lexcel in 1997, the Law Society has been closely monitoring the operation of the scheme and developments in the field of practice management. As a result, a number of amendments have been made to the scheme following extensive consultation with practices, assessors and various key individuals and interest groups within the profession and the Law Society.

The Lexcel standard has been rearranged into eight more balanced sections in place of the former six. There are new sections dealing with policies, client care, and supervision and risk management. The opportunity has also been taken to address issues that were not so pressing in 2000 at the time of the last revisions: computer use and combating money laundering are the most obvious examples. It is hoped that the changes will improve the benefits that practices receive from implementing the standard, as well as improving client confidence in the scheme.

An important change is the removal of the need for documented procedures in the case of a number of provisions. It is recognised that if compliance can be shown by other means, this may sometimes be appropriate.

A fuller comparison of the new contents of the standard appears as an appendix to this *Guide*.

The philosophy of assessment

The objective of Lexcel is to enhance the service given by a practice to its clients and to improve the management of the practice and the morale and motivation of its staff. In the case of firms in private practice this should enhance profitability.

Assessments are carried out to provide objective assurance that the core requirements of the PMS are being adhered to by the practice.

The assessor will seek to identify whether and how the practice is working to their core requirements. The guidance set out in the Assessment Criteria is intended to assist a practice in understanding and working towards the core requirements. The prescriptive aspects are contained in the requirements but the guidance itself is illustrative, and practices may demonstrate that they comply with the core requirements by other means.

Joint assessments to ISO9000 or Investors in People

For those practices wishing to apply for joint assessment of Lexcel with either ISO9000 or with Investors in People, a table has been produced showing how these standards overlap. Copies are included in the Lexcel information pack which is available from the Lexcel Office on 020 7320 5749.

Further information about ISO9000 is available from the relevant assessment centres or bodies. Copies of the ISO9000 Standard are available from:

> The British Standards Institution
> 389 Chiswick High Road
> London W4 4AL
>
> tel: 020 8996 9000
> fax: 020 8996 7400
> Standards Sales Information Line: 020 8996 9001

Further information about Investors in People is available from Regional Quality Centres or Learning and Skills Councils (LSCs), or from:

> Investors in People UK
> 7–10 Chandos Street
> London W1M 9DE
>
> tel: 020 7467 1900
> fax: 020 7636 2386

Details of those Investors in People and ISO9000 bodies which also offer Lexcel are available from the Lexcel Office on 020 7320 5749.

Lexcel and the Community Legal Service Quality Mark

The Legal Services Commission and the Lexcel Office will continue to consider the relationship between the new version of Lexcel and the Community Legal Service Quality Mark (CLSQM) in the light of operational changes to the CLSQM.

Lexcel assessment is directed at the wider needs of the profession. Practices that wish to consider CLSQM may be expected to comply with a number of additional requirements over and above those demanded by Lexcel. Compliance with the CLSQM is mandatory for those practices seeking to offer publicly funded work.

Who may apply for accreditation?

Lexcel is normally granted to a whole practice. All offices or branches of a practice will normally be expected to apply for certification at the same time.

Subject to satisfying the conditions set out below, local government, and commerce and industry practices may also apply for certification. The practice must:

- Have a defined structure and policies.
- Develop and maintain a marketing and business plan.
- Document responsibility for financial management procedures.
- Document the office facilities needed to provide a service to clients.
- Adopt arrangements for the recruitment, development and welfare of its personnel.
- Have supervision and operational risk management systems in place.
- Have a documented policy for client care.
- Have file and case management systems in place.

Where applicable, guidance on the application of Lexcel in local government practices, commerce and industry practices and sole practitioners is given in the guidance section of each requirement. Sole practitioners will also be able to obtain a Lexcel booklet entitled 'Lexcel: a Guide for Sole Practitioners', which contains useful information on how to implement the Standard.

Charges

A registration fee is payable directly to the Law Society and is based upon the number of partners (or fee-earners for local government, and commerce and industry practices) in the practice. The assessment body will charge the practice a fee based upon the duration of the assessment, which is influenced chiefly by the number of people in the practice and the number of branches.

Tables setting out assessment duration guidelines are included with the Lexcel information pack which is available from the Lexcel Office on 020 7320 5749.

Please bear in mind that the level of fees may vary between assessment bodies and it is advisable to obtain a number of quotes. Enquiries might also be made to see when an assessment will be possible and whether a single assessor or a team will be involved. The relevant bodies will be able to give an idea of their charges. If the intention is to apply for Investors in People at the same time as Lexcel, the practice may qualify for financial assistance. Further details are available from Regional Quality Centres or Learning and Skills Council.

II Applying for accreditation

The application process

This section sets out the steps that a practice will need to take in order to apply for Lexcel certification alone or jointly with another standard.

Preparing for the application

The practice seeking Lexcel certification will need to satisfy itself that it complies with the mandatory requirements of the PMS. Using the Self-Assessment Checklist (supplied with the Lexcel information pack) the practice can check the extent to which it meets these requirements. Any weaknesses identified should be put right.

During the self-assessment process, the practice will need to refer to the Assessment Criteria.

It may be necessary to repeat the self-assessment process a number of times before arriving at a satisfactory result.

The commitment scheme

The scheme has been developed to encourage firms to register their genuine commitment towards applying for Lexcel accreditation.

Previous experience has shown that firms are hesitant to apply for Lexcel until they are absolutely sure that the practice will fully comply with all the PMS. Quite often this is due to a lack of confidence, rather than an inability to meet the requirements of the standard. The aim of the commitment scheme is to enhance motivation and provide a definitive assessment deadline for a firm to work towards.

To register on the commitment scheme, a firm needs to complete a registration form, which can be obtained from the Lexcel Office. Once the form has been returned, a commitment scheme certificate will be issued to the firm. The Lexcel Office will then make periodic contact with the practice to provide support, establish that progress is still being made, and ensure that the intended assessment date will be met.

A further benefit available to the firms registered on the commitment scheme is the availability of a pre-application assessment.

Pre-application assessment

Historically, practices have employed Lexcel consultants and assessors to conduct diagnostic tests or 'dummy assessments' (at additional expense) to check Lexcel compliance. Any areas of compliance identified from this dummy or diagnostic assessment could not be credited to the practice once it had applied for Lexcel. This means practices incur additional expense in time and cost, since the assessment must be repeated following application. The pre-application assessment allows firms to undergo a dummy assessment, but to receive credit towards the final assessment for any of the PMS requirements that are met, thus reducing the burden of time and cost on the practice. To receive further information, please contact the Lexcel Office.

Choosing an assessment body

Details of Lexcel assessment bodies taking part in the scheme are included in the Lexcel information pack.

If the intention is to apply for Lexcel only, then it should make little difference which assessment body the practice chooses, as Lexcel will be assessed in a standard way. However, as mentioned previously, different assessment bodies have different fee structures.

The choice of assessment body will depend to a large extent on future plans for certification. If the practice currently has, or intends to apply for ISO9000 then it makes sense to choose an ISO9000 assessment body. If the preference is for Investors in People, then the practice should apply to its Regional Quality Centre or Learning Skills Council.

Applying for assessment

When the practice has satisfied itself that it meets the Lexcel requirements it should contact the Lexcel Office and request an information pack. The application pack includes status enquiry forms that gives the Lexcel Office the authority to check the practice's indemnity insurance and disciplinary records prior to the certificate being awarded.

The Law Society will consider the results of these checks before allowing a practice to proceed with the assessment. Practices should apply well in advance to ensure the checks are completed in time for their proposed assessment.

With the application form, the practice should enclose:

- some background information about the practice (a copy of the practice's brochure, should one exist, will normally be sufficient);
- a copy of the Self-Assessment Checklist, completed;
- for non-private practices, a letter authorising the application;
- signed status enquiry forms for the practice and all relevant personnel (relevant personnel are defined as all fee-earners, whether admitted as solicitors, or non-admitted, such as legal executives, barristers or trainee solicitors; non-fee-earning staff do *not* have to complete the status enquiry forms);
- details of any indemnity insurance or disciplinary history relevant to the application.

III The assessment process

The assessment

The Lexcel assessment is designed to ensure that:

- all the PMS core requirements are addressed within the practice;
- documentary evidence of this exists;
- procedures and processes are understood throughout the practice;
- the practice applies them and does so consistently.

The assessment process is entirely transparent.

The assessment criteria

The 'Assessment Criteria' section provides information concerning each mandatory requirement of the PMS. It contains:

- guidance on the manner in which a practice may meet the requirements;
- key issues to consider in each section;
- examples of typical documentation which may be used to show that the practice meets the requirement;
- examples of what would constitute a major or minor non-compliance in a particular area.

Planning the assessment

The assessor will arrange dates for the assessment with the practice's nominated Lexcel contact. During the assessment the assessor will visit each practice location and have meetings with the practice's representative, as required, to review progress.

The assessor will respect client and business confidentiality. Subject to this, the assessor will, on site:

- inspect documentary evidence and look at other relevant records;
- interview a representative cross-section of principals and staff to confirm that the necessary processes are in place and are understood;
- conduct case management audits with a selection of fee-earners.

Lexcel assessors undergo a quality-assured training programme to ensure that they apply the Lexcel standard according to national guidelines. However, they also need to be able to exercise sufficient flexibility to use their professional judgement in the context of each assessment. Consistency of assessment is monitored by the Law Society and anomalies are investigated.

It is important that an appropriate distinction is maintained between assessment and consultancy. If a practice uses a consultant to advise on implementation of the standard, that individual must not carry out the Lexcel assessment for the practice.

Assessors must confine themselves to the requirements of Lexcel when conducting an assessment and must not assess procedures which fall outside it.

Assessors are required to respect the duty of confidentiality which solicitors owe to their clients. The section on 'Client confidentiality and the contents of files' (page 13) gives detailed information on the practical issues that may affect assessments.

Practices may not be able to allow inspection of some or all files. If a client has refused to allow disclosure to an assessor, the practice may not be able to show the assessor a letter of refusal as the letter would contain the client's name. Assessors will need to have an understanding of the way in which they can identify files where clients' consent has been obtained, at an early stage.

When seeking certification, the onus is on the practice to satisfy the assessor that it meets the standard. If the practice cannot allow access to case files, it will have to work with the assessor to identify other ways in which satisfactory evidence can be established. It is likely that alternative methods will take longer to assess, and may increase the cost of any assessment. The assessor should advise the practice accordingly.

What happens during the assessment

Assessments typically include the following processes:

a: The assessor becomes familiar with the systems by which the applicant practice is implementing the Lexcel standard.
b: The assessor seeks objective evidence that the required systems and procedures are in effective operation.

The most significant part of the time spent during the assessment will be on the premises of the practice applying for certification. Assessors differ in that some familiarise themselves with the systems on the premises while others carry out some familiarisation off-site. It is common practice, however, to conduct an initial 'desk-top' audit of the office manual before the visit. Assessors may also spend time following the assessment in completing their report and reporting back to the Law Society. Assessors should ensure that practices are aware that any costs involved in so doing are included in the cost quotation for the assessment.

The processes involved in the assessment will be as described above regardless of where they take place.

Obtaining a cost quotation for the assessment

The assessor will need sufficient information from the practice before a quotation can be prepared. Relevant information would include: the number of categories of law offered by the practice; the number and location of sites; numbers of fee-earners, partners, solicitors; numbers of support staff; whether the practice holds any other quality certification; whether the assessment is Lexcel alone or will be combined with Investors in People or ISO9000.

Since the length and cost of an assessment will be significantly affected if the assessor cannot see case files, assessors will need to establish whether this is likely to be a significant factor at an early stage.

The cost quotation *should not* include the annual registration fee paid by the practice to the Law Society. Details of the registration fee can be obtained from the Lexcel information brochure.

Duration of assessment

The main factor affecting the length of assessment is the number of fee-earners. Other significant factors include: numbers of support staff; number and type of sites; degree of differentiation in work patterns between departments; degree of documentation available to support the systems; whether the auditor has access to case files; familiarity of the practice being audited with quality systems, e.g. ISO9000, Investors in People, or the Community Legal Service Quality Mark.

The time estimates given below are guidelines only and are not prescriptive. The actual time taken for assessments is monitored by the Law Society and the guidelines are reviewed in the light of experience. In the course of monitoring, any anomalies will be investigated.

The guidelines below include all the work leading up to the assessor's recommendation at the end of the assessment on the applicant's premises. They include preparation and final reporting to the Law Society.

Geographical location of offices and degree of centralisation of systems will affect the duration of assessments in multi-office practices.

The likely duration of assessment can be ascertained by adding the total obtained from Table 1 (overleaf) to the total obtained from Table 2. It is very unlikely that the length of assessments can be reduced at the bottom end of the scale. The Lexcel Assessment Panel has rebuked assessors for such conduct in the past, which may in extreme cases require a re-visit.

Assessors are reminded that the duration of assessments may be reduced where a practice has been assessed against a quality standard such as Investors in People, ISO9000, CharterMark or the Specialist Quality Mark (SQM) within six months of having their Lexcel assessment. An overlap table can be obtained from the Lexcel office, which details the overlaps between Lexcel and other quality standards.

Table 1: Duration indicator – by number of fee-earners

Fee-earners in office	Person days: main office	Additional person days: branch offices
1–5	1	0.5
6–10	1.5	0.5
11–20	2	1
21–30	2.5	1
31–40	3	1.5
41–50	3.5	2
50+	4	3

Table 2: Duration indicator – by number of support staff

Support staff in office	Person days: main office	Additional person days: branch offices
1–30	0.5	0.5
31+	0.75	0.75

Example: estimating duration of assessment

Main Office has 59 fee-earners and 40 support staff, Branch Office A has 15 fee-earners and 5 support staff and Branch Office B has 4 fee-earners and 2 support staff.

Duration at Main Office:	fee-earners – 4 days; support staff – 0.75 day
Duration at Branch Office A:	fee-earners – 1 day; support staff – 0.5 day
Duration at Branch Office B:	fee-earners – 0.5 day; support staff: 0.5 day
Total duration:	*7.25 days*

Interview sample sizes

Assessors will interview individuals during the course of the assessment. Those interviewed may have a designated role, such as supervisor, senior partner, trainee, newly recruited staff member, etc., or they may be selected on a random basis to verify that a procedure is in effective operation.

Samples will depend on the number of legal categories offered by a practice, the numbers of people working within each department and the degree of compliance observed in the initial sample. If an assessor notes apparent non-compliance, the sample may need to be larger than the initial sample to demonstrate a high degree of compliance. The Law Society may also direct that sample sizes may need to be increased at assessment, up to the recommended maximum guidelines for the size of that practice, where the results of the status enquiry checks indicate this is necessary.

The interview sample sizes given in Table 3 are guidelines. Assessors will make decisions based on the circumstances of the practice being assessed, such as those set out above.

Actual sample sizes will be monitored by the Law Society and the guidelines will be revised in the light of experience. In the course of monitoring, any anomalies will be investigated.

Table 3: Interview sample size guidelines

Total number of partners, principals, fee-earners and support staff in the practice	Sample (%)	
	Fee-earners	Support
1–5	70	40
6–15	50	30
16–25	35	15
26–50	25	10
51–75	15	7
76–100	12	5
101–125	8	3
126–500	6	2.5
501–1000	3	1
1001+	2	0.5

Case file samples

An assessor should audit at least five open files for each fee-earner in the sample. If the fee-earner undertakes more than one category of work, the assessor should look at files from all categories if possible.

Fewer files may be audited if the individual has a small number of files. This is typically because the fee-earner is senior and conducts a small number of complex cases, or because the fee-earner is junior and is developing a caseload under supervision.

The number of files audited may need to be increased if any fee-earner has conduct of a large number or percentage of the practice's total open file stock, or if initial assessment appears to indicate a high level of non-compliance.

Files selected should cover all the areas of law in which the practice offers services. A practice with SQM, for example, would not normally need to have those areas of overlap with the SQM examined.

The time taken to audit files will vary according to whether the assessor has direct access to them. The assessment will be quicker if the assessor can identify key issues for him/herself rather than having to ascertain the information from the fee-earner during an interview.

An increasing number of practices use computerised case management systems, so that a case record may be held partly on computer and partly on paper. Where this is so, and the assessor has access to case files, he or she will wish to see the computer records as well as the paper file.

Inspection of documentation

During the self-assessment process, the practice must have identified internal documentation showing how it meets the Lexcel requirements. It should make this documentation available to the assessor on request. A major part may be in the practice's office manual. Note that to have an office manual is a mandatory Lexcel requirement, though it can be in electronic format.

Documents submitted as evidence that the practice complies with a requirement should be self-evident, current and in use generally within the practice.

The assessor will study the documentary evidence submitted. Practices need not produce information that is commercially sensitive or client confidential. Indeed, to protect practice or client confidentiality, a practice may submit documents in such a form that anonymity is assured.

Assessment interviews

There are three main reasons for conducting interviews:

- to clarify points that may arise during the review of written evidence;
- to obtain more evidence (where the documentation only forms part of the evidence required to demonstrate compliance, or where documentation is not appropriate);
- to check that relevant personnel understand processes and procedures and apply them consistently.

The assessor may request a listing for each location, of principals and staff with details of names, job titles, departments and, if possible, length of service. The assessor will choose a representative cross-section of personnel for interview from the list supplied with the application. The assessor will notify the practice of the names of those selected for interview before any site visit. The numbers and roles of the personnel selected for interview will depend upon the size of the practice, its type and its structure.

Conscious of a practice's operational requirements, the assessor will fix the times of interviews for the convenience of those concerned. The assessor will agree to replacements for personnel who are, for operational reasons, unavailable for interview or reschedule the interview.

Interviews will be informal and confidential. Assessors will request that practices provide a quiet and secure room so that the interviews may take place in private.

Case management audits

The assessor will identify a selection of case files. The assessor will question the relevant fee-earner about these files, to check that all requirements of the case management standard are being met. This review will give the fee-earner an opportunity to explain how the procedures are working.

Client confidentiality and the contents of files

A number of the requirements set out in the Assessment Criteria concern the relationship between a practice and its clients and the way in which the practice maintains a record of that relationship. The lists of 'Typical Documentation' for those requirements include client care letters, attendance notes, client correspondence and case files. These are all documents confidential to the client, which the practice cannot disclose to an assessor without prior consent of the client. Solicitors owe a duty of confidentiality to clients in law and in conduct.

Practices are encouraged to obtain consent from their clients to disclosure of the contents of these documents to assessors. However, if a practice considers that it is not practical to ask for that consent, the assessment of the relevant requirement will be carried out on the basis that evidence will be gathered by the assessor through asking a fee-earner to find relevant documents in the case file, and evidence of compliance will be given by the fee-earner confirming that a document of the sort needed to show compliance is in fact present on the file. Care should be taken to avoid disclosing confidential information concerning the client's identity and affairs.

The following notes A to E apply if a practice proposes to allow assessors to inspect case files.

A. *Need for consent*

The best evidence that the client's consent has been given is a note on the file to that effect signed by the client. It may, however, be sufficient for consent to be obtained by 'exception reporting', i.e. clients are invited to notify the practice only if they wish to withhold their consent. Practitioners should be aware that this latter method of seeking consent has not been tested in the courts and so no guarantee can be given that it would be adequate; the ultimate decision must be one for the practice, depending on all the circumstances.

Subject to the above, the Law Society recommends:

a: the client must be notified of the possibility of inspection by quality assessors and the reasons for such inspection; and
b: either:

    i: the client must expressly consent to the inspection and must be informed that he or she can withdraw consent at any time; or
    ii: the client must be informed that he or she should notify the practice at any time if the client wishes to withhold consent; and

c: the solicitor (who is under a continuing duty to act in the best interests of the client) must at all times consider whether the client should have his or her file protected from inspection, whether or not the client has previously consented to its disclosure.

B. Obtaining consent

Solicitors practices which seek certification to Lexcel, or to other externally assessed standards, will normally have a written procedure for taking instructions. These will provide that every client receives a letter, or other document, confirming the practice's terms of business, basis of charging and named contact in the event of any problem with the service provided. This would normally be an ideal opportunity to provide the information and to seek the consent referred to above.

The precise manner in which consent is requested will vary according to the individual circumstances of the client and the nature of the retainer. For example, it would be inappropriate to seek consent to disclosure at the outset of the retainer:

a: if particular sensitivity is required in handling the matter, e.g. when preparing a deathbed will, in a domestic violence emergency or when seeing a person very recently bereaved;
b: in cases of urgency when it is not practical to give the client a proper opportunity to consider the question of confidentiality.

In other cases, it might be possible to obtain the client's consent in respect of a series of future transactions to be carried out on the client's behalf or as part of standing terms of business with a regular client.

C. Initial assessment

When an initial assessment takes place there may be clients whose files were opened before the practice started notifying clients of the possibility of inspection. If the proportion of these files means that they need to be included in the initial inspection, a letter must be written to all clients informing them of the possibility of the inspection, and either:

a: seeking the client's express consent to the inspection, and informing the client that he or she may withdraw consent at any time; or
b: advising the client of his or her rights to notify the practice at any time if the client wishes to withhold consent to inspection.

D. No consent

If:

a: the client refuses consent; or
b: it is appropriate to treat the file as one for which consent has been refused

the practice must tell the assessor that the file is not available for inspection.

E. *Withholding certain files*

Circumstances in which it may be appropriate to treat the file as one for which consent has been refused include:

a: if the case involves allegations about behaviour which might seriously prejudice the client's reputation or which might offend public decency, e.g. serious criminal charges and some matrimonial and child care proceedings;
b: if the client lacks the capacity to appreciate properly the consequences of giving consent (e.g. a minor, a client with difficulty understanding written English or suffering mental incapacity);
c: if the case involves matters of current or future financial, commercial or market sensitivity (price-sensitive information).

Non-compliances

A non-compliance is recorded where an assessor cannot find evidence that a requirement of the standard is being met. There are two types of non-compliance which may be recorded:

- **minor:** where the non-compliance can be corrected within 21 days *and* the assessor is able to accept documentary evidence sent by the practice that corrective action has been carried out;
- **major:** where the non-compliance will take longer than 21 days to correct *or* the assessor has to visit the practice again in order to establish that corrective action has been carried out.

In some circumstances assessors may note areas for improvement. For example: where a non-compliance cannot be fully rectified as an activity has not been carried out at the correct time; where non-compliances have been identified within the practice due to an individual who has left the practice, although subsequent corrective action has been taken; where there is evidence that a system may be breaking down although no non-compliance is identified; or as suggestions for improving, or recording best practice.

Assessors are also actively encouraged to note areas of good practice and congratulate the organisation where appropriate.

Accreditation

After the assessment has been completed there will be a meeting with the relevant members of the practice at which the assessor will provide feedback on the assessment.

The assessor will inform the practice of his or her recommendation at the end of the assessment visit.

Four recommendations are possible:

a: The assessor requires documentary evidence of corrective action within 21 days of the assessment before a recommendation for certification can be made.

b: A re-visit to check corrective action is required within three months of the assessment before a recommendation for certification can be made.
c: Certification premature – further full assessment is required (with an indication of the likely timescale).
d: Certification/continue certification.

It is accepted that the assessment is carried out on a sampling basis and an assessor is unlikely to observe all non-compliances within the practice. The recommendation for certification is based on the findings relating to the sample.

The assessor will produce a written report and recommend whether to grant a certificate. The report will include a summary of the evidence collected and state whether the practice meets all the PMS core requirements. The report will be sent to the Law Society's Lexcel Office, which will decide whether to grant Lexcel certification. In some circumstances the report will need to be referred to the Lexcel Assessment Panel who will decide whether to grant Lexcel certification.

Annual maintenance visits

Following the initial assessment the Law Society issues a certificate to confirm that the practice meets the Lexcel requirements. The certificate is valid for three years subject to annual maintenance visits to ensure that the Standards are still being met. A full reassessment is carried out after three years.

Annual maintenance visits (AMVs) should be held before or during the month of the anniversary of the issue of the certificate. The **whole** process must have been completed each year by the end of the month of the anniversary of the issue of the certificate. Practices are therefore advised to have their AMV and reassessments carried out prior to, or early in the month of, the anniversary of assessment to give time for corrective action, if necessary.

If a simultaneous monitoring visit falls due for Investors in People or ISO9000 before the Lexcel AMV, the Lexcel assessment can be brought forward to bring the two into alignment. However, practices will need to keep the earlier date for their subsequent AMV and reassessment or there would be a gap of more than one year between assessments.

Practices will have a maximum of one month's leeway on either side of the due date for the annual maintenance assessment or reassessment to take place, subject to the above paragraphs.

During an AMV, compliance against all the Lexcel requirements will be reviewed. However, the number of case files reviewed and interviews conducted will be approximately half of the number in the guidelines for an initial assessment.

Factors affecting the duration of the annual maintenance assessment will include the number and type of non-compliances previously identified and the degree of change to the practice structure or staff since the last visit.

The procedures for status enquiry checks is different for AMVs. Checks will only be carried out for any new starters since the date of the practice's initial assessment (or previous AMV). However, status enquiry checks would be carried out for all fee-earners at the full re-assessment.

However, the Law Society will be entitled to carry out further status enquiry checks about the practice at its discretion at any time during the duration of the Lexcel certificate. This is to maintain the overall integrity of the system, and retain a safeguard for further checks at the Assessment Panel's discretion.

The Law Society will therefore only require status enquiry forms from:

a: any new partners and admitted fee-earners;
b: any new non-admitted fee-earners; or
c: fee-earners if they have changed status, e.g. non-admitted fee-earners have become admitted or admitted fee-earners have become partners.

Practices will be asked to enclose a staff list, when returning the AMV form, indicating new starters since the original assessment or last AMV, together with their status enquiry forms.

Practices are reminded that they are under a continuing duty to inform the Lexcel Office immediately of any circumstances involving the practice, or any individual working at the practice involved in fraud, serious professional misconduct or a flagrant breach of the PMS.

Mergers and de-mergers

Where the practice has recently merged with another practice, or opened a new branch or branches, those parts of the practice which have not previously been assessed will be subject to a full assessment. Such assessment will take place either concurrently with the AMV, or at a time to be agreed between the Law Society and the practice. A Lexcel certificate will be awarded for each new branch once all the branches of the practice have been successfully assessed. The additional certificates will be valid for the same duration as the original certificate to enable the future AMVs or full assessments to coincide for the whole practice.

Where a branch has de-merged from the original practice, a fresh application will be required from the new practice. The new practice must surrender any certificate and logos from the date of de-merger. A fresh assessment will be required for the new practice, although credit will be given in relation to the previous award including status enquiry checks and the results of the previous assessment. The extent of this credit depends on the individual circumstances of the practice, and the time elapsed from first assessment or AMV.

Fraud/dishonesty discovered during an assessment

If an assessor suspects as a result of findings during an assessment that there may be fraud, dishonest activity or serious breaches of the Solicitors' Professional Conduct Rules within the practice, the assessor must without delay contact the Lexcel Office for advice as to how to proceed.

Withdrawal or suspension of certification

The Law Society's Lexcel Assessment Panel may decide to defer, withdraw, withhold or suspend certification in respect of the whole of any practice if the practice is found, or suspected to be, in flagrant breach of Lexcel, or to have committed a fraud or serious professional misconduct.

Practices and assessors are reminded that an assessment should *not* be carried out without clearance to proceed first having been granted by the Law Society. Without this clearance the practice runs the risk of having to pay for the cost of assessment and not being awarded Lexcel by the Lexcel Assessment Panel.

The Panel may require a full reassessment as a condition of reviewing a suspended or withdrawn certificate.

Appeals and complaints

If a practice wishes to appeal against a recommendation not to award or renew a certificate, it has the right of appeal to the Lexcel Appeals Panel. Details of the Lexcel appeal process can be obtained from the Lexcel Office.

Similarly, the Lexcel Office will consider complaints about the way in which the assessment has been conducted, or the assessment bodies involved.

2.1 Practices will develop and maintain a marketing and a business plan.
2.2 Practices will document the services they wish to offer, the client groups to be served, how services are to be provided (including any special features) and the way in which services are designed to meet client needs.
2.3 The documents, required by section 2.1 must be reviewed every six months and the review must be documented. The services and marketing plan or documentation required by section 2.2 must be produced or reviewed at least annually and must be current at the time of any assessment.

3. FINANCIAL MANAGEMENT

3.1 Practices will document responsibility for financial management procedures.
3.2 Practices will be able to provide documentary evidence of their financial management processes, including:
   a: Annual budget (including, where appropriate, any capital expenditure proposed).
   b: Variance analysis conducted at least quarterly of income and expenditure against budgets.
   c: Annual profit and loss or income and expenditure accounts (certificated or audited accounts).
   d: Annual balance sheet.
   e: Annual cash or funds flow forecast.
   f: Quarterly variance analysis at least of cashflow.

   Financial management data is best evidenced by showing all appropriate data or paperwork to assessors, but practices may decline to do so if they wish. In such cases the assessor will consider other evidence that is available, including correspondence from the practice's auditors and interviews with the partners and/or managers.

3.3 Practices will have a time recording process which enables the accurate measurement of time spent on matters for billing purposes and/or management analysis of the cost effectiveness of work and the efficiency of the practice.

c. ~~Consider any~~ report and advise on such circumstances without delay, informing the risk manager if appropriate.
d: Inform the client in all cases where an adverse costs order is made against the practice in relation to the matter in question.

At the end of the matter the fee-earner must:

e: Undertake a concluding risk assessment by considering if the client's objectives have been achieved and if the client could fairly complain or make a claim for damages in relation to the service provided.
f: Notify the risk manager of all such circumstances in accordance with documented procedures without delay.

7   CLIENT CARE

7.1   Practices will have a documented policy for client care, which will include:

  a: The practice's commitment to provide services to clients in an appropriate manner.
  b: Procedures to ensure compliance with Practice Rule 15 and its accompanying code in relation to client care and costs information.

7.2   Practices will have processes to ensure that clients are informed in writing of the terms of business under which instructions are received and will be handled, including:

  a: The name and status of the fee-earner and the person(s) responsible for overall supervision.
  b: Whom the client should approach in the event of a problem with the service provided.
  c: The basis under which charges will be calculated including the best information possible on the likely overall costs of the matter.

The information required by this section should usually be provided in writing unless there are professional considerations that make this unsuitable in any particular matter.

There must be a record of any standing terms of business with regular clients, such as many commercial clients. The practice must be able to produce such terms in relation to the issues covered by this section.

8.9 Practices will have a documented procedure to:

   a: List open and closed matters, identify all matters for a single client and linked files where relevant and all files for particular funders.
   b: Ensure that they are able to identify and trace any documents, files, deeds, wills or any other items relating to a matter.
   c: Safeguard the confidentiality of matter files and all other client information.
   d: Ensure that the status of the matter and the action taken can be easily checked by other members of the practice.
   e: Ensure that documents are stored on the matter file(s) in an orderly way.

8.10 Practices will have a documented procedure for using barristers, expert witnesses and other external advisers who are involved in the delivery of legal services, which will include provision for the following:

   a: Use of clear selection criteria, which do not discriminate on grounds of race, colour, ethnic or national origins, sex, creed, disability, sexual orientation or age.
   b: Where appropriate, consultation with the client in relation to selection, and proper advice to the client on choice of advocate or other professional.
   c: Clients to be advised of the name and status of the person being instructed, how long she/he might take to respond, and where disbursements are to be paid by the client, the cost involved.
   d: Maintenance of records (centrally, by department or office) on barristers and experts used, including evidence of assessment against the criteria.
   e: Evaluation of performance, for the information of other members of the practice.
   f: Giving of instructions, which clearly describe what is required and which, in litigation matters, comply with the rules of court and any court orders.
   g: Checking of opinions and reports received to ensure they adequately provide the information sought (and, in litigation matters, comply with the rules of court and any court orders).
   h: Payment of fees.

8.11 Practices will have documented procedures to ensure that, at the end of the matter, the practice:

   a: Reports to the client on the outcome and explains any further action that the client is required to take in the matter and what (if anything) the practice will do.

obviously in the areas of equal opportunities and anti-discrimination. For private practice firms it is a breach of the regulations not to have adopted these policies, while employed practices are likely to be subject to organisation-wide policies. In other cases practices will need to address the requirements and decide the right approach for them.

Key issues

- Management structure.
- Business model.
- The role of quality in management.
- Responsibility for quality management.
- Reviews of the quality programme.
- Anti-discrimination.
- Equality of opportunity.
- Avoiding money laundering.
- Combating mortgage fraud.
- What is the most appropriate format for the necessary documentation? One document or a series of linked documents?
- Staff involvement in the preparation of policies covered in this section and communication and training thereafter.
- If and how to communicate relevant policies to clients and others that the practice deals with.

1.1 Practices will have documentation setting out the legal framework under which they operate.

For many practices this will be one of the most fundamental considerations – the basis on which the practice is formed. In the case of partnerships there is always the risk of a breakdown of working relationships or other difficulties between the members of the firm and it will be good practice to have a partnership deed, dealing with such issues as:

a: Management and voting rights.
b: The authorisation of individual partners or managers to bind the practice in contract.

In-house practices in law and industry, are likely to provide evidence in the corporate plans of the umbrella organisation.

Example of major non-compliances

- Consideration has not been given to the most appropriate business structure for the practice, and the size or composition of the practice would make it impracticable to do this within 21 days.

Example of minor non-compliances

- There has been no review or adequate review of the structure.

1.3   **Practices will have a risk management strategy or framework.**

Example of major non-compliances

- There is no risk management strategy or framework documented, and it would be impracticable to address this within 21 days.

Example of minor non-compliances

- There is a risk management strategy or framework, but it is not comprehensive.

1.4   **Practices will have a written quality policy. This is a high level document setting out the organisation's commitment to quality and overall policy. Practices will also have documented procedures as set out in this standard, which will be distributed and published throughout the practice showing:**

   a: The role that the quality system plays in the overall strategy of the practice.
   b: Who has responsibility for the management of the quality system.

Example of minor non-compliances

- There is no designated individual who has responsibil[ity...]
  there is evidence that such an appointee does not have su[fficient...]
  requirements of the role.

1.6 **There must be a review of the operation of the quality sy[stem...] process for people within the practice to suggest impro[vements. The] review must show the part that the quality system is int[egral to the] strategy of the practice over the next 12 months at least.**

If the quality system is to be a living system that develops within [the practice there must be] regular reviews to see how it needs to be changed. The requirem[ent is] that, at least annually, the practice should be able to show a process w[hereby] its procedures have been considered and amended if and where appr[opriate.] complaints received (see 7.3) and clients' perceptions of services provided (s[ee 7.4) are] a good starting point for a review of the quality system. In addition, many practices will seek input from the heads of departments or teams, which may be combined with a formal system of staff suggestions for improvements. In-house practices should be able to provide evidence that they have been gathering relevant data on the operation of the quality system within the department as well as participating in any organisation-wide quality reviews, if the latter are restricted to limited quality issues, such as response times. Such structures do not need to be documented as procedures, though in many cases practices are likely to choose to do so in order that the process is transparent within the practice.

Example of major non-compliances

- There is a process in place by which people within the practice can suggest improvements to the quality system, but there is insufficient evidence that it is in effective operation.

Example of minor non-compliances

- There has been no review or adequate review of the operation of the quality system within the previous 12 months where the system has been in place for at least that period of time.

1.7 **Practices will document procedures on non-discrimination, and have regard to guidance from the Law Society on non-discrimination in accepting instructions from clients, the use of experts and counsel and the provision of services to clients.**

All firms in private practice are required to adopt the model policy of the Law Society which is reviewed from time to time. In local authorities, other public sector bodies, and those in commerce and industry, practices may be subject to the policies of the umbrella organisation. Assessors will expect these to meet the above requirement except where a practice can demonstrate that they conflict with a statutory requirement or guidance from a statutory body, and that the practice meets those requirements. Whereas, formerly,

Example of major non-compliances

- There is evidence that procedures on equality and diversity are not being adhered to, and therefore are not in effective operation.

Example of minor non-compliances

- The practice has not adopted the Law Society's policy on anti-discrimination or it cannot be produced.

1.9 **Practices will have documented procedures to ensure compliance with money laundering legislation. The documented procedures should cover:**

    a: **The appointment of a 'Nominated Officer', usually referred to as a Money Laundering Reporting Officer (MLRO).**
    b: **Reporting of suspicious circumstances within the practice and by the MLRO to the authorities.**
    c: **Identification checking.**
    d: **Partner and staff training in anti-money laundering awareness.**
    e: **The proper maintenance of records.**

Any exemptions to these requirements must be stated in the practice's documented procedures.

The extension of the anti-money laundering regime to all 'criminal conduct' where there is 'criminal property' under the Proceeds of Crime Act 2002 has received extensive consideration in the legal press. Certain provisions under the Terrorism Act 2000 are also involved. The provisions of the Money Laundering Regulations 2003 are mandatory for most firms in private practice and it is a criminal offence not to have implemented the necessary provisions, regardless of whether money laundering is actually occurring within the firm.

Local authorities, other public sector bodies, and those in commerce and industry, will need to consider whether and if so, how, these provisions apply to them.

The implementation of the Money Laundering Regulations 2003 will need to be in line with current Law Society guidance. Practices should bear in mind that sections 330 and 331 of the Proceeds of Crime Act 2002 provide that in deciding whether a person has committed an offence of failure to report 'the court must consider whether he followed any relevant guidance which was at the time ... issued by the supervisory authority or any other competent authority'. Since the Law Society is within this range of organisations the fact that professional guidance has been followed may well provide an effective defence to a prosecution.

Example of major non-compliances

- The practice has not addressed some or all of the requirements of the Money Laundering Regulations 2003 where they apply, or the procedures are used so inconsistently that they could not be said to be in effective operation.

Example of minor non-compliances

- Procedures dealing with the avoidance of money laundering liability are not documented where required, although they are in operation, or documented procedures do not address one or more of the areas that are required to be covered.

1.10 Practices providing services to clients in relation to property transactions will have documented procedures in relation to the avoidance of involvement in mortgage fraud.

Private practice firms providing conveyancing services will need to have clear guidelines in relation to procedures to be followed in the event of suspicions of mortgage fraud. The requirements of the *Council of Mortgage Lenders Handbook* will also be a concern for most firms providing conveyancing services.

Full guidance on avoiding mortgage fraud can be obtained by contacting the Law Society Ethics Department.

Example of major non-compliances

- There are no procedures for avoiding mortgage fraud in a practice that provides conveyancing services to purchasers or the procedures are so poorly observed that they are not in effective operation.

Example of minor non-compliances

- Procedures for avoiding mortgage fraud are not documented in a practice that provides conveyancing services to purchasers, although they are in operation, or the documented procedures do not address one or more of the areas that are required to be covered.

1.11 Practices will have a documented policy in relation to data protection compliance issues.

In 2002 Elizabeth France – the then outgoing Information Commissioner – revealed that only some 25% of law firms in private practice had registered under the Data Protection Act 1998. A more active regime of enforcing the need to register and observe the data protection principles was announced.

Registration with the Information Commissioner's Office, where it is necessary to do so, commits the organisation to the data protection principles and the necessary internal controls that will be needed. Practices must register if they record and process data that identifies an individual, which includes any expression of opinion.

Example of major non-compliances

- There is no policy in relation to data protection compliance or the policy is so poorly observed that it is not in effective operation.

Example of minor non-compliances

- The policy in relation to data protection compliance is not documented, although it is in operation, or it does not address one or more of the areas that are required to be covered.

1.12 Practices will have a documented policy in relation to the health and safety of partners, staff and visitors to the practice.

There are general duties on employers and organisations to ensure a safe working environment. In accordance with the applicable legislation, practices should adopt a policy that they are taking adequate steps to ensure that they meet their obligations. More detailed procedures on this point appear at 4.2.

Example of major non-compliances

- There is no policy in relation to health and safety or the policy is so poorly observed that it is not in effective operation.

Example of minor non-compliances

- The policy in relation to health and safety is not documented or does not address one or more of the areas that are required to be covered.

2 STRATEGY, THE PROVISION OF SERVICES AND MARKETING

Section 2 deals with the need for a business plan and for due consideration to be given to marketing. Underlying these provisions is a requirement that Lexcel awarded practices need to consider effective strategies in order to remain successful.

Private practice firms might choose one all-embracing document for these requirements or the plans could be broken into a series of departmental plans. All will depend on the style, size and culture of the practice. The in-house practice might need to refer to organisation-wide plans, perhaps supplemented by further details on planning within the department.

Whatever the choices made, it is a requirement that plans are committed to some form of documentation. If this is not made available to the assessors some other evidence of its existence and adequacy will be needed.

Key issues

- Format of business and marketing plans.
- In private practice, the aspirations of the partners.
- Realistic objectives for the practice.
- Scope of research of internal and external factors.
- Extent of staff involvement in compilation of plans.
- Extent to which plans are shared with and communicated to staff.
- What marketing would be appropriate and what is intended from it.

2.1 Practices will develop and maintain a marketing and a business plan.

A business plan should consist of:

a: Analysis of the factors, both internal to the practice and externally, that are relevant to the future development of the practice.
b: Key objectives for the forthcoming 12 months at least from the date of the document or review of any such document to provide a background against which the practice may measure its performance.
c: Some outline or detailed objectives covering a further two years at least which evidence a consideration of the factors relevant to the future of the practice.
d: For items (b) and (c) above a finance plan, evidencing due consideration of the overall financial implications of the strategy or strategies to be adopted within the practice and setting some financial goals or objectives if not appearing elsewhere in the business plan.

Some form of strategic document or business plan is required by this provision. In some practices this may be achieved through a combination of different documents – perhaps a main business plan for the firm along with a series of departmental plans. In local authority and in-house practices, the assessor would expect to see a service plan or documented references to the corporate plans of the umbrella organisation. The assessor will expect the practice to have documented what it seeks to achieve, within the limits imposed by corporate or statutory prescription. It is for each practice to choose the format and style of the documentation. It follows that the length and complexity of the documentation will vary between similar practices.

Factors that will determine the complexity of the strategic documentation will include:

- The size of the practice – sole practices and smaller firms will often have simpler strategies and less need for complex documentation.
- The amount of change that is anticipated over the period of the plan – a practice seeking to consolidate or stabilise its current operations will probably have less to address than one that is expanding.
- The management style of the partners or managers.
- The organisational requirements in local authorities or other in-house departments.

Whatever the style and format of the documentation, assessors will seek evidence of analysis of significant factors – both internal and external to the practice – which will be likely to have an impact on the future of the practice. This analysis could take various forms, but could include:

- staff survey;
- internal 'brainstorming' sessions;
- assessment within the practice of 'SWOT' factors (strengths, weaknesses, opportunities and threats);
- consideration of proposed legislative changes or Government plans;
- consultation of local plans;
- organisation-wide plans for in-house departments.

Performance objectives are intended to provide hard data as to whether the plan has succeeded or not. Wherever possible, objectives should be 'smart', i.e.:

> **S**pecific
>
> **M**easurable
>
> **A**chievable
>
> **R**ealistic
>
> **T**ime-limited

Objectives may relate to gross fee income, size of the organisation, or any performance ratios felt to be relevant, including client satisfaction.

The standard recognises that objectives for the current or next 12 months should in most cases be more detailed than those for the medium-term future.

It is a requirement that the financial implications of the strategy are shown to have been considered. This will result either in evidence being available of such consideration or the establishment of financial objectives within the business or departmental plans. A finance plan is best seen as a management overview of the financial implications of the strategy in question. It is separate from, but perhaps ancillary to, more detailed budgets.

However marketing is dealt with, the documentation should cover:

a: Areas of work that the practice wishes to develop, expand, reduce or cease to provide.
b: The benefits that the practice hopes to achieve from its marketing or promotional activity.
c: Any promotional methods that will be employed and responsibility for them.
d: A budget for promotional activities.

The standard does not require all recognised practices to market themselves actively – merely that they should consider the appropriate marketing activity for the practice. The practice content with its current supply of work, or which feels that instructions may need to be turned away because of excess demand, would not be expected to involve itself in promotion that is likely to further increase the flow of potential instructions. If a decision is made not to engage in active marketing, it must be documented in order to meet this requirement. On the other hand, a practice that sets out in its main strategy a desire to develop all or some of its practice areas would need to show that the marketing steps that will be needed have been considered.

Example of major non-compliances

- There is no marketing and/or business plan and the size or composition of the practice would make it impracticable to address this within 21 days.

Examples of minor non-compliances

- There is no marketing documentation available at the assessment when it is clear that marketing activity is undertaken by the practice.
- There is some shortcoming in the documentation which is available at the assessment, such as:
  - Lack of evidence of analysis of relevant factors to inform the business plan.
  - No objectives or objectives which are too vague for the practice to measure its performance at some future stage.
  - Inadequate consideration of the financial implications of the strategy or strategies described.

2.2 Practices will document the services they wish to offer, the client groups to be served, how services are to be provided (including any special features) and the way in which services are designed to meet client needs.

It is important that the practice should consider and record the extent or scope of its services and also any limitations to them. This will be useful to:

- clients wishing to check if the practice can deal with their concerns;
- other external persons such as referrers of work;
- staff, as on induction training.

Since, in most cases, it will be clients and potential clients who have most interest in this provision, the requirements will often be met by lists and details of services as contained in brochures or on websites.

The sort of special features which will commonly be listed will be the languages that advice can be offered through, the availability of home visits, wheelchair access to the offices, etc.

Practices providing publicly funded services should list the contract categories that are offered and any policy established on the acceptance of instructions given any limitations to matter starts.

Local authority departments might describe or append service agreements with colleague departments, or external authorities that are advised through contractual arrangements.

Example of major non-compliances

- The practice has not considered or documented any of the requirements of 2.2, and the size or composition of the practice would make it impracticable to address this within 21 days.

Example of minor non-compliances

- No list of services is available or some element (e.g. special features, when provided) is missing.

2.3 **The documents required by section 2.1 must be reviewed every six months and the review must be documented. The services and marketing plan or documentation required by section 2.2 must be produced or reviewed at least annually and must be current at the time of any assessment.**

Practices must be able to show that all strategic and marketing documentation is kept under continual review. There will need to be a substantive review at least annually and an interim review at least six-monthly. The evidence of such reviews could be partnership strategy papers or partnership or management group minutes. Sole practitioners must also be able to demonstrate that reviews have taken place as required, for example by way of dated notes or appendices to plans.

Issues for practices

- Type, length and style of desired documentation.
- Possible involvement of external advice.
- Staff involvement and communication to the staff.
- Feasible marketing activity and its budget.
- Most effective format of review.

Assessment guidelines

Plans which are shortly to come into operation or which are already implemented for the current 12 months will be acceptable.

It is not a requirement of the standard that staff must be consulted on and informed of the business plan or other documentation described in this section. It is, however, increasingly regarded as good business practice to involve staff in the business planning process and to keep them informed of the practice's plans and progress.

The contents of all business or marketing plans can be retained as being confidential to the practice, if it so chooses. In such circumstances the assessor will seek evidence of the existence and understanding of such plans from interviews. Interviews are likely to be at partner or senior manager level as these are the people most likely to be involved in business strategy.

Example of major non-compliances

- No reviews have taken place.

Example of minor non-compliances

- A review has taken place but it has not been documented.

3 FINANCIAL MANAGEMENT

This section requires there to be clear management responsibility for financial management and various controls to monitor the use of available funds and, in the case of private practice, business performance.

It is recognised that many in-house departments will not need to set the targets and to monitor performance as required by this section. Local authority and other public institution practices should consider, however, any recharge arrangements and their application to legal work performed within the department. Where services are provided to authorities on a contracted out basis many of the controls associated with private practice become appropriate.

Key issues

- Responsibility for financial controls and performance.
- Preparation of financial reports and future budgets.
- Responsibility for monitoring performance against budgets.
- Time recording within the practice: when it is required and who undertakes it.

3.1 Practices will document responsibility for financial management procedures.

In an increasing number of private practice firms it may be an employee who has responsibility for monitoring and correcting financial performance issues, or it may be shared responsibility between an employee and the partners or a finance or managing partner.

There is no requirement as to the seniority of the person or persons concerned.

In the local authority practice responsibility for financial performance may lie outside the department, e.g. a designated contact in the finance department.

Example of major non-compliances

- There are no documented procedure and staff are unclear about who is responsible for financial management.

Example of minor non-compliances

- Nobody has been designated as having responsibility for financial management or it is not clear from the documentation available or interviews within the practice who has such responsibility.

3.2 Practices will be able to provide documentary evidence of their financial management processes, including:

a: Annual budget (including, where appropriate, any capital expenditure proposed).
b: Variance analysis conducted at least quarterly of income and expenditure against budgets.

c: Annual profit and loss or income and expenditure accounts (certificated or audited accounts).
d: Annual balance sheet.
e: Annual cash or funds flow forecast.
f: Quarterly variance analysis at least of cashflow.

Financial management data is best evidenced by showing all appropriate data or paperwork to assessors, but practices may decline to do so if they wish. In such cases the assessors will consider other evidence that is available, including correspondence from the practice's auditor and interviews with the partners and/or managers.

In private practice the production of a profit and loss account and a balance sheet are commonplace. Firms could often improve, however, in the area of management accounting, i.e. planning for future performance rather than reporting on the past.

Assessors will take into account that many firms will not necessarily engage their auditors to advise on management accounting issues. They should therefore enquire as to the extent of the accountants' involvement in the firm in considering any assurance from such advisers that the requirements of this section have been addressed.

Example of major non-compliances

- There is no system of establishing and undertaking variance analysis of future budgets or income and/or expenditure in circumstances where they could fairly be excluded (e.g. local authority department where financial matters are controlled outside the legal department).

Example of minor non-compliances

- One or more of the elements of 3.2 are not evident and/or a quarterly variance analysis of a budget or cash flow statement is overdue.

3.3 Practices will have a time recording process which enables the accurate measurement of time spent on matters for billing purposes and/or management analysis of the cost effectiveness of work and the efficiency of the practice.

Computerised time recording has become the norm for most types of legal practice in recent years. It is not compulsory that any such system is computerised: in some smaller firms file-based or manual systems are still in use and this will be acceptable.

Most private practitioners see time recording as a matter of collecting billing data and therefore decline to record non-chargeable time. Likewise, many in-house lawyers or those in private practice working to fixed fees will not time-record. In non-private practice, time recording and billing systems may not be linked as billing is governed by inter-departmental agreements. The provision in 3.3 reflects the growing view that time recording should be seen as management data first and billing information second. It is nonetheless acceptable that a practice could take the view that it will only time-record on those matters that will need to be billed or costed on a time recorded basis (if any) and decline to time-record elsewhere. Where some matters or types of matter are not normally subject to time recording, practices may wish to carry out a time recording exercise on a sample basis. This would provide a benchmark to ensure that fixed fee or percentage-based fees are viable.

Example of major non-compliances

- There is no system of time recording where time is nonetheless a factor in charges to clients (or client departments in employed practice).

Example of minor non-compliances

- There is a system of time recording in existence but one or more fee-earners who are required to record time in this way is or are not doing so. However, if the assessor identifies extensive non-compliance with a time recording system, to the extent that the system could not be said to be in effective operation, that could amount to a major non-compliance.

4 FACILITIES AND INFORMATION TECHNOLOGY

Lawyers have always required office premises and related facilities from which to operate. More recently the importance and use of computers has become a major consideration for all practices. Of equal concern is the growing volume of compliance requirements in relation to data control and computer use.

In-house lawyers may be subject to organisation-wide policies and procedures in relation to all or most of this section of the standard.

Key issues

- The needs of the firm and all its personnel in relation to office accommodation, having regard to:
  - The importance of a comfortable and secure working environment.
  - Health and safety responsibilities.
  - The projection of an appropriate image to clients.
  - The maintenance of effective 'back-office' services.
- Maintaining client confidentiality and providing an effective service through computer communication systems.
- Compliance with requirements in relation to e-mail use and storage, data protection registrations and any related requirements of the firm's insurers.
- What the firm would do should a catastrophic event occur – e.g. the office is burned: business continuity plan.

4.1 **Practices will document the office facilities needed to provide a service to clients, including:**

   a: **The use of premises and equipment, including security and related health and safety issues.**
   b: **Photocopying, including maintenance and support.**
   c: **Arrangements for clients to visit the offices, including reception, directions and car parking, if appropriate.**
   d: **Staff facilities.**
   e: **Mail, fax and other communication arrangements.**
   f: **Procedures for the handling of financial transactions.**

Some practices may choose to address these requirements through one document, while others may comply with a series of documents, whether co-ordinated or not. Practices may choose the style and complexity of documentation that suits them best, but in most cases these provisions will be set out in the practice's office procedures manual. It is important that the arrangements required above should be accessible to all personnel within the practice.

Practices are required to have a policy on health and safety (1.12) which must be subject to at least an annual review (4.2). The sort of arrangements that might additionally be documented under this section might include how and when risk assessments are conducted, arrangements for eye tests for screen users, fire drills, testing of fire extinguishers, etc.

Many practices will have arrangements in place on the maintenance of photocopying equipment and contractual arrangements for external copying of large or multiple copies. Computer support contracts become increasingly significant as more work is entrusted to data format or conducted via e-mails.

The importance of client reactions to the offices has often been stressed. The state of the reception area, the professionalism of the welcome and the availability of refreshments should be seen as an important element of the client care policy of the practice. Issues to be addressed might include:

- How clients will be informed of delays.
- How and when refreshments will be offered and served.
- The provision of up-to-date magazines, newspapers and publicity matter on the firm.
- Ensuring that floral displays are kept fresh.

In most firms the provision of confidential facilities for clients who need to have documents signed or other short communications within the reception area should be considered. In too many practices confidential information will be overheard by other clients awaiting an appointment.

The efficient use of communication facilities might require training for those personnel concerned, for example, familiarisation with the features of the practice's telephone system is likely to form part of induction.

In most practices the accounts procedures will be a significant element of the overall practice manual and should provide worked examples of entries for payments in, cheque payments, payments of petty cash, transfers, etc. Breaches of the Solicitors' Accounts Rules are a significant risk for firms in private practice and the availability of clear instructions forms an effective safeguard in this respect and can assist in minimising wasted time between accounts and fee-earning personnel.

Examples of major non-compliances

- There is no documentation dealing with office facilities or it fails to address most or all of the issues.
- There is evidence of widespread ignorance of the facilities dealt with under 4.1 or of a significant amount or aspect of them.

Examples of minor non-compliances

- Documentation does exist in relation to office facilities but it fails to deal with a limited number of the issues referred to or fails to do so adequately.
- There is evidence that staff are not fully aware of relevant facilities or processes covered by 4.1.
- There is evidence that the documented procedures are not being followed, to a limited extent.

4.2 Practices will conduct a documented review of health and safety issues at least annually. They must show that it has received due consideration by top management and implementation has been acted upon or is planned, as appropriate.

There is a requirement in the Health and Safety at Work Act 1974 for an annual review of health and safety in all organisations employing five persons or more. The review might form part of an annual review of the business plan or be one element of the annual review of all risk assessment data (see 6.7f). Sole and small practices which may not be caught by the legislation must still comply with this requirement although it is likely that the documentation they produce will be relatively short and straightforward. Practices can choose the degree of detail that they work into such a review. However, the report must show a genuine consideration of the principal issues affecting health and safety in professional offices, to include:

- Equipment.
- Safe handling and use of substances.
- Information, instruction and supervision on health and safety issues.
- Any training required.
- Accidents, first aid and work-related ill-health.
- Monitoring of conditions and systems of work.
- Emergency procedures, fire and evacuation of premises.

Examples of major non-compliances

- There has been no review of health and safety within the previous 12 months and the size of the practice makes such a review unlikely within the period of 21 days.
- There is no evidence that top management has considered any review and/or there is a failure to implement or plan to act upon its findings.

Example of minor non-compliances

- The annual review has taken place but is not documented.

4.3 There should be a business continuity plan envisaging the nature of catastrophic events that could beset the practice and the contingency plans that should be put into effect should they become necessary.

The need for business continuity planning arises from the practice's responsibilities to its clients and the need to comply with requirements imposed by legislation, practice rules and insurers. An increasing number of indemnity insurers are insisting upon the existence of a recently reviewed business continuity plan as a condition of insurance.

The business continuity plan should address the following issues:

a: An analysis of the practice's information technology systems required both to enable it to function and to deliver its advertised services to clients.
b: An analysis of the data it holds relating to: the practice; its personnel; its clients and business partners.

c: A description of the facilities and information technology systems it has in place for the storage and retrieval of data in the event of a disaster that prevents the operational activities of the practice.
d: Procedures for the identification and location of key personnel whose services will be available in the event of disaster and training and education in respect of their responsibilities.
e: The availability of 'standby systems' as a temporary measure in the event of disaster; or, where a decision is taken to outsource business continuity planning strategies to a managed or application service provider, evidence that proper consideration has been given to: selection of an appropriate provider; the contract of service; the cost; compliance with the Data Protection Act 1998; and the resolution of disputes.

Example of major non-compliances

- There is no business continuity plan in existence.

Example of minor non-compliances

- During interviews it becomes apparent that a limited number of staff are not aware of the business continuity plan.

4.4 Practices will have a plan for IT use setting out the use of IT facilities within the practice and any planned changes. The IT plan should cover:

a: Responsibility for IT purchasing, installation, maintenance, support and training.
b: The current and planned applications within the practice of IT.
c: A data protection compliance statement in relation to staff, clients and others and registration with the Information Commissioner.
d: Compliance with all appropriate regulations and requirements.
e: User safety (see also 4.2 above).
f: Appropriate use of e-mail and attachments, both externally and internally, including storage of messages and the implications of not observing such procedures.
g: Computer data and system back up, to the extent not covered in any disaster recovery plan.

The IT plan must address at least a period of the current or next 12 months and may form part of the practice's overall strategy documentation, the office manual, or a separate document.

Practices must demonstrate a regular review of the use and development of information technology systems. This does not require a particular level of computerisation and assessors will not judge the appropriateness of the information technology plan. They will, however, need to be satisfied that the use of information technology for delivering the practice's services has received due consideration by partners or managers. Each practice must decide how to address the issues set out in this section.

In section 4.4f (e-mail), a policy should specify: suitable business use; suitable personal use; the legal implications of e-mail (e.g. defamation and harassment); security issues and standards (e.g. viruses and 'spam' communications); criteria for the use of e-mail notices (e.g. disclaimers, etc.); whether the practice will accept service electronically; and procedures for electronic storage of e-mail.

A policy regarding use of the internet should specify: the general policy of the practice; suitable business use; suitable personal use; the legal implications of using the internet (e.g. downloading copyright or obscene material); and security standards.

A policy regarding the practice website should specify the practice's policy on: the management of site content (e.g. facilities for disabled users); the use of disclaimers; jurisdiction and applicable law in respect of site content; linking to other sites; copyright issues; and privacy of data collected from site visitors. Practices may wish to consider applying to the Legal Services Commission for its 'Quality Mark for Websites'.

A policy regarding electronic legal services should specify: the key legal, regulatory, professional and codified provisions to be observed; the procedures to be observed for on-line contracting; and the method of handling of electronic payments.

In section 4.4c (data management), a policy should specify: the different types of data that will be collected; the need for compliance with the eight data protection principles of the Data Protection Act 1998; and the assignment of responsibility for training and implementation.

In section 4.4d (legal and regulatory compliance), practices will need to ensure that at least one member of senior management has a working knowledge and understanding of the application of provisions with compliance implications for the practice's use of information technology and internet technologies. Further details are contained in the *Office Procedures Manual*.

Examples of major non-compliances

- The firm's website does not supply the information specified by the E-commerce (EC Directive) Regulations 2002.
- The firm has not notified itself as a 'data controller' under the Data Protection Act 1998.
- There is no documentation dealing with the use of information technology or it fails to address most or all of the issues referred to.

Example of minor non-compliances

- There is an IT plan but one or more of the elements that should be covered have not been addressed or have not been addressed adequately.

4.5 Practices will document arrangements for legal research and library facilities, whether in the practice or externally and whether through books or periodicals or computer-based services. A process must exist for the updating and sharing of legal and professional information.

This provision does not require the practice to have its own law library, though many do. What is important is that fee-earners have reasonable access to legal research tools, which in many practices will increasingly be web-based. There should be reasonable controls regarding location of reports, books, periodicals and other journals, along with distribution arrangements for updating material if appropriate.

The reference to knowledge management means that consideration needs to be given to the sharing of know-how, be it notes of research from within the firm, materials from courses attended, discussions at team or departmental meetings, counsels' opinions that might be of general interest within the practice, the accessibility of precedents and also, subject to data protection principles, client information as in a marketing database.

Example of major non-compliances

- There are no legal research or library facilities.

Example of minor non-compliances

- Arrangements for library and research facilities do exist but are not documented.
- Arrangements for library and research facilities do exist but fail to meet relevant needs, for example they do not cover certain areas of the practice, or are not fully up to date.

4.6 **Practices will maintain an office manual collating information on office practice, which must be available to all members of the practice. Practices will document their arrangements to:**

  a: Note each page with the date and/or issue.
  b: Review the manual at least annually.
  c: Update the manual and record the date of amendments.

5 PEOPLE MANAGEMENT

The observation is commonly made that legal service providers are 'people businesses'. It follows that compliance with section 5 on arrangements for the management of personnel will be important to any plan to improve performance within the practice.

Section 5 concentrates on the devices needed for effective management and control of staff. Certain provisions extend to partners in the case of private practice, particularly job descriptions and appraisals which previously extended to employed staff only.

Assessors are now more specifically required to examine the effectiveness of arrangements in relation to people management than was the case under previous versions of the Lexcel standard.

Key issues

- Responsibility for developing and maintaining an effective personnel policy for the firm, in particular:
    - Who is responsible for recruitment.
    - Who drafts any job descriptions or other such documentation and who is required to approve it.
    - Who conducts induction training.
    - What should go onto a personnel file for each person within the practice and who should have access to it, taking into account the rights of employees as data subjects.
    - Who co-ordinates performance appraisals.
    - Who is responsible for training and who controls the budget.
    - Who checks for compliance with annual CPD requirements.

5.1 **Practices will have a plan for the recruitment, development and welfare of their personnel, including:**

   a: **Likely recruitment needs, whether for the practice as a whole, its departments or offices, which may form part of the practice's overall business plan or departmental or other operational plans.**
   b: **Training and development.**
   c: **Welfare and entitlements.**

The requirement in 5.1 is that practices should set out in their strategic documentation their plans for the recruitment, development and treatment of partners, managers and staff.

For guidance on the formulation of a recruitment plan see the *Lexcel Office Procedures Manual*.

The standard recognises that practices will have different ways of addressing the planning required by this provision. Some practices may include personnel requirements as a heading or part of a general business plan; others may have a separate 'staff plan'; or it may fall to heads of department or team leaders to address their requirements in operational plans for which they are responsible.

The length and complexity of the plan or plans will be for each practice to determine. However, assessors will want to see sufficient evidence of the issues raised by this provision receiving adequate consideration. A sole practitioner or small practice may have no plans to recruit staff. Where such is the case, a record of the decision must be made in order to satisfy requirement 5.1a.

The plan(s) will be confidential to the practice and need not be disclosed to the assessor. Practices that decline to show the documentation to assessors will have to convince them by other means that the personnel plan does exist and covers the necessary areas for compliance.

Good communication is an essential ingredient of management. The responsibility to foster it lies with partners, supervisors and line managers. A practice which satisfies this requirement will have taken steps to develop team spirit and will achieve greater efficiency through regular communication involving all members of the practice. Briefing arrangements may be of a formal or informal nature, including, for example, staff meetings, intranet and e-mail. The assessor will examine how effectively these communication processes operate by interviewing a cross-section of staff. Communications processes should be two-way and the assessor should look for evidence of this.

Non-private practices will need to demonstrate that staff are kept informed of any issues within the wider corporate body that affect them directly as well as its overall policies.

Where a sole practitioner practises without any staff, requirement 5.1b only applies to the sole practitioner and 5.1c does not apply.

Examples of major non-compliances

- There is no plan (documented or otherwise) covering the areas required by this section.
- The plan has not been put into effect.

Examples of minor non-compliances

- There is a documented plan covering most of the issues addressed by this section but one or more elements is missing or dealt with inadequately.
- The practice has arrangements dealing with the requirements of this section but they are not documented.
- Some limited elements of the plan have not been implemented.

5.2 Practices will list the tasks to be undertaken by all personnel within the practice – including partners – and document the skills, knowledge and experience required for individuals to fulfil their role satisfactorily, usually in the form of a person specification and job description.

All personnel within the practice – including partners – will need to have a job description or other such documentation in place. This requirement applies equally to sole practitioners. The precise format of the job documentation will be at the discretion of the practice, but typically should recite the job title and then cover the jobholder's place in the organisation, reporting lines, the main purpose(s) of the role and a list of specific responsibilities.

It is good practice to review the job description regularly; many practices do so at each appraisal meeting.

An assessor may request to see the job description of any individual within the practice.

Example of major non-compliances

- There are no job descriptions/person specifications for personnel within the practice or a substantial number of them do not exist.

Examples of minor non-compliances

- There are job descriptions/person specifications for most personnel within the practice but there is a limited number of personnel who do not have such documentation in place.
- A number of job descriptions do not bear sufficient resemblance to the duties of the jobholder and are in clear need of amendment or redrafting.

5.3 Practices will have procedures to deal effectively with recruitment into the practice, including:

   a: The identification of vacancies.
   b: The drafting of consequential job documentation, usually in the form of a job description.
   c: Methods of attracting candidates and applicants.
   d: Selection methods used.
   e: Storage of interview notes.
   f: Provision of information by way of feedback to unsuccessful candidates.
   g: Any use of medical examination and/or references.
   h: Confirmation of job offers.
   i: Maintenance of communication during the pre-joining period and starting instructions.

Effective recruitment into the practice will clearly make a substantial contribution to the quality of service by the organisation. It is an increasing trend that recruitment and selection are open processes which are seen to be as objective and non-discriminatory as possible.

Practices should ensure that the responsibility for recruitment is documented; in many firms there are different arrangements for the recruitment and selection of professional staff, secretaries and trainees.

There is no requirement that firms should necessarily employ techniques such as psychometric testing in personnel selection, take up references or conduct medical tests, but if they do the arrangements will need to be documented.

Practices should always maintain records of interview notes, not least so that any later claim of unfairness in the process can be rebutted or defended. The Data Protection Employment Practices Code (part 1) provides that interview notes should not be kept for longer than a year.

Example of major non-compliances

- There are no procedures for recruitment and selection or they are clearly inadequate in some material regard, for example practising certificates and professional standing are not checked when recruiting solicitors.

Examples of minor non-compliances

- There are procedures covering most of the issues addressed by this section but one or more elements are missing or are dealt with inadequately.
- There is a limited number of instances when the procedures have not been observed.

5.4 Practices will conduct an appropriate induction process to cover:

    a: The practice's aims.
    b: Management structure and the individual's job responsibilities.
    c: Terms and conditions of employment, personal and banking details for personnel records.
    d: Initial and future training requirements.
    e: Key policies, including equality and diversity and client care and office procedures.

It is recognised that the full induction process may be staggered over a period of time and may consist of the provision of reading materials, face-to-face meetings or the use of interactive materials on the firm's intranet. There is no need for a documented procedure setting out how induction training is provided, but assessors will need to see sufficient evidence that the induction process does cover the areas listed and is in effective operation.

Practices will need to ensure that personal details are taken at an early stage of the jobholder's time with the practice. These would typically cover banking details, next-of-kin and any medical condition.

Example of major non-compliances

- There is no induction training process or there is evidence that it is not in effective operation.

Examples of minor non-compliances

- There is an induction training process but a limited number of people who should have received induction training have not done so.
- Induction training has occurred as required but did not cover relevant topics.

5.5 The induction process must occur within a reasonable period of time of taking up the role.

In many firms there may be an initial induction meeting to be followed by more substantive induction training at a later date. It is important, however, that the new joiner is brought up to speed with his or her role as soon as practicable. Undue delays in doing so will limit the new joiner's effectiveness for the practice and may cause anxiety for the person concerned.

Example of minor non-compliances

- There is an induction training process but a limited number of people who should have received induction training have not done so within a reasonable time frame.

5.6 Appropriate induction processes must apply when existing personnel transfer roles within the practice.

Assessors will not necessarily expect the same degree of induction training for those transferring roles within the firm. The practice should examine which areas of the new role will need explanation and training, and may rely on earlier training or experience for more familiar elements.

Example of major non-compliances

- There is no induction training process for people who transfer roles within the practice.

Example of minor non-compliances

- There is an induction training process but a limited number of people who have transferred roles within the previous 12 months have not received induction training.

5.7 Practices will operate a process for:

  a: An annual review at least of responsibilities, objectives and performance for all partners and staff members.
  b: Written appraisal records, which will be confidential to the jobholder and named persons under the practice's data protection policy and may be inspected as evidence of compliance only with the consent of the jobholder.
  c: An annual review at least of the training and development needs of all personnel within the practice, recorded in an individual training and development plan.

An effective appraisal scheme is core to the performance management programme of most organisations. This does not necessarily mean, however, that the same documentation should be in use for all personnel or that the process should be unduly bureaucratic. Partner schemes, in particular, may be subject to quite different arrangements from the staff scheme or schemes.

The requirement in this section for written records and documented procedures is to ensure that difficult issues are addressed and that there is a written record of the discussions and agreements emerging from the process.

In most practices the setting of objectives will coincide with the annual appraisal meeting, but it does not necessarily have to. It is commonplace for financial objectives emerging from the budget, for example, to be settled before the start of the financial year and then reviewed in the appraisal meeting or even at ongoing departmental or office meetings.

Sole practitioners will need to review and document their own responsibilities and objectives.

It is good practice to review the individual's job description in an appraisal meeting, but it is not essential to do so.

Practices need not use the term 'appraisal' at all as long as they have procedures that meet the specified requirements. Some use terms such as 'performance review' or 'development review'. There is no standard appraisal scheme, but for sample forms see the *Office Procedures Manual* which contains a range of possible paperwork for adoption by practices. The publication also includes further guidance on the conduct of appraisal interviews.

Appraisal records are sensitive and will need to be subject to controls under data protection compliance considerations. The practice should make clear who has access to records and for how long they are retained. Assessors may only examine appraisal records with the express consent of the jobholder in question.

It is common practice to review training needs for jobholders within the appraisal meeting, perhaps in conjunction with other training reviews throughout the year. The appraisal process can therefore generate a training plan, whether on an organisation-wide, or departmental level. Sole practitioners need to document their own individual training and development plans.

Examples of major non-compliances

- There is no process for the setting of objectives and responsibilities and/or performance appraisal.
- There are no substantive records of appraisal meetings.
- There is no process whereby training and development needs are reviewed and planned.
- The processes that are adopted by the practice are clearly and materially ineffective, for example, because they have not been implemented in relation to a significant number of partners or staff.

Example of minor non-compliances

- There are systems for all the elements required by this section but in a limited number of instances these have not been followed.

5.8 Practices will ensure that appropriate training is provided to personnel within the practice in accordance with its policy on training and development. Training may be arranged on an in-house or external basis and may be on-line or through more traditional means. Where appropriate the training should be recognised for CPD purposes under the scheme operated by the Law Society of England and Wales or other professional bodies.

Training will typically be heavily linked to the appraisal scheme.

Assessors will seek evidence that:

a: Training needs are being assessed in an appropriate manner.
b: Agreed training needs are being provided for.
c: The effectiveness of training activity is monitored, and that unmet needs are addressed.
d: Management and IT skills are being considered as well as technical and legal issues.
e: Appropriate training records are maintained.

Practices should bear in mind the need for compulsory CPD in relation to the Law Society and other professional regulatory bodies. A firm committed to quality will see more to training than mere CPD compliance, but it is always a consideration nonetheless. There are also a number of requirements for designated supervisors and caseworkers in the SQM and LSC contracts that practices will need to consider if they hold a contract for publicly funded work.

Examples of major non-compliances

- There is no discernible training process within the practice.
- The process adopted by the practice is clearly and materially ineffective, for example, because it has not been implemented in relation to a significant number of partners or staff.

Example of minor non-compliances

- There are training processes within the practice that are substantially effective but some element required by this section has not been adequately addressed.

6 SUPERVISION AND OPERATIONAL RISK MANAGEMENT

Recent changes in the indemnity insurance market for solicitors have led to much greater interest in the areas of supervision and risk management in private practice. Many firms will be concerned to reduce the incidence or risk of claims and complaints against the practice, thereby improving the profile of the firm in relation to insurance renewals.

For the purposes of this section, operational risk management is the control and reduction of prosecutions, claims and client complaints against the practice. Areas such as health and safety or occupiers' risks are not covered here: they are the domain of section 4 on facilities and information technology.

Effective supervision will be a concern wherever there is a commitment to delivering a quality service. The role of partners or senior managers is often seen as being increasingly one of supervision rather than simply fee-earning. For many firms the contribution by junior fee-earners will be key to profitability. This, in turn, requires more emphasis on supervision than has generally been the case in the past.

Assessors should be aware of Practice Rule 13, which is not directly part of the Lexcel standard, but which is important for a general understanding of the framework within which solicitors are required to operate. This provides that every office where the solicitor practises from needs to be 'properly supervised'. This now includes a requirement that anyone assuming the responsibility for supervising that office should be trained to do so as set out in the Rule unless they were already in place as the office supervisor as at 23 December 1999, in which case phasing-in arrangements still apply.

6.1 Practices will have a written description of their management structure which designates the responsibilities of individuals and their accountability. This will be updated within three months of any change.

The description of management structure may take many forms, from the simple list of responsibilities commonly found in the introductory sections to the office manual to an organisational chart showing the role of departments and administrators in the overall reporting structure. In-house departments are required to show how the legal department fits into the parent organisation and the main reporting structures within the department. The management structure in a sole practice may be very simple as there may be only one person who is responsible for everything. All the functions for which the sole practitioner is responsible need to be listed.

Example of major non-compliances

- There is no description of the management structure or it does not reflect the reality within the practice.

Example of minor non-compliances

- There is a written description of the management structure but it is defective or inadequate to a limited extent, e.g. various key roles are not identified.

6.2 There will be a named supervisor for each area of work undertaken by the practice. A supervisor may be responsible for more than one area of work. The supervisor must have appropriate experience of the work supervised and be competent to guide and assist others.

Practices are required to designate a named supervisor for each area of work that they undertake. In many cases it will not be apparent from the full list of services provided; it will be a matter of judgement in every case as to whether a limited supply of work is a distinct aspect of work in its own right or merely an incidental part of a larger area of the practice's work. One example would be that change of name deeds would usually be seen as being incidental to certain areas of practice and not a distinct area of specialisation.

There are two separate limbs to the competences that supervisors must show: technical experience and supervisory skills. In relation to the first of these there are no particular requirements in the Lexcel standard, for example, for supervisors to be members of a specialist panel if one exists for that area of work, or to maintain a minimum number of hours of work per annum on that specialisation. Likewise, there is no requirement that supervisors must be of a certain status such as partner or senior manager.

By contrast, assessors will seek evidence of appropriate experience and training. The standard of experience will vary between those who 'self-supervise' and those who are responsible for large departments within a practice, especially if staffed by more junior personnel. Where a sole practitioner does not have solicitor or other experienced lawyer colleagues, or there is only one solicitor practising in a particular area of law within a larger practice, he or she is self-supervising. In such circumstances, the solicitor will need to demonstrate how supervisory skills are applied to his or her own professional development (for example, in planning the work programme and analysis of training needs).

Supervisors might wish to consider preparing a brief profile of their experience and recent training in the event that the assessor wishes to explore this with them.

Examples of major non-compliances

- There is no supervisor for all or some of the areas of the practice's work.
- One or more of the supervisors does not have the necessary experience of the work supervised to be able to guide and assist others.
- There is objective evidence that one or more of the supervisors does not have sufficient skills or experience of supervision to be able to guide and assist others, e.g. interview evidence with personnel in that department or a pattern of non-compliances on files inspected which were not known about.

Example of minor non-compliances

- One or more areas of work within the practice do not have designated supervisors but there are personnel who do perform the function and their role is merely not noted.

6.3 **Practices will have processes to ensure that supervision of all staff, both legal and support staff, is effective. Issues which should receive consideration may include:**

a: Checks on incoming and outgoing post, including e-mails and faxes.
b: Departmental, team and office meetings and communication structures.
c: Reviews of matter print-outs in order to ensure good financial controls and the appropriate allocation of workloads.
d: The exercise of devolved powers in publicly funded work.

Assessors will seek evidence from interviews that any arrangements for supervision are adequate. Particular attention will be paid to the availability of supervisors in multi-office practices. In most cases there must be more to availability than the supervisor simply being contactable by phone, though this might be adequate where it is senior personnel only who are supervised.

The proper allocation of work is a significant tool for quality control. This may be evidenced by a partner's signature to a matter opening form in private practice. Many practices will benefit from reviewing how introductions are referred internally where normal controls can sometimes be bypassed. In high volume areas of the practice, fee-earners will often be authorised to accept or decline instructions. However, the nature and number of open files will often be subject to discussion at supervision meetings.

Examples of major non-compliances

- One or more supervisors could not be seen to have been sufficiently available to attend to the needs for supervision that exist.
- There is no observable process for the appropriate allocation of work in one or more areas of the practice.

Example of minor non-compliances

- There are adequate processes for the availability of the supervisor and for the allocation of work but there has been a limited number of instances where they have not been observed.

6.4 **Practices will have processes to ensure the effective supervision of legal work, to include:**

a: The availability of adequate supervision.
b: Appropriate procedures to allocate new work and reallocate existing work if necessary.

Section 6.4 should probably be seen as the acid test of supervision: is it effective in the way that it operates within the practice? Assessors will compile evidence of the effectiveness of supervision from interviews with those who are supervised and from files inspected.

Common supervisory tools include those in requirement 6.3, as well as 'one-to-one' review meetings at regular intervals.

With the exception of file reviews (see 6.6) it is not mandatory that any particular supervisory tool is in place. The onus is on the practice to show that it operates appropriate supervision in each area of the practice, given the seniority and experience of those working in that area, the complexity of the work undertaken and the past record of mistakes, claims and complaints. There will often be quite different arrangements for separate areas within the same firm.

Assessors will make enquiries as to the effectiveness of supervision particularly in multi-office practices.

Supervision of support staff should ensure that people have suitable equipment and back-up facilities (see also 4.1); workloads are monitored; systems of work are appropriate; staffing, training and development, health and welfare needs of staff are met; and that staff have the opportunity to receive feedback and raise any issues of concern to them.

Example of major non-compliances

- There are clear inadequacies in the arrangements for supervision in one or more areas of work within the practice.

Example of minor non-compliances

- Although largely adequate, there is a limited number of instances where supervision has been inadequate or ineffective.

6.5 Practices will have processes to ensure that all those doing legal work check their files regularly for inactivity to avoid client dissatisfaction and possible claims arising from delay.

It is important that files are checked regularly by those handling them to ensure that client dissatisfaction and possible claims arising from delay do not occur. This requirement is ancillary to independent file reviews since those are normally carried out by someone who has not had conduct of the matter. In addition, file reviews tend to be selective and will not therefore check whether all matters are being progressed in an appropriate manner. Typical arrangements will include a weekly to monthly trawl by the fee-earner of the contents of their filing cabinet and/or e-mail records or a check of an accounts department print-out of all matters per fee-earner, especially if it is a report that highlights time elapsed since time recorded on that matter.

Examples of major non-compliances

- There are no processes for checking for inactivity in one or more areas of the practice.
- There are processes for checking for inactivity but they are widely ignored by a significant number of persons within one or more of the practice areas and there is evidence of delay in progressing matters.

Examples of minor non-compliances

- There are processes for checking for inactivity but they are being ignored by a limited number of personnel in one or more areas of the practice.
- The documented processes are being generally complied with but are not effective in preventing delay arising from inactivity in a limited number of instances.

6.6 Practices will have procedures for regular, independent file reviews, of either the management of the file or its substantive legal content, or both. The number and frequency of such reviews will be documented. There is no requirement that designated supervisors should conduct all such reviews in person, but they will need to show that they control or monitor the process and that the process is effective.

In relation to file reviews, practices will have procedures to ensure that:

a: A record of the file review is kept on the matter file and centrally, whether for the practice or office as a whole or by team or department.
b: Any corrective action which is identified in a file review must be actioned within 28 days and verified by the reviewer.
c: There is a review at least annually of the data generated by file reviews which will contribute to the review of risk assessment data (section 6.7f).

The main requirement in section 6.6 is for regular independent file reviews. These reviews need not be undertaken by the designated supervisor in person although they often will be; where the supervisor does not undertake all reviews in person it will need to be apparent that they will occur under the supervisor's control. The supervisor may delegate some of the checking to a non-fee-earner where he or she has appropriate experience and training.

File review arrangements will need to extend to all personnel, including partners and senior managers. The frequency and depth of reviews may reflect the seniority and experience of the file handlers. In most practices more file reviews are required for those with limited experience – perhaps up to three years' post-admission experience in the case of solicitors.

Ideally, file reviews are undertaken by someone other than the person with conduct of the case. However, in sole practices and where there is only one fee-earner practising in a category of law, it may not be possible to identify anyone who could comment on legal issues. Where such is the case, a supervisor, fee-earner in another category, suitably trained manager or administrator may carry out the file review. If a sole practitioner is the only fee-earner, the process of case management and client care activity can be reviewed by a member of support staff. Another option is that file reviews could be outsourced, as where there are reciprocal arrangements with fellow local sole practitioners. It will be important to ensure that client confidentiality is controlled in such cases, however, and that no conflict of interest arises from the operation of such arrangements.

The review will generally embrace technical and procedural issues but may be limited to procedural review only. This will be most common in sole or very small practices where there is no prospect of another person within the practice having the necessary expertise to assess the technical content of the file.

It is common practice to employ pro forma sheets for file reviews: for an example see the *Office Procedures Manual*. They will also highlight corrective action that is needed and record when it has been closed out. Corrective action will usually be checked by the reviewer on the files actually reviewed, or fee-earners may confirm that it has been carried out, but in some cases the corrective action might be checked at a future file review. One example could be the systematic failure of a fee-earner to send out satisfactory Practice Rule 15 initial information: it may be more expedient to check that this problem has been addressed by looking at a batch of files opened after the corrective action has been requested.

File review data should be assessed and will need to be seen as risk assessment data for the annual risk review required by the following section.

Example of major non-compliances

- There are no adequate file review arrangements in one or more departments of the practice.

Example of minor non-compliances

- There are file review arrangements in the practice but there is some inadequacy in their operation in one or more areas of the practice, for example:
    - There are limited instances of file reviews not being conducted as required in the case of some fee-earners.
    - The file review records are missing or incomplete with some fee-earners.

6.7 For the purposes of this section, operational risk management is the control and reduction of prosecutions, claims and client complaints against the practice. Practices will ensure that procedures are in place to:

   a: Designate one overall risk manager for the practice with sufficient seniority, to be able to identify and deal with all risk issues which may arise.
   b: Establish appropriate reporting arrangements to ensure that risk issues are appreciated and addressed.
   c: Maintain lists of work that the practice will and will not undertake including any steps to be taken when work is declined on grounds that it falls outside acceptable risk levels. This information should be communicated to all staff and should be updated regularly.

- d: Maintain details of the generic risks and causes of claims associated with the area(s) of work that is/are undertaken by the practice. This information must be adequately communicated to all staff.
- e: Manage instructions which may be undertaken even though they have a higher risk profile than the norm for the practice including unusual supervisory and reporting requirements or contingency planning.
- f: Conduct at least an annual review of all risk assessment data generated within the practice, including claims records, an analysis of client complaints trends and data generated by file reviews. The practice should identify remedial action which should then be reviewed at management level in the practice.

This section addresses the need for clear management of operational risk in legal practice. It is based on the recommendations of the Turnbull report on the management of risk prepared by the Institute of Chartered Accountants for the Stock Exchange and now widely adopted in the business world at large.

The main requirement is that one designated person should have overall control of the risk exposure of the practice. This is not to say that that person needs to have all of the responsibility: in many firms different personnel will have the roles of handling complaints, claims and money laundering reporting, for example. In such instances the overall risk manager might be the managing or senior partner in private practice, or one of those with a particular responsibility. The overall risk manager should have sufficient seniority and influence within the practice to be able to ensure that risk matters are treated with the importance that they will usually deserve. In many firms these critical responsibilities are combined under the auspices of a compliance partner, sometimes the senior partner.

Assessors should appreciate that section 6.7 is likely to be of greater importance to private practice firms than to in-house practices. In many governmental or local authority practices the parent body will not have insurance in place and will, in effect, self-insure. Assessors should note that in-house practices may not be able to decline instructions (see also guidance in relation to 8.2). However, there may still be risks which may need to be managed, for example adopting an effective media strategy in potentially sensitive matters. Therefore, in the interests of providing a reliable and satisfactory service to clients, the requirements of this section must still be addressed.

There are a number of authoritative works on risk management. Copies of the Solicitors' Indemnity Fund Self Assessment Questionnaire can be purchased from the Law Society bookshop.

One familiar suggestion in risk management is that the organisation should be more selective in the work that it takes on. There should be evidence that consideration is always given to whether the practice has sufficient resources and expertise to meet the client's reasonable expectations. Work that is beyond the competence of the practice, where mistakes are more likely to happen, should be declined and, if possible, referred elsewhere.

Practices will need to compile and keep under review lists of the risks implicit in the work that they undertake. This should be based primarily on the experience of the practice.

Where work is accepted into the practice even though it has a higher risk profile than the norm there should be special procedures to ensure that particular care is taken with it. One example is a matter that might seem to be quite straightforward, but where the potential loss in the event of a negligence claim would be at the upper end of the firm's maximum liability cover and might even exceed it. These risks should be known about from the start and be carefully managed throughout.

It is important that the practice learns from its experience and continues to look to improve its profile where possible. There needs to be an annual documented review, therefore, of all risk assessment data. This will include:

- Complaints data.
- Information on claims and notifications to the practice's insurers.
- File review data.
- Client survey findings and any other information which might be helpful.

The format of this report is for each practice to determine for itself. It may be presented as an item at a regular strategic meeting or be independent from it. Steps should be taken to share the findings with all personnel within the practice.

Example of major non-compliances

- There are no processes in effective operation to manage risk associated with work accepted, declined or undertaken by the practice.

Examples of major non-compliances in relation to this section are more likely where there is a general failure of various of the requirements listed within the section or a number of failures within one or more of the departments.

Examples of minor non-compliances

- There is no overall risk manager in place but such an individual could readily be appointed.
- There are processes in effective operation which cover the requirements of this section but they are not documented or the documentation is defective.
- The practice has not listed the areas of work that it will undertake and decline in one or more of its practice areas.
- There are no lists of generic risks associated with an area or areas of the practice's work or they have not been reviewed in the last 12 months.
- There are no arrangements to manage work of an unusually high risk profile in one or more of the areas of work of the practice.
- No annual review of risk assessment data has been compiled in the last 12 months but it should be possible to compile this from the data available within 21 days.

6.8 **Operational risk needs to be considered in all matters before, during and after the processing of instructions. Before the matter is undertaken the adviser must:**

   a: **Consider if a new client and/or matter should be accepted by the practice, in accordance with section 8.2 below.**
   b: **Assess the risk profile of all new instructions and notify the risk manager in accordance with procedures under 6.7 of any unusual or high risk considerations in order that appropriate action may be taken.**

During the retainer the fee-earner must:

c: Consider any change to the risk profile of the matter from the client's point of view and report and advise on such circumstances without delay, informing the risk manager if appropriate.
d: Inform the client in all cases where an adverse costs order is made against the practice in relation to the matter in question.

At the end of the matter the fee-earner must:

e: Undertake a concluding risk assessment by considering if the client's objectives have been achieved and if the client could fairly complain or make a claim for damages in relation to the service provided.
f: Notify the risk manager of all such circumstances in accordance with documented procedures without delay.

The essence of section 6.8 is that risk needs to be considered before, during and after the work is performed for the client.

An initial risk assessment should be based on the instructions received. Special risk will then need to be referred to the risk manager via a procedure established for doing so. This could either be a risk notice or a section in the matter opening form highlighting 'high' or 'unusual' risk associated with the instructions or the client.

During the retainer the ongoing risk profile should be considered. If the risk to the client or the firm changes materially – e.g. third parties are joined onto litigation, materially adding to costs risks, or counsel's opinion is obtained casting doubt on advice already provided to the client – the client will need to be informed and consulted without delay. Adverse costs orders need to be reported immediately as they will usually have to be paid forthwith.

At the end of the matter the fee-earner should consider if the client could fairly claim or complain about the service provided. This is not as simple as looking at whether the transaction or litigation succeeded or not, but rather whether the client could feel that they were not as effectively represented as they might reasonably have expected. In such circumstances there will need to be a procedure for a report to be made to the risk manager. All such reports could be addressed initially to a departmental supervisor, such as the head of department.

Examples of major non-compliances

- Risk is routinely overlooked before, during or after the matter is undertaken in one or more of the areas of work undertaken by the practice, such that risk management procedures are not in effective operation.
- Reports of risk are made but are not being acted upon or assessed by the risk manager or someone to whom he or she delegates responsibility to do so.

Examples of minor non-compliances

- There are limited instances in one or more areas of the practice of risk not being considered before, during or after the matter is undertaken.
- Reports of risk have in some instances been overlooked or not acted upon.

7 CLIENT CARE

The importance of client care has received extensive coverage in recent years. For the individual practice the significance is readily apparent: in a competitive profession the quality of service to the client will bear heavily on whether to instruct that firm again on future occasions. For the profession more widely, the threat remains that if standards of client service are judged inadequate, the reputation of the profession may be adversely affected.

Assessors will not simply seek evidence of client care procedures being in place, but will also want to see evidence that there is a culture within the practice that recognises the importance of client care and seeks to improve service standards wherever possible. Practices should be truly client-centred: a token approach to client care systems will not be adequate. To make this a reality, top management will need to recognise its role in giving a clear lead on the standards of service delivery that will be expected.

Key issues

- The current approach to client service and where improvements could be made.
- Adoption of a client care policy.
- Extent of involvement of staff and/or clients in the development of a client care policy.
- Compliance with Practice Rule 15 and the Solicitors' Costs Information and Client Care Code.
- How precedent letters on costs information and client care issues could be improved.
- Whether current complaints procedure meets the guidelines established by the Office for the Supervision of Solicitors.
- Who should take responsibility for client surveys and when and how they should be carried out.

7.1 Practices will have a documented policy for client care, which will include:

a: The practice's commitment to provide services to clients in an appropriate manner.
b: Procedures to ensure compliance with Practice Rule 15 and its accompanying code in relation to client care and costs information.

The requirement for a client care policy is in line with recommendations from the Office for the Supervision of Solicitors. Its recommendations on the development and adoption of a client care policy can be found in 'Keeping clients', a client care guide for solicitors. This can be viewed on the Law Society website **www.clientcare.lawsociety.org.uk**. It will be for each practice to determine its approach to the style and format of documentation and, in particular, whether it forms part of a more general policy document or is produced separately. Given the extensive overlaps between related management concerns the client care policy might be styled as the 'risk management' or the 'quality' policy in many firms.

The sort of issues that should be addressed, whatever the description of the documentation, will include:

- Responsibility for client care.
- General approach of the firm.
- Actions that will be taken to test and improve client care.
- Specific procedures as required by the other provisions of this section.

Examples of major non-compliances

- The policy on client care is so defective that it is not in effective operation or it seriously fails to address a number of the relevant issues of client care in that practice.
- Interviews within the practice, perhaps in conjunction with other data, suggest that there is insufficient commitment to the policy by most personnel in the practice. It would be possible to record a major non-compliance against a department where there was evidence of a lack of commitment to client care by a majority of personnel within it.

Examples of minor non-compliances

- There are processes in effective operation which cover the requirements of this section but they are not documented or the documentation is defective.
- There is a documented policy on client care but it does not cover or deal adequately with some element that is relevant to the practice.
- Interviews within the practice, perhaps in conjunction with other data, suggest that there is insufficient commitment to the policy in some quarters.

7.2 **Practices will have processes to ensure that clients are informed in writing of the terms of business under which instructions are received and will be handled, including:**

   a: **The name and status of the fee-earner and the person(s) responsible for overall supervision.**
   b: **Whom the client should approach in the event of a problem with the service provided.**
   c: **The basis under which charges will be calculated including the best information possible on the likely overall costs of the matter.**

   The information required by this section should usually be provided in writing unless there are professional considerations that make this unsuitable in any particular matter.

   There must be a record of any standing terms of business with regular clients, such as many commercial clients. The practice must be able to produce such terms in relation to the issues covered by this section.

Practices are reminded of the risks of not informing clients of the status of the fee-earner handling their matter: see *Pilbrow* v. *Peerless de Rougemont* [1999] 3 All ER 355 where the Court of Appeal ruled that the provision of advice by a non-solicitor, where advice from a solicitor had been specifically requested, meant that no fees were recoverable by the firm for the work done for the client.

The obligation in the Lexcel standard in relation to initial information on complaints by clients is limited to the need to ensure that clients are aware of whom they should approach in the event of a problem with the service provided. This does not necessitate the full complaints procedure to be set out in initial correspondence. In many cases it would be inappropriate to do this, especially if the client is in some distress at the time of instructing the practice.

This requirement reflects the relevant provisions of the Solicitors' Costs Information and Client Care Code which, in turn, sets out how practices will comply with Practice Rule 15 where appropriate.

Assessors will take into account that 'employed solicitors' (i.e. in-house practices) are not obliged to follow rules 3–6 of the Code, which deal with the provision of initial and continuing costs information to clients, but should 'have regard' to these provisions (2e of the Code). A local authority that provides advice and services to other separate authorities may well be in much the same position as a private practice and would need to address these requirements.

In cases of apparent conflict between the Lexcel standard and the provisions of the Code the latter should take precedence. In particular, assessors are reminded of the provisions of 2b of the Code which provides that strict compliance with its requirements will not be required in every case, such as:

- repetitive work for a repeat client where the client has already been provided with the relevant information, although such clients will need to be informed of changes (e.g. changes to charge out rates that will apply to this work in future); or
- in all cases where compliance with the Code would be 'at the time insensitive or impractical'.

Commercial departments may well establish standing terms of business with their key, regular clients. The practice must be able to produce such terms in relation to the issues covered by this section. Situations where assessors may not expect the Code to be complied with immediately could include probate instructions where a recent death has occurred or complex instructions where some initial investigatory work will be needed in order to provide the client with helpful and reliable information. In such circumstances the Code envisages that 'relevant information should be given as soon as reasonably practicable' (2b:ii).

In most situations the provision of hourly rates without reference to the likely total time that may be incurred on the matter will not amount to the 'best information possible on the likely overall costs of the matter'. Hourly rates would not usually be quoted to clients where these do not form the basis on which fees will be calculated, such as in fixed fee work or domestic conveyancing work that will be charged on an estimate basis. Practices are referred to the provisions of rule 4c–e of the Code on what might amount to 'best information possible' and to:

4f–g: The basis of the firm's charges.
4h–i: Further information required.
4j: The client's ability to pay and the source of funding.

4k: Cost benefit and risk.
5: Additional costs information for private paying and publicly funded clients, including potential liability for third party costs.

Example of major non-compliances

- The practice fails in a significant number of instances to confirm any or all of the issues dealt with by this section where it would be appropriate to do so or it fails to do so in any practice area (e.g. one department consistently fails to do so).

Examples of minor non-compliances

- There are a limited number of instances where all or some of the issues dealt with by this section are not confirmed to clients where it would be appropriate to do so.
- There are arrangements to agree standing terms of business with regular clients but these are not sufficiently accessible to people within the firm needing to consult them.

It is envisaged that where a very limited number of files only do not comply with these requirements this would be noted as an area for improvement in the report.

7.3 Practices will operate a written complaints handling procedure that:

 a: Is made readily available and accessible to clients when it is apparent that they may wish to have recourse to it.
 b: Defines what the practice regards as a complaint and sets out how to identify and respond to complaints.
 c: Records and reports centrally all complaints received from clients.
 d: Identifies the cause of any problem of which the client has complained, offering any appropriate redress, and correcting any unsatisfactory procedures.

 Practices must conduct reviews at least annually of complaints data and trends, such review(s) forming part of the review of risk assessment under 6.7f above.

It is a requirement of the Solicitors' Costs Information and Client Care Code 1999 that:

> 'Every principal in private practice must ... have a written complaints procedure and ensure that complaints are handled in accordance with it; and ensure that the client is given a copy of the complaints procedure on request.' (7b)

A precedent complaints procedure can be obtained from the Practice Standards Unit by contacting tel: 01527 883264. The leaflet is called 'Handling complaints effectively'.

Practices will need to determine how they will define what a 'complaint' is. A wide definition of 'any expression of client dissatisfaction, however it is expressed' will result in more numerous instances of having to report to the practice's system. An unduly restrictive definition – e.g. that it has to be in writing – may not be regarded as adequate by the Office for the Supervision of Solicitors. Assessors should be satisfied that the approach adopted by the practice is appropriate for its client base.

Reports to the central system could be pro forma or by e-mail or another format. The complaints handler need not be the risk manager of the practice but often the roles will be undertaken by the same person. Where there are separate roles of complaints handler and risk manager it is a requirement that the reporting of one to the other should be clearly documented (see 6.7b).

It may be more difficult for sole practitioners to provide clients with an opportunity to express dissatisfaction to someone who is not actually involved with the matter if there is no other lawyer or senior member of staff. Where there is another senior member of staff he or she may respond to any complaint in relation to the principal. In some areas, and where there is no risk of conflicts of interest, sole practitioners act as complaints officers for each other's firms. In addition, some local Law Societies operate an independent informal mediation service between their members and clients.

The annual review of complaints data may form part of a review of the business plan. Whatever approach is adopted for the review it will be necessary for the practice to show that the report has received proper attention from senior management.

Examples of major non-compliances

- The complaints handling process is seriously deficient in some major regard so that it cannot be said to be in effective operation.
- The records of complaints are so badly or inadequately maintained that the complaints handling system cannot be said to be in effective operation.
- There is widespread ignorance of the practice's approach and procedures on complaints handling amongst people within the practice.

Examples of minor non-compliances

- There is a complaints handling process which is in effective operation but it is not documented or the written complaints handling procedure is deficient in some way, e.g. it fails to define what the practice regards as a 'complaint'.
- There has been no annual review of complaints data outside the 12 months stipulated.

7.4 Practices must conduct an annual review to check that the practice's commitment to provide quality services is being met in the perception of clients.

Some form of client survey to test satisfaction with the services provided must have occurred within the 12 months preceding the assessment or annual maintenance visit. This need not be continuous nor need it involve all parts of the practice. There must, however, be adequate data on which the practice can assess the effectiveness of the delivery of its services.

The practice should specify how and when clients will be requested to provide feedback and the methodology it will use to analyse it. The findings and outcome should be documented. Any client feedback data could be added to the review of risk assessment data under 6.7 and the review of the quality system under 1.6.

Example of major non-compliances

- There has been no client survey conducted over the 12 months preceding the assessment or the annual maintenance visit. In any such instances some form of survey will need to be collected, and considered by senior management, before the non-compliance can be closed out.
- The information collected in the 12 months preceding the client survey or the annual maintenance visit, having regard also to evidence collected in previous years, is not adequate for the firm to assess how well it is delivering its services.

Examples of minor non-compliances

- The client survey data has not received appropriate attention from top management.

8 FILE AND CASE MANAGEMENT

The final section of the Lexcel standard may prove to be the most time-consuming to implement. The practice will need to review how its legal files are organised and set down clear standards that must be adhered to. Those fee-earners who are most set in their ways may struggle to comply with any new requirements, but the improvement of file standards may well be the single greatest benefit to come from a Lexcel programme. This section is best viewed as tracking the life of a file from start to finish: from first enquiry to eventual archiving.

Key issues

- Handling of client enquiries.
- Acceptance of new clients and new matters from existing clients.
- Arrangements for conflicts of interest.
- How instructions are taken, recorded on file and confirmed.
- Planning the progress of a matter.
- Ensuring that matters are progressed in an appropriate manner.
- The giving, monitoring and discharge on undertakings.
- Traceability of files, papers, deeds and other documents – also items that come into the firm's possession or control.
- How counsel and other experts are chosen, instructed, evaluated and paid.
- File closing and archiving.

8.1 Practices will document how client enquiries in relation to possible instructions are handled, with particular regard to:

a: The treatment of telephone enquiries.
b: Clients who enquire in person in the reception area, including confidentiality.
c: Enquiries by correspondence and e-mail.

There will be very different considerations for practices in relation to initial enquiries. A firm that attracts work from callers off the street will probably need more elaborate arrangements than the in-house department where work is transferred by e-mails from colleague departments.

Many firms let themselves down at the first enquiry stage by having no clear arrangements for handling enquiries about possible instructions. It is all the more important to plan how enquiries will be handled in areas such as domestic conveyancing where telephone quotations are an important source of work for most firms.

Similar considerations apply to clients who enquire in person in the reception areas. When seeking information about the potential client's enquiry, it is nevertheless important to ensure that confidentiality is respected (see also 8.9c). Sadly, all practices open to public access should consider staff safety and how threatening or abusive behaviour should be dealt with.

In relation to enquiries by correspondence or e-mail, practices might establish a minimum response time, in which case this will be taken into account by assessors. There might also be a general enquiries file that all such messages are stored in. Many conveyancing departments keep notes of all enquiries in order to monitor success rates from quotations provided.

Example of major non-compliances

- There are documented arrangements for handling initial enquiries but they are not in effective operation or the arrangements do not reflect actual practice within the firm to a significant extent.

Examples of minor non-compliances

- There are arrangements for handing initial enquiries which are in effective operation but they are not documented.
- There are documented arrangements for handling initial enquiries but they do not reflect actual practice within the firm to a limited extent.
- The documented arrangements are defective in some regard, e.g. there are no documented arrangements for telephone enquiries or clients who call in person or enquiries by correspondence or e-mail.

8.2 Practices will document how decisions will be made whether to accept new instructions from existing clients or instructions from clients who have not instructed the practice before.

In most firms greater attention will be paid to the acceptance of new clients than new instructions from existing clients. Where there is any policy of declining work, for example in relation to the financial viability of the work or past experience with that client, this must be documented. Practices may not decline to act for reasons that would amount to a breach of policies of the Law Society in relation to anti-discrimination or equal opportunities.

Assessors should be aware that there is no 'cab-rank' principle in relation to work accepted by solicitors in private practice.

Assessors will accept that in-house practices may not be able to decline instructions. Where acceptance of instructions may cause difficulty (see also requirement 6.7), they should have systems to draw such issues to the attention of senior decision-makers within the umbrella body. However, where in-house practices act for legally separate entities, they must comply with the Employed Solicitors Code and procedures for dealing with such clients should reflect those of private practices.

The reasons why a practice might decline work should be set out in the office manual and could include:

- Work is not of a specialisation that the firm undertakes.
- Work would not be sufficiently profitable or meet firm's strategy.
- Work could be of a type that the firm does not wish to be associated with (e.g. pornography).

- Conflict of interest, professional or commercial.
- Past record of unsatisfactory experience with this client.
- An individual or department is operating at capacity.

Practices will need to consider who can decide if and when work should be declined, whether from existing or new clients, and document if and how this will be relayed to the potential or existing client. It should be noted that *The Guide to the Professional Conduct of Solicitors 1999* provides that a firm should not accept work where a solicitor has insufficient time, experience or skills to deal with instructions. The 1999 edition of the *Guide* provides at page 245 under the chapter on 'Retainer' that 'a solicitor must not act, or continue to act, where the client cannot be represented with competence and diligence'.

Example of major non-compliances

- There are documented arrangements for evaluating whether to accept instructions from new or existing clients but the arrangements are not in effective operation or they do not reflect actual practice within the firm to a significant extent.

Examples of minor non-compliances

- There are documented arrangements for evaluating whether to accept instructions from new or existing clients but they are defective in some way, e.g. it is the practice's policy to accept instructions in respect of intellectual property matters but this is not documented.
- There are documented arrangements for evaluating whether to accept instructions from new or existing clients but these have not been followed to a limited extent, e.g. it is the practice's policy that accepting a certain type of matter must be authorised by a partner and this has not been followed in one particular case.

8.3 Practices will document their arrangements to ensure that conflicts of interest are identified and acted upon in an appropriate manner. Although this is a particular consideration when receiving instructions it may also be an issue later in the matter, as when third parties are subsequently joined in proceedings.

A conflict of interest would prohibit a practice from acting for a given client. Where two established clients wish to deal with or claim against each other it is likely that the firm will not be able to act for either. The limited circumstances where a conveyancing department could act for seller and purchaser are provided for in Practice Rule 6 and its accompanying guidance in *The Guide to the Professional Conduct of Solicitors 1999*.

In some departments conflicts of interest will not arise or will be very unlikely, e.g. the practice offers a service in immigration law and would never act for the Home Office. It follows that very different procedures might be in place for different departments within the same firm. Conflicts of interest are remote in in-house legal practices since the department will, in effect, represent one client only.

Although conflict most obviously arises as an issue at the outset of a matter it could develop at any stage and fee-earners need to be alert to the dangers of conflicts developing once work has started on the matter.

Practices may choose to extend arrangements on conflicts of interest to include commercial considerations. This is most likely with larger commercial practices where a particular client may seek an exclusivity agreement (that the firm will not represent other businesses in that sector).

Examples of major non-compliances

- The documented procedures are used so inconsistently that they are not in effective operation in one or more departments within the practice.
- There is little or no evidence that conflict of interest procedures have been followed and therefore the practice cannot demonstrate that they are in effective operation.

Examples of minor non-compliances

- Procedures for considering conflicts of evidence are in effective operation but they are not documented.
- There is a limited number of instances of fee-earners who are not giving due consideration to conflicts of interest.
- There is a limited number of instances of fee-earners who are not following the documented procedures for conflict checking.

8.4 At the outset of the matter the fee-earner will establish:

a: As full an understanding as possible of the client's requirements and objectives (where incomplete this must be supplemented subsequently).
b: A clear explanation of the issues raised and the advice given.
c: What the fee-earner will do and in what timescale.
d: Whether the fee-earner is the appropriate person to deal with the matter or whether it should be referred to a colleague.
e: Method of funding, including the availability or suitability of insurance, trade union benefits, conditional or contingency fee arrangements or costs insurance products.
f: Whether the intended action would be merited on a cost benefit analysis and whether, in public funding cases, the guidance in the funding code would be satisfied.

The issues covered in a–f above must be confirmed to the client, ordinarily in writing, unless it would be appropriate not to do so under the Solicitors' Costs Information and Client Care Code. In all cases a note of these issues must appear on the matter file.

The importance of a clear start to the matter file should be readily apparent. Likewise, a clear note at the start of the matter file setting out all pertinent details and the instructions received should always be a priority. The fee-earner must note not only the instructions but also the client's objectives. All too often there is no clear note of the first meeting or conversation. Confusion, errors and embarrassment can result from this.

If a contemporaneous letter or e-mail to the client confirms all issues that would have been covered in the first meeting or communication it could be accepted as an adequate note of the meeting. The date and time of any meeting must be referred to, however, and this is best achieved through an attendance note. The availability of computer time records might also be taken into account.

It will not always be possible to confirm all details with confidence at the outset (e.g. timescale) in which case the advice might be outline and confirmed as soon as it becomes clearer.

In relation to 8.4d, a document confirming the name and status of the person who has conduct of the matter (see 7.2a) is acceptable evidence that the issue of suitability has been considered.

Some practices may operate general files in relation to some instructions. For example, in-house practices may have general files in which they record enquiries from instructing departments. Where such is the case, assessors will expect to see criteria which set out when a matter specific file should be opened. Similarly, in private practice, telephone only duty solicitor attendances in crime are usually filed together by date rather than by opening an individual matter file.

In private practice, rule 4j of the Costs Information and Client Care Code provides that, 'the solicitor should discuss with the client how when and by whom any costs are to be met'. This rule goes on to place an obligation on the fee-earner to consider the various methods of funding that could be available to the client, including those mentioned in 8.4e. It is important that solicitors cover these matters and note them on file in order to minimise the risks of a 'lost opportunity claim' in which the client later asks why the possibility of relying on existing legal expenses insurance or other source of funding was not raised earlier. It is good practice to confirm the client's instructions on the availability of insurance, trade union benefits, etc. in a letter to the client.

In publicly funded (legal aid certificate) matters the funding code provides a two-stage test. First, the practitioner must assess the prospects of success, ranging from 'very good' (above 80%) to 'unclear' (where representation will be refused). If prospects are borderline, a Representation Certificate will be refused unless there is a significant wider public interest (i.e. the case will benefit a group of individuals wider than the client) or the case is of overwhelming interest to the client (i.e. it is about life, liberty, or the roof over his/her head).

If the case can be quantified, the cost benefit must then be determined in relation to the prospects of success. For example, if prospects are very good, likely damages must exceed likely costs, whereas if prospects are moderate, likely damages must exceed likely costs by a ratio of 4:1. In unquantifiable cases, such as claims other than for damages, having regard to all the circumstances, the likely benefits must justify the likely costs such that a reasonable private paying client would be prepared to bring or defend the case. In 'public interest' cases, having regard to all the circumstances, including the prospects of success, the likely benefits to the client and others must justify the likely costs.

In all matters in private practice it is important that the fee-earner considers whether the likely outcome will justify the likely expenditure by the client (see rule 4k of the Costs Information and Client Care Code). Although this rule does not apply to in-house lawyers consideration should always be given even by the non-private practice adviser as to whether a court might make a costs order to reflect its disapproval of the use of the court's time on the matter in question.

In-house practices may comply with the requirements of this section by way of a document which is distributed to client departments. Such a document may also cover other procedures, e.g. charges (see 7.2c and 8.5), complaints (see 7.2b), document and deed storage arrangements (see 8.9b and 8.11d). Any exceptions to this overall agreement must be confirmed in writing to the client department.

Examples of major non-compliances

- The documented procedures required by 8.4a–f are used so inconsistently that they are not in effective operation in one or more departments within the practice.
- There is little or no evidence that the procedures have been followed and therefore the practice cannot demonstrate that they are in effective operation.

Examples of minor non-compliances

- There are procedures for all the requirements of this section which are in effective operation but they are not documented.
- There are documented procedures for all the requirements of the section but one or more elements of them is/are not being followed in a limited number of instances or by a limited number of fee-earners.

8.5 Practices will ensure compliance with the requirements of the Solicitors' Costs Information and Client Care Code in relation to initial costs information and, in particular, the provision of the 'best information possible on the likely overall costs of the matter, including a breakdown between fees, VAT and disbursements' (4a). Where there are special circumstances making the provision of this information inappropriate the special considerations must be noted on the matter file. In relation to standing agreed terms with regular clients see section 7.2.

This section should be read in conjunction with section 7.2. It stresses the need for full costs information at the outset of a matter save where exempt under section 2 of the Code, such as where repetitive work is done for a repeat client who has already been provided with the required information.

In some cases it may not be possible to give an estimate of total costs at the outset, for example in a medical negligence matter where an expert's report may be required to establish that the client has a cause of action. In such cases, an estimate of the cost of initial steps should be provided.

Where time forms the basis on which costs will be calculated, practices may provide information about hourly rates and the likely number of hours to be taken or may provide an estimate as a range of costs, e.g. between £500 and £1,000. In such matters, giving clients a list of hourly rates without providing a calculation of likely costs is unlikely to be acceptable.

Examples of major non-compliances

- There are no arrangements for the confirmation of initial costs information in one or more departments of the practice.
- The documented procedures are used so inconsistently that they are not in effective operation in one or more departments within the practice.

Examples of minor non-compliances

- There are arrangements for the confirmation of initial costs information which are in effective operation but they are not documented or the documentation is defective.
- There are arrangements for the confirmation of initial costs information but there are a limited number of files or fee-earners who are not complying with all or some of the requirements.

8.6 **Practices will ensure that the strategy for the matter is always apparent on the matter file and that in complex cases a separate case plan is developed. Save in exceptional cases the client must be consulted upon and kept informed of the strategy in the matter and any planned changes to it.**

All matters must have a clear strategy. In most cases this will be apparent and will need only a letter to the client confirming what the practice proposes to do. In other, more complex, matters a separate case plan is required. In publicly funded (legal aid) matters, any case requiring an individual high cost case contract (whether civil or criminal) must have a separate case plan.

Examples of situations where assessors would not expect clients to have been consulted on changes to the case plan or strategy could include cases where the firm acts for a minor or in certain mental health cases. However, where a litigation friend or guardian has been appointed to act on someone's behalf, an assessor will expect him or her to be consulted and informed.

It is important the client is kept abreast of proposals on the strategy for the matter and, save in exceptional matters (for example, those involving minors where someone is acting on their behalf), is in agreement with it.

Examples of major non-compliances

- There are no observable processes setting out the strategy for matters in one or more departments of the practice.
- There are numerous instances of there being no strategy on matters.
- There are numerous instances of the client not being informed or consulted on the strategy where they could reasonably expect to be so involved.

Examples of minor non-compliances

- There is a limited number of files where no strategy is apparent.
- There is a limited number of files where the client has not been consulted on and/or informed of the strategy and/or changes to it.

8.7 Practices will have documented procedures to ensure that matters are progressed in an appropriate manner. In particular:

   a: Key information must be recorded on the file.
   b: Key dates must be recorded on the file and in a back-up system.
   c: A timely response is made to telephone calls and correspondence from the client and others.
   d: Information on cost is provided at least every six months and, in publicly funded matters, the effect of the statutory charge, if any, is provided to the client in accordance with the Solicitors' Costs Information and Client Care Code.
   e: Clients are informed in writing if the person with conduct of their matter changes, or there is a change of person to whom any problem with service should be addressed.

Section 8.7 requires practices to ensure that matters are progressed effectively. All too often matters 'drift' when the initial work has been done. Delay remains one of the principal causes of complaint to the OSS.

Whether 'key information' is shown on the file will depend on any particular arrangements in place for the practice. It has become increasingly common to have a file summary sheet, which could be combined with a progress check in various areas of work, but this would probably be too basic for very substantial files running to numerous lever arch files. On the other hand, a very straightforward matter with few documents, attendance notes or correspondence, may not need a schedule or file summary sheet. The standard for this section is that the file (with any accompanying data records which form part of the practice's filing system) should tell the story of what is going on in that matter. Very often this will be achieved through systematic noting of all actions and conversations in relation to that matter by way of attendance notes.

Key dates should be seen as any date, which, if missed, could give rise to a claim against or a loss by the practice. There are key dates in all areas of legal work: it is for every practice to determine its list of relevant key dates. All key dates must be noted on the file (which could include data records where these form part of the filing arrangements in question). They will often be highlighted in any file summary sheet, but do not necessarily need to be so. However, where they are not, they must still be readily apparent to anyone reading the file or accessing the data record.

The back-up system for key dates is increasingly likely to be a computer-based system, but the fee-earner's personal diary may be accepted if it does not leave the practice's premises. Where a hard copy diary is used for this purpose a departmental or team diary would generally be seen as being preferable.

In assessing whether sufficient information has been given on the progress of matters and a timely response has been made to telephone calls or correspondence the assessor will take into account any instructions or preferences that the client has expressed in this regard (8.7c–e). Where a firm stipulates response times (e.g. all telephone calls from clients to be returned within 24 hours) they will be assessed on this basis.

The requirement to provide a costs update every six months reflects rule 6a of the Costs Information and Client Care Code. It should be remembered that there is no need to provide a routine costs update every six months if the client has agreed otherwise. This agreement could be implied in work that has an annual cycle, e.g. annual trusts and investment work. Section 8.7 gives effect to sections 6c–d in the Costs Information and Client Care Code.

Checking for inactivity could take various forms including a weekly or monthly trawl through the filing cabinet or a print-out review by the fee-earner or his/her supervisor, especially if this highlights time lapsed since time was last recorded to that matter.

If a solicitor practises as the only fee-earner, it is not necessary to have a documented procedure to inform clients about any change in the person with conduct of the matter.

Examples of major non-compliances

- There are no processes covering the majority of requirements of the section in relation to progressing matters.
- The documented procedures are used so inconsistently that they are not in effective operation in one or more departments within the practice.

Examples of minor non-compliances

- There are processes covering the requirements of the section in relation to progressing matters which are in effective operation but they are not documented or the documentation is defective in some respect.
- There are documented procedures for all the requirements of the section but one or more elements of them are not being followed in a limited number of instances or by a limited number of fee-earners.

8.8 Practices will document procedures for the giving, monitoring and discharge of undertakings.

An undertaking is defined in *The Guide to the Professional Conduct of Solicitors 1999* as 'any unequivocal declaration of intention addressed to someone who reasonably places reliance on it and is made by: (a) a solicitor or a member of a solicitor's staff in the course of practice; or (b) a solicitor as "solicitor", but not in the course of practice'. Failure to honour an undertaking is described in the *Guide* as being, prima facie, professional misconduct which could be dealt with at a disciplinary tribunal and enforceable by the courts through their inherent jurisdiction.

It should be noted that:

- An undertaking need not be described as such.
- In private practice an undertaking will be binding on the partners even if they did not know of or sanction it.

- In certain circumstances liability could arise from an undertaking given in the solicitor's private life.

Given the potential liability that could be suffered, practices will wish to consider when and how undertakings should be provided. Common arrangements will be to distinguish routine and non-routine undertakings and apply different safeguards to them. Conveyancing departments are likely to specify who can provide routine undertakings on exchange and completion of contracts. Consideration should be given to the procedure for authorising undertakings required by a court as practicalities may require special arrangements.

There is no requirement for a central register of undertakings though some practices find this helpful. Many practices check that any undertaking has been discharged as part of their file closure procedures (see also 8.11).

Examples of major non-compliances

- There are no processes for the giving, monitoring and discharge of undertakings.
- The documented procedures are applied so inconsistently that they are not in effective operation in one or more departments within the practice.

Examples of minor non-compliances

- There are processes in effective operation which cover the requirements of this section but they are not documented or the documentation is defective.
- There are documented procedures for all the requirements of the section but one or more elements of them are not being followed in a limited number of instances or by a limited number of fee-earners.

8.9 Practices will have a documented procedure to:

   a: List open and closed matters, identify all matters for a single client and linked files where relevant and all files for particular funders.
   b: Ensure that they are able to identify and trace any documents, files, deeds, wills or any other items relating to a matter.
   c: Safeguard the confidentiality of matter files and all other client information.
   d: Ensure that the status of the matter and the action taken can be easily checked by other members of the practice.
   e: Ensure that documents are stored on the matter file(s) in an orderly way.

Most practices will be able to identify the funders of matters (e.g. the Legal Services Commission, named trade unions or legal expense insurers) through a computer coding system.

Conveyancing departments should be able to link sale and purchase files for the same client in linked transactions.

As a general rule all papers relating to a matter should be capable of being traced by being on the file. When a file is contained in a number of folders/lever arch files, there should be some method by which they can be shown to belong to the same matter. This could be by use of the client/matter reference number and an indication on each part, e.g. 1 of 2; 2 of 2, etc. or 'correspondence from 01.01.03 – 09.09.03' or by listing on a schedule, kept in a prominent part of the file. Where there are ancillary papers or other records (e.g. X-rays or medical records in clinical negligence work) they should be linked to the file in question by tagging or use of the client/matter numbering system.

Consideration should be given to all the circumstances where safeguarding the confidentiality of the client could be at risk (e.g. files being worked on during a train journey, files left in unattended cars, etc.). Where clients are seen in the reception area there should be arrangements for consultations, even if very short, to be conducted out of earshot of other clients or visitors in the reception area.

The state of matter files is important under this section. Showing key information on a file summary sheet or colour coding of notes of meetings, reviews or letters to the client are helpful options. Where computer case management systems are used, the assessor will need to check the procedures for naming and storing documents and for taking regular back-ups.

Assessors will judge the tidiness of files under 8.9e. In order to comply with this requirement, attendance notes need to be filed in date order and papers need to be secured within the file. Attendance notes in cardboard folders should be secured on 'treasury tags' or other fastenings. More substantial documents may be placed together in file pockets, plastic wallets or similar.

Examples of major non-compliances

- There are no processes for one or more of the requirements of the section in relation to file status.
- The documented procedures are used so inconsistently that they are not in effective operation in one or more departments within the practice.

Examples of minor non-compliances

- There are processes in effective operation which cover the requirements of this section but they are not documented or the documentation is defective.
- There are documented procedures for all the requirements of the section but one or more elements of them are not being followed in a limited number of instances or by a limited number of fee-earners.

8.10 Practices will have a documented procedure for using barristers, expert witnesses and other external advisers who are involved in the delivery of legal services, which will include provision for the following:

   a: Use of clear selection criteria, which do not discriminate on grounds of race, colour, ethnic or national origins, sex, creed, disability, sexual orientation or age.
   b: Where appropriate, consultation with the client in relation to selection, and proper advice to the client on choice of advocate or other professional.

- c: **Clients to be advised of the name and status of the person being instructed, how long she/he might take to respond, and where disbursements are to be paid by the client, the cost involved.**
- d: **Maintenance of records (centrally, by department or office) on barristers and experts used, including evidence of assessment against the criteria.**
- e: **Evaluation of performance, for the information of other members of the practice.**
- f: **Giving of instructions which clearly describe what is required and which, in litigation matters, comply with the rules of court and any court orders.**
- g: **Checking of opinions and reports received to ensure they adequately provide the information sought (and, in litigation matters, comply with the rules of court and any court orders).**
- h: **Payment of fees.**

Where outsiders to the practice are involved in the service provided, checks should be in place to ensure that the practice's commitment to quality is still assured.

It is necessary for the practice to maintain lists of counsel and other experts used. This may be one list for the practice as a whole or it could be devolved to the departments or teams within the practice to maintain their own lists.

Lists are never closed: it should always be possible to add newcomers. The list will be a useful first point of contact; where counsel or an expert are used for the first time, checks should be made as to their suitability, and a note made on file of why they have been instructed. When appropriate, consideration should be given as to whether to include that provider on the approved list.

Many practices might be interested to maintain a non-approved list. The combination of the rights of the data subject and the law of defamation mean that this should be very carefully controlled. However, such a list can avoid counsel or an expert being instructed subsequently, when he or she has already failed to meet the practice's quality standards.

There will need to be procedures for how instructions are provided and checked. The client's consent to the instruction of an outsider would usually be needed, not least so that they can express any preference and understand the implications for the fees that they will or may have to pay.

Procedures for paying fees are likely to differ depending on the way cases are funded.

Examples of major non-compliances

- There are no processes for the requirements of the section in relation to the use of counsel and experts.
- The documented procedures are used so inconsistently that they are not in effective operation in one or more departments within the practice.

Examples of minor non-compliances

- There are processes in effective operation which cover the requirements of this section but they are not documented or the documentation is defective.

- There are documented procedures for all the requirements of the section but one or more elements of them are not being followed in a limited number of instances or by a limited number of fee-earners.

8.11 Practices will have documented procedures to ensure that, at the end of the matter, the practice:

a: Reports to the client on the outcome and explains any further action that the client is required to take in the matter and what (if anything) the practice will do.
b: Accounts to the client for any outstanding money.
c: Returns to the client any original documents or other property belonging to the client if required (save for items which are by agreement to be stored by the practice).
d: If appropriate, advises the client about arrangements for storage and retrieval of papers and other items retained (in so far as this has not already been dealt with, for example in terms of business) and any charges to be made in this regard.
e: Advises the client whether they should review the matter in future and, if so, when and why.
f: Archives or destroys files in an appropriate manner.

It is essential that matters are closed effectively. In most firms a reminder and checklist is provided for the issues covered in this section either on the file summary sheet (see the *Office Procedures Manual*) or in an archiving instruction sheet.

Those with conduct of cases should also remember to conduct a final risk assessment to consider if there are circumstances that should be reported to the practice's risk manager. If a sole principal is the person responsible for risk management, a note of any such circumstances should still be made in relation to his or her own files as this information contributes to the annual review of risk (see also 6.7f). In private practice noting issues of concern at the end of a matter might necessitate a report to the firm's insurers.

The Law Society does not advise on any particular period for the retention of files before they are destroyed but practices should note that the Money Laundering Regulations 2003 require certain records to be kept for at least 5 years. The Legal Services Commission stipulates as a term of its criminal and civil contracts that files must be retained for six years after closure.

Examples of major non-compliances

- There are no processes for the requirements of the section in relation to file closure and archiving.
- The documented procedures are used so inconsistently that they are not in effective operation in one or more departments within the practice.

Examples of minor non-compliances

- There are processes in effective operation which cover the requirements of this section but they are not documented or the documentation is defective.

- There are documented procedures for all the requirements of the section but one or more elements of them are not being followed in a limited number of instances or by a limited number of fee-earners.

Appendix

Summary of substantive changes in Lexcel 2004 version

2004 Lexcel		2000 Lexcel
Structures and Policies	1	–
Constitutional framework	1.1	–
Business framework considered and reviewed	1.2	–
Risk management strategy or framework	1.3	–
Written quality policy	1.4	–
Management responsibility for quality	1.5	–
Review of operation of quality system	1.6	–
Non-discrimination policy	1.7	B.2
Equal opportunities and diversity	1.8	D.8
Money laundering compliance	1.9	–
Mortgage fraud prevention	1.10	–
Data protection compliance	1.11	–
Health and safety policy	1.12	E.1
Strategy, the Provision of Services and Marketing	2	
Marketing and business plan(s)	2.1	B.1a, B.1c
Service plan	2.2	B.1b
Review of plans above	2.3	B.1d

2004 Lexcel		2000 Lexcel	
Financial Management	3		
Responsibility for financial procedures	3.1	C.1	
Financial processes	3.2	C.2	Need for documented procedures removed: processes now acceptable
Annual budget	a		
Variance analysis of budgets	b		
Profit and loss accounts	c		
Balance sheet	d		
Cashflow/funds forecast	e		
Variance analysis of cash/ funds flow	f		
Time recording	3.3	C.3	Need for documented procedures removed: processes now acceptable
Facilities and IT	4	E	
Use of premises and equipment	4.1a		
Photocopying	b		
Clients visiting offices	c		
Staff facilities	d		
Mail, fax and communication	e		
Finance procedures	f		
Document review of health and safety	4.2	E.1b, E.1c	
Business continuity plan	4.3		
Information technology plan	4.4		Formed an element of B.1a
Purchasing, etc.	a		
Current and planned applications	b		
Data protection compliance	c		
Compliance	d		
User safety	e		
E-mail use and storage	f		
Computer data and system back-up	g		Formed an element of E.1a

2004 Lexcel		2000 Lexcel	
Legal research and library; updating of information	4.5	E.3	
Office manual	4.6	E.2	
People Management	5		
Recruitment and development plan	5.1		Recruitment and development plan was an optional element under D.1.1
Recruitment needs	a		
Training and development	b		Training and development planning was a requirement of D.5
Welfare and entitlements	c		
Job documentation	5.2	D.1	Now extends to partners also
Recruitment	5.3	D.2	Required documented arrangements or recruitment areas to be covered now more specific
Verification of vacancies	a		
Drafting of job documentation	b		
Methods of attracting candidates	c		
Selection methods	d		
Storage of interview notes	e		
Information to unsuccessful candidates	f		
Other information sources	g		
Confirmation of job offer	h		
Maintenance of communication pre-joining	i		
Induction process	5.4	D.3	Required documented arrangements process now acceptable. Contents of induction made more specific
Practice aims	a		
Management structure and individual's responsibilities	b		
Terms and conditions; personal details	c		
Initial and future training	d		

APPENDIX

2004 Lexcel		2000 Lexcel	
Key policies	e		
Induction process to be held in reasonable time of taking role	5.5		
Induction on changing roles internally	5.6		
Process for annual review of responsibilities, objectives and performance	5.7a	D.4a, D.4b	Now applies to partners also and does not need to be a documented procedure
Process for appraisal records	b	D.4c	
Process for training review	c	D.5b	
Provision of appropriate training	5.8	D.5	
Supervision and Operational Risk Management	6		
Written description of management structure; update within 3 months	6.1	A.1	
Named supervisor for each area of work	6.2	A.1	
Process for effective supervision	6.3	D.7	
Supervision of legal work	6.4	F.10	
Adequate supervision	a	F.10a	
Allocation of work	b	F.10, F.10b	
Checking for inactivity	6.5	–	
File reviews	6.6	F.10c	
Record of file review on file and centrally	a	F.10d	
Corrective action	b	F.10	28 day rule now introduced
Review of file review data	c	–	
Operational risk management	6.7		

2004 Lexcel		2000 Lexcel
One overall risk manager	a	F.1f (i)
Reporting arrangements	b	F.1f
Lists of work not undertaken	c	F.1f (v)
Generic lists	d	F.1f (ii)
Unusual risk matters	e	F.1f (iv)
Risk assessment data reviews	f	F.1f (vi)
Operational risk	6.8	
Client acceptance	a	–
Risk profile of new instructions	b	F.4f
Change to risk profile	c	F.5c
Addressee costs orders	d	F.5f
Concluding risk assessment	e	F.7f
Notify risk manager	f	F.7g
Client Care	7	
Client care policy	7.1	–
Commitment to provide services	a	
PR15 compliance	b	F.3
Terms of business	7.2	F.3
Role and status of fee-earner and supervisor	a	F.4a (v)
Problem with service	b	F.4c
Basis of charges and best information possible	c	F.3
Written complaints handling procedure	7.3	F.11
Available to clients	a	F.11b
'Complaint' defined	b	F.11a
Report and review complaints	c	F.11c
Response to complaints	d	F.11d
Annual review	7.4	–

2004 Lexcel			2000 Lexcel	
Case and File Management	8			
Handling of client enquiries	8.1		E.1	Implicit in E.1
Telephone enquiries		a	–	
Client enquiries at reception		b	–	
Written enquiries		c	–	
Decisions on new clients	8.2		–	
Conflicts of interest	8.3		F.16	
Outset of matter	8.4			
Client requirements and objectives		a	F.4a (i)	
Explanation and advice		b	F.4a (ii)	
What fee-earner will do		c	F.4a (iii)	
If matter to be transferred to colleague		d	–	
Method of funding		e	F.3 (iii)–(x)	
Cost benefit analysis		f	F.4e	
Initial costs information	8.5		F.3	In particular F.3 (i)
Strategy and case plan	8.6		F.4a (iv)	
Progressing matters	8.7			
Key information on file		a	F.9c	
Key dates on file and on back-up system		b	F.1d, F.4d	
Timely response		c	F.5d	
Costs updates		d	F.5e	
Change of person handling matter		e	–	
Undertakings	8.8		F.1e	
Matter management	8.9			
List open and closed files		a	F.1a, F.2	
Traceability		b	F.6	
Confidentiality		c	–	
Status apparent		d	F.9a	
Orderly filing		e	F.9b	
Use of barristers and other outside advisers	8.10		F.8	

2004 Lexcel		2000 Lexcel
Selection criteria	a	F.8a
Consultation with client	b	F.8c (b)
Name and status of adviser instructed	c	–
Records on advisers	d	F.8c
Evaluation of performance	e	–
Clear instructions	f	F.8d
Checking of opinions	g	F.8e
Payment of fees	h	F.8f
End of matter	8.11	F.7
Report on outcome	a	F.7a
Account for monies	b	F.7b
Return of documents	c	F.7c
Storage and retrieval	d	F.7d
Future review	e	F.7e
Archive and destruction	f	

Index

Accounts procedures 47
Accreditation
   annual maintenance visits 1, 16–17
   appeals 18
   application process 5
   assessment *see* Assessment
   commitment scheme 5
   generally 15–16
   mergers and de-mergers 17
   preparing for application 5
   recommendations as to 15–16
   suspension of certificate 18
   who may apply 3–4
   withdrawal of certificate 18
Annual maintenance visits 1, 16–17
Annual registration fee 4, 9
Appeals 18
Appraisal scheme 23, 56–7
Assessment
   application form 6
   applying for 6
   case file samples 11
   case management audits 7, 12
   charges 3
   choosing an assessment body 6
   commitment scheme 5
   complaints 18
   confidentiality *see* Client confidentiality and the contents of files
   consultancy distinguished 8
   cost quotation 8, 9
   de-mergers 17
   'desk-top' audit 8
   diagnostic assessments 5–6
   dishonesty, discovery of 17
   dummy assessments 5–6
   duration 4, 9–10
   fraud, discovery of 17
   generally 1
   inspection of documentation 7, 12
   interviews 7, 10–11, 12
   mergers 17
   philosophy of 2
   planning 7–8
   pre-application assessment 5–6
   process 7–18
   purpose of 7
   self-assessment 5, 8, 12

Assessment bodies 6
Attendance notes 84
Audits
   case management audits 7, 12
   'Desk-top' audit 8

Barristers *see* Counsel
Billing systems 21, 44–5
Business continuity plan 22, 46, 48–9
Business plan 21, 38–40
   review 41–2

Case file samples 11
Case management *see* File and case management
Case plan 80
Catastrophic events 22, 46, 48–9
Certification *see* Accreditation
Changes to Lexcel 2, 88–94
Charges, registration fee 4, 9
Client care
   annual review 26, 72–3
   client survey 72–3
   complaints handling procedure 26, 71–2
   costs information 25, 26, 27, 69, 70, 78, 79–80, 82
   generally 25–6, 68
   policy 25, 68–9
   status of fee-earner 25, 69
   terms of business 25, 69, 70
Client confidentiality and the contents of files
   exception reporting 13
   generally 8, 12, 13
   initial assessment 14
   need for consent 13
   no consent 14
   obtaining consent 14
   typical documentation 13
   withholding files 15
see also File and case management
Commitment scheme 5
Communication facilities 22, 46, 47
Community Legal Service Quality Mark (CLSQM)
   generally 3, 9
   joint assessment of Lexcel with 9

Complaints
complaints handling procedure 26, 71–2
recommendation not to award/renew certificate 18
Conflicts of interest 26, 76–7
Consultancy, assessment distinguished 8
Continuing professional development 58
see also Training and development
Costs
cost benefit analysis 77, 78–9
cost quotation 8, 9
costs information 25, 26, 27, 69, 70, 78, 79–80, 82
initial costs information 79–80
time recording 21, 44–5
update 82
Counsel
list of 85
non-discrimination 20, 84
use of 27, 33, 84–5

Data management 50
Data protection compliance 21, 22, 36–7, 46
appraisal records 57
De-mergers 17
'Desk-top' audit 8
Diagnostic assessments 5–6
Disciplinary record 1, 6
Dishonesty, discovered during assessment 17
Dummy assessments 5–6

E-mail
enquiries by 74
policy on 49–50
use and storage 22, 46, 49–50
Electronic legal services 50
Enquiries, handling 26, 74–5
Experts
list of 85
non-discrimination 20
use of 27, 33, 84–5

Facilities and information technology
accounts procedures 47
business continuity plan 22, 46, 48–9
catastrophic events 22, 46, 48–9
communication facilities 22, 46, 47
confidentiality 46, 47
data management 50
data protection compliance 21, 22, 36–7, 46
documentation 46–7
e-mail 22, 46, 49–50, 74
electronic legal services 50
facilities for clients 22, 46–7
generally 22, 46
health and safety review 22, 46–7, 48
internet use 50
IT plan 22, 49–50
legal and regulatory compliance 50
legal research facilities 22, 50–1
library facilities 22, 50–1
maintenance and support contracts 47
office accommodation 22, 46, 47
updating and sharing legal information 22, 50–1
website 50
Fees, registration fee 4, 9
File and case management
acceptance of instructions 20, 26, 29, 33–4, 75–6
attendance notes 84
case file samples 11
case management audits 7, 12
case plan 27, 80
checking for inactivity 24, 62–3, 82
closing of files 25, 27–8, 86
computerised systems 11
confidentiality 74, 84
conflicts of interest 26, 76–7
cost benefit analysis 77, 78–9
costs information 26, 27, 78, 79–80, 82
costs update 82
counsel, use of 27, 33, 84–5
end of the matter procedures 86–7
experts, use of 27, 33, 84–5
file reviews 24, 63–4
final risk assessment 86
funders 83
generally 26–8
initial enquiries 26, 74–5
key dates 27, 81
key information 27, 81
opening a matter file 26, 77–9
progressing matters 27, 81–2
publicly funded matters 78
responses to client 27, 81–2
retention of files 28, 86
risk assessment 25, 86
sale and purchase files 83
staff safety 74
state of matter files 84
strategy 27, 80–1
tidiness 84
tracing files 83–4
undertakings, giving, monitoring and discharge of 27, 82–3
see also Client confidentiality and the contents of files

Financial management
  billing systems 21, 44–5
  generally 21, 43
  local government practices 43
  management accounting 44
  procedures 21, 43
  processes 21, 43–4
  public sector bodies 43
  responsibility for procedures 21
  time recording 21, 44–5
Fraud
  discovered during assessment 17
  mortgage fraud 21, 36

Health and safety
  policy 21, 37, 46
  review 22, 46, 48

Incorporated practices 31
Indemnity insurance 59
  records 1, 6
Induction process 23, 55–6
information technology see Facilities and information technology
Initial enquiries, handling 26, 74–5
Inspection of documentation 7, 12
see also Client confidentiality and the contents of files
Instructions, acceptance of 20, 26, 29, 33–4, 75–6
Internet use 50
Interviews 7, 12
  reasons for 12
  sample sizes 10–11
Investors in People (IIP)
  generally 1, 3, 9
  joint assessment of Lexcel with 2–3, 9
  monitoring visits 16
  Regional Quality Centres 1, 3, 6
ISO 9000
  assessment bodies 6
  generally 1, 3, 9
  joint assessment of Lexcel with 2–3, 9
  monitoring visits 16
IT see Facilities and information technology

Job descriptions 23, 53–4

Learning and Skills Councils 3, 6
Legal research facilities 22, 50–1
Library facilities 22, 50–1
Limited liability partnership 31
Local government practices 3, 4, 31, 33, 43

Major non-compliances 15
Management accounting 44
see also Financial management
Marketing plan 21, 38–40
  review 41–2
see also Strategy, the provision of services and marketing
Mergers 17
Minor non-compliances 15
Money laundering legislation, compliance with 20–1, 35–6
Money Laundering Reporting Officer (MLRO) 20, 35
Mortgage fraud 21, 36

Non-compliances, generally 15
Non-discrimination
  acceptance of instructions 20, 29, 33–4
  counsel and experts, selection of 20, 84

Office accommodation 22, 46
  client reactions 47
Office manual 12, 22, 46, 51, 75
Operational risk management
  closing of files 25, 86
  designated person 24, 64, 65
  generally 24–5
  lists of work 24, 64, 65
  meaning 24, 59, 64
  procedures 24, 64–6
  reporting arrangements 24, 64
  risk assessment 24, 25, 26, 66–7
  risk management strategy or framework 31
  risk manager 24, 25, 64, 86

Partnership deed 29–30
People management
  annual review 23, 56–7
  appraisal scheme 23, 56–7
  communication 53
  continuing professional development 58
  generally 22–3, 52
  induction process 23, 55–6
  job descriptions 23, 53–4
  person specifications 23, 53–4
  recruitment 23, 52–3, 54–5
  training and development 23, 52–3, 58
  welfare and entitlements 52–3
Person specifications 23, 53–4
Plan, meaning 19
Policy
  meaning 19
see also Structures and policies

Practice, meaning 20
Pre-application assessment 5–6
Procedure, meaning 19
Process, meaning 19
Property transactions 21, 36
Public sector bodies 31, 33, 43

Quality system 20, 31–2
  designated individual 20, 32–3
  quality policy 20, 31, 32
  review of operation 20, 33

Recruitment 23, 54–5
  plan 52–3
Regional Quality Centres 1, 3, 6
Registration fee 4, 9
Revisions to Lexcel 2, 88–94
Risk management see Operational risk management

Self-assessment 5, 8, 12
Services plan 21, 40–2
  review 21, 41–2
see also Strategy, the provision of services and marketing
Sole practitioners 4
  appraisal 57
  death or incapacity 30
  legal framework 30
  recruitment plan 53
Strategy, the provision of services and marketing
  business plan 21, 38–40
  generally 21, 38
  marketing plan 21, 38–40
  review of documentation 21, 41–2
  services documentation 21, 40–2
  SMART objectives 39
Structures and policies
  appropriate business structure 20, 30–1
  data protection compliance 21, 36–7
  generally 20–1, 29
  health and safety policy 21, 37, 46
  incorporated practices 31
  legal framework documentation 20, 29–30
  limited liability partnership 31
  local government practices 31
  money laundering legislation compliance 20–1, 35–6
  Money Laundering Reporting Officer (MLRO) 20, 35
  mortgage fraud 21, 36
  non-discrimination 20, 33–4
  partnership deed 29–30
  property transactions 21, 36
  public sector bodies 31
  quality policy 20, 31, 32
  quality system see Quality system
  risk management strategy or framework 20, 31
  sole practitioners 30
  unlimited liability partnership 30, 31
Supervision
  checking for inactivity 24, 62–3, 82
  description of management structure 24, 59–60
  file reviews 24, 63–4
  generally 24, 59
  legal work, of 24, 61–2
  named supervisor 24, 60–1
  support staff, of 24, 61
  work allocation 24, 61
Suspension of certification 18

Telephone enquiries 26, 74
Terms of business 25, 69, 70
Time recording 21, 44–5
Training and development 23, 52–3, 58
  annual review 23
  CPD 58
  induction process 23, 55–6

Undertakings
  definition 82
  giving, monitoring and discharge of 27, 82–3
Unlimited liability partnership 30, 31

Website 50
Welfare and entitlements 52–3
Withdrawal of certification 18
Work allocation 24, 61

Lexcel Office Procedures Manual

Related titles from Law Society Publishing

Excellent Client Service
Heather Stewart
1 85328 777 6

Managing Cyber-Risks
Rupert Kendrick
1 85328 771 7

New Partners' Guide to Management
Simon Young
1 85328 776 8

Profitability and Law Firm Management
Andrew Otterburn
1 85328 820 9

Quality Management for Law Firms
Matthew Moore
1 85328 715 6

Setting Up and Managing a Small Practice (2nd edition)
Martin Smith
1 85328 792 X

Solicitors' Guide to Good Management (2nd edition)
Trevor Boutall and Bill Blackburn
1 85328 732 6

Titles from Law Society Publishing can be ordered from all good legal bookshops or direct from our distributors, Marston Book Services (01235 465656 or e-mail law.society@marston.co.uk). For further information or a catalogue, contact our editorial and marketing office at publishing@lawsociety.org.uk

Lexcel Office Procedures Manual

Edited by:
Matthew Moore

Contributors:
Michael Dodd
Rupert Kendrick
Charlotte Points
Simon Young

WEB4LAW

The Law Society

All rights reserved. The purchaser may reproduce and/or store the contents of the disk that accompanies this publication for the firm's internal practice management purposes only. The publication may not be reproduced in whole or in part for resale or commercial use, or for distribution otherwise to any third parties.

Neither the Law Society, Web4Law Ltd nor the individual contributors accept any responsibility whatsoever for loss or damage howsoever arising from the use of this publication by any person. The publication must not be construed as giving specific advice and it is incumbent on each legal practice to satisfy itself as to the appropriateness of any of the draft procedures, seeking specialist advice if it needs to do so.

© The Law Society 2004

First edition published in 1997 as *The Office Procedures Manual*
Second edition published in 2001 as the *Lexcel Office Procedures Manual*

This third edition published in 2004 by the Law Society
113 Chancery Lane, London WC2A 1PL

ISBN 1–85328–916–7

Typeset by Columns Design Ltd., Reading, Berkshire
Printed by TJ International, Padstow, Cornwall

Contents

Foreword to the third edition x
Preface xi
Notes on contributors xiii

1	**Firmwide policies**	**1**
1.0	Introduction	1
1.1	The legal status of the firm	1
1.2	Reviewing the business structure	2
1.3	The firm's commitment to quality	2
1.4	Responsibility for maintenance of the quality assurance system	3
1.5	The process of review of the quality assurance system	4
1.6	Non-discrimination with regard to services	5
1.7	Non-discrimination with regard to personnel	7
1.8	Money laundering	9
1.9	Mortgage fraud prevention	15
1.10	Data protection	17
1.11	Health and safety	19
Appendix 1A	Money laundering regulations: Client identity check (ML1)	20
Appendix 1B	Money laundering regulations: Form ML2	22
Appendix 1C	Money laundering regulations: Report Form (ML3)	23

2	**Planning**	**25**
2.1	Developing and maintaining the business plan	25
2.2	Documenting the services the firm is to offer	28
2.3	Producing a marketing plan	30
2.4	Reviewing the firm's plans	32
2.5	The process of review	32

3	**Financial management**	**33**
3.1	Responsibility for financial management	33
3.2	Computer system	33
3.3	Management reports	34
3.4	Income and expenditure budgets	34
3.5	Cash flow	34
3.6	Receipts of cash and cheques	35
3.7	Receipts for cheques and cash	35
3.8	Cheque requisitions	35
3.9	Transfers	36
3.10	Payment out of client monies	36
3.11	Write-offs	36
3.12	Petty cash	36
3.13	Issue of bills and cheques	37

3.14	Amendments to cheques	37
3.15	Receipts from third parties	37
3.16	Client Ledger Balances Report	37
3.17	Investigation and clearance of ledger queries	38
3.18	Credit control	38
3.19	Reserving and write-off of debts	40
3.20	Billing guides or draft bills	41
3.21	Time recording	41

4 Facilities and information technology — 43

I   Reception and telephone facilities — 43
- 4.1 Premises — 43
- 4.2 The client appointment procedure — 44
- 4.3 Telephone calls — 45
- 4.4 Facsimile (fax) — 47

II Post and communications — 47
- 4.5 Incoming mail — 47
- 4.6 Outgoing mail — 48

III Information technology — 49
- 4.7 Management of the firm's IT system — 50
- 4.8 E-mail — 51
- 4.9 Internet use — 54
- 4.10 Electronic delivery of legal services — 55

IV Health and safety — 55
- 4.11 Introduction — 55
- 4.12 Legislative background — 56
- 4.13 External advice — 57
- 4.14 The role of personnel in health and safety issues — 57
- 4.15 Risk assessments — 57
- 4.16 Circulating information — 58
- 4.17 First aid — 59
- 4.18 Accident book — 59
- 4.19 Central heating — 59
- 4.20 Working on VDUs — 59
- 4.21 Smoking — 60
- 4.22 Control of Substances Hazardous to Health (COSHH) — 60
- 4.23 Teleworkers — 60
- 4.24 Personal security arrangements — 61
- 4.25 Security of premises and property — 61
- 4.26 Electrical equipment — 61
- 4.27 Fire instructions — 61

V Office facilities — 63
- 4.28 Photocopying — 63
- 4.29 Office equipment — 63
- 4.30 Business continuity — 64

VI Library		65
4.31 Library		65
Appendix 4A	Detailed fire instructions (sample)	66

5 People management — 67
5.1 Personnel plan		67
5.2 Job descriptions		68
5.3 Recruitment		69
5.4 Contracts of employment		73
5.5 Induction		73
5.6 Objective setting and performance appraisal		73
5.7 Training		77
Appendix 5A	Personnel plan outline (5 years)	80
Appendix 5B	Job description: partner	81
Appendix 5C	Job description: partner – longer format	82
Appendix 5D	Job description: fee-earner	84
Appendix 5E	Job description: partner – showing breakdown of office time	85
Appendix 5F	Job description: para-legal	86
Appendix 5G	Job description: legal secretary	87
Appendix 5H	Job description: receptionist	88
Appendix 5I	Job description: legal cashier	89
Appendix 5J	Job description: office junior	90
Appendix 5K	Job description: trainee solicitor	91
Appendix 5L	Person specification: general	92
Appendix 5M	Contract of employment format	93
Appendix 5N	Interview assessment form	97
Appendix 5O	Competency based interview paperwork	99
Appendix 5P	Reference request	101
Appendix 5Q	Induction training form	102
Appendix 5R	Partner review/appraisal form – small firm	103
Appendix 5S	Partner review/appraisal report form [with optional ratings]	104
Appendix 5T	Pre-appraisal questions for appraisee	106
Appendix 5U	Alternative pre-appraisal questionnaire	107
Appendix 5V	Fee-earner appraisal with ratings – short form	109
Appendix 5W	Appraisal form without ratings	111
Appendix 5X	Competency based appraisal form	114
Appendix 5Y	Staff appraisal form with ratings	117
Appendix 5Z(1) Training request form		120
Appendix 5Z(2) External course evaluation form		121
Appendix 5Z(3) Post-course review		122

6 Supervision and risk management — 123
6.1 Supervision	123
6.2 Systems of supervision	125
6.3 Work allocation	125
6.4 Maintaining progress	125
6.5 Devolved powers	126

6.6	File reviews	126
6.7	Managing risk	127
6.8	Reporting risk	129
Appendix 6A	Sample organisational chart	131
Appendix 6B	Consideration of devolved powers	132
Appendix 6C	File review form	133
Appendix 6D	Risk notice	134

7 Client care — 135

7.1	Policy on client care	135
7.2	Dress and demeanour	136
7.3	Client confidentiality	137
7.4	Fee-earner responsibilities	137
7.5	Receptionists' responsibilities	137
7.6	Confirmation of instructions	138
7.7	Complaints handling	139
7.8	Client surveys	142
Appendix 7A	Client care letter – general format	144
Appendix 7B	Terms and conditions	146
Appendix 7C	Sample complaints procedures	151
Appendix 7D	Client complaint report form	153
Appendix 7E	Client complaints register	154
Appendix 7F	Client survey form	155
Appendix 7G	Staff survey form	157

8 Case and file management — 159

I   Preliminary issues — 159

8.1	Client enquiries	159
8.2	File opening	160
8.3	Acceptance of instructions	161
8.4	Authorisation	162
8.5	Miscellaneous files	162
8.6	Conflicts of interest	163

II   Taking instructions and early action — 164

8.7	Taking instructions	164
8.8	Terms of business	165
8.9	Consent to inspection	165
8.10	Welfare benefits	166
8.11	Key dates	166
8.12	Case planning	167

III   File maintenance — 168

8.13	File maintenance	168
8.14	File summary sheets	168
8.15	Attendance notes	168
8.16	Traceability and confidentiality	169

IV	*Progressing matters*	169
8.17	Maintaining progress	169
8.18	Case plan and costs updates	169
8.19	Undertakings	170
8.20	Experts and counsel	171
V	*Matter closing*	172
8.21	File closing	172
8.22	Final review	173
8.23	Archiving	173
Appendix 8A	Format of departmental appendix (conveyancing)	174
Appendix 8B	Costs and funding checklist	175
Appendix 8C	File opening form	176
Appendix 8D	File summary sheet – general	177
Appendix 8E	Experts/counsel recommendation form	178

Index 179

Foreword to the third edition

I spent fifteen years as a managing partner of a 22-partner, six-office firm with the usual mix of different – and difficult – personalities and partners. How I wish that a model manual, such as this, had been available to me then.

Large firms understand that you have to have management structures and disciplines: and that if you have them, you may as well document them to ensure that you all sing from the same hymn sheet. As President of the Law Society in 1996–97 I urged all firms, however small, to recognise the value to them of improved management. 'But I am a lawyer not a manager', was often the complaint. If you struggle as a business, your professionalism faces an unequal struggle.

The Society has committed itself to support for high street practices in various ways. Few will provide as much practical help as the new edition of this Manual produced with the accumulated expertise of Matthew Moore and a team of contributors from Web4Law.

There is a new awareness within the profession of the need to give active consideration to risk management. If nothing else, the importance which will be attached to it by commercial insurers when offering professional indemnity renewal terms each summer will force all firms to review these procedures. I was delighted therefore to see the help given in these pages on this topic. Recent developments such as the Proceeds of Crime Act and the new Money Laundering Regulations have imposed important new obligations upon solicitors in relation to combating money laundering, and this new edition of the Manual also provides helpful guidance on this pressing issue.

Above all, the attraction of this manual is that it avoids wasteful re-invention of the wheel by hard-pressed firms. Health and safety, discrimination, complaints, personnel issues, are all areas on which we have to have firm policies. This manual provides precedents and acts as an invaluable checklist.

Use this guide selectively to suit your firm but make sure that it is seen as a friendly working tool – not as an inconvenient imposition. If everything in it does not need to be available to all staff, extract those sections. A complementary partners' manual is used by many firms and may be an appropriate home for some items. If everybody does not have their own copy, make sure that all staff have instant access to the index. Treat updates as a positive exercise rather than a chore. An amended index accompanying the update papers reminds staff of the manual and ensures that it remains a living reference aid, not a forgotten volume on the shelf.

John Harvey Jones, the management trouble-shooter, revelled in the aphorism:

'The great thing about not *planning is that failure comes as a complete surprise!'*

Unless you have adopted that as your firm's mission statement, you will read on from here and share my pleasure at the solutions and suggestions you will find.

Tony Girling
President of the Law Society 1996–97

Preface

This is the third edition of the Law Society's *Office Procedures Manual* that I have been involved with. Its aim has always been to provide a template from which solicitors can prepare a manual for their firm. It has consistently been stressed that this publication is a precedent for firms to work from and not a draft – the more red ink that is used within the firm, the better.

The legal office does not feel intrinsically a more dangerous place than it was ten years ago, but there is no denying that it is certainly very much more heavily regulated. This latest version has much more of an air of a compliance manual about it than the simpler treatment of office life that was possible until just a few years ago. This means that there are many more pitfalls in not having the right systems in place and also increased penalties for the unwary in the event of non-compliance.

A number of recent developments illustrate the increased pressure that solicitors are now under to get their systems right. As the full force of the new money laundering regime has unfolded, solicitors have had to come to terms with the fact that they could be convicted and face custodial sentences for mere oversight of wrongdoings on the part of their clients. The Government has chosen to go beyond the provisions of the Second EU Directive on Money Laundering and impose criminal sanctions on firms in the regulated sector for failure to address the regulations. Regardless of whether money laundering is actually happening, non-compliance with these administrative regulations counts as criminal behaviour. We already have solicitors who have been convicted of offences under the Proceeds of Crime Act and, sadly, there are likely to be more to follow.

Even as late as 2000 – the date of the last edition of this work – the widespread use of e-mail was largely confined to commercial firms. Many practices were making valiant, but doomed, efforts to restrict its use. Quicker and more reliable communication has brought many advantages for practitioners, but also increased stress and much greater risk of errors. The whole issue of computer use has attracted extensive regulation, much of it inspired by the much tougher regime on data protection now in place. Again, those who own or manage firms face the risk of criminal penalties for simple errors of oversight.

Finally, we are now looking at some radical changes to workplace culture as a result of the Council Directive 2000/78/EC and the Employment Equality (Religion or Belief) Regulations and the Employment Equality (Sexual Orientation) Regulations. The legal duties owed to employees continue to grow and the employment lawyer has probably never been busier with in-house instructions from the firm itself. The prospects are for yet more regulation in the future and not less. The net effect is that office manuals are here to stay and will continue to need to develop. Ongoing review of the firm's procedures is vital.

There are, of course, risks with a publication of this nature. Wherever possible the latest source of advice or regulation should be consulted. This is particularly the case with the money laundering offences where the all-important guidance is bound to develop as the authorities and courts get to grips with what they will regard as culpable behaviour by professional advisers.

This edition follows the revised Lexcel standard of the Law Society very much more closely than its predecessors. I was very pleased to be invited to work with the Lexcel office on the re-drafting of the standard and I am confident that practices will find the new version a better model to work with in many regards. Lexcel has gained in popularity largely as a result of the need to have effective controls over all elements of office life, especially with the needs of indemnity insurance in mind. The provisions of the Community Legal Services Quality Mark (the SQM) are also referred to for those firms that continue to provide a legally aided service.

As with the two previous editions, I have been pleased to work with my co-author – Mike Dodd – who has many years' experience of most areas of practice management. There is a wider team of contributors now and each has brought greater expertise to bear on the publication. Simon Young has brought his considerable experience as a managing partner and now as the representative of the Law Management Section on the Law Society Council to the title. His areas of particular expertise in partnership law and practice and business structures have been particularly welcome. Charlotte Points is a personnel professional with extensive experience of the management of people within law firms. Rupert Kendrick – a fellow director in Web4Law – is an acknowledged expert on IT use in legal practice. It has been an excellent team to work with.

In addition to the contributors I am grateful to Mike Frith for his helpful advice on the section dealing with client care, and for permission to work from various of his precedents. Tony Girling has again contributed a much appreciated Foreword, along with some draft terms and conditions for the client care section and a considerable amount of practical suggestions throughout. Jo Plumstead of Anglia Polytechnic University provided some much appreciated points on employment law issues. We hope that this edition will be genuinely helpful to firms whether they are embarking on their first office manual or simply revising an older version. Either way, let the red ink flow.

Matthew Moore
matt@web4law.biz

Notes on contributors

This publication has been written by Web4Law Ltd (**www.web4law.biz**), a law firm quality and risk management consultancy whose members are the trainers in the Lexcel scheme for the Law Society.

Matthew Moore (LL.B, MCIM, MCIPD, C.Dip.AF): Originally a solicitor in private practice, Matthew has over 15 years' experience of law firm management consultancy and training. He was part of the committee that reviewed the Lexcel Standard in 2003 and was a contributor to the third edition of the *Lexcel Assessment Guide* that accompanies this Manual. He is the author of *Quality Management for Law Firms*, published by the Law Society, and is a director of Web4Law.

Michael Dodd (DMS, FIMgt): Mike has more than 25 years of law firm practice management experience and in recent years has provided consultancy support to many firms seeking quality standards accreditation.

Rupert Kendrick (LL.M): Rupert was for many years a partner in a medium-sized law firm in the Home Counties. After a ten-year spell in legal publishing, he was awarded a masters degree in Advanced Legal Practice (Legal Practice Management) which examined the implications for law firms marketing themselves on the Internet. He is the author of *Managing Cyber-Risks*, published by the Law Society, and is a director of Web4Law.

Charlotte Points (BA, MSc, Grad.IPD): Charlotte spent over ten years as head of Personnel and Training at a large regional law firm and is now a consultant and trainer on a wide range of personnel and HR development issues. She has particular expertise in assessments for recruitment and promotion.

Simon Young (MA Cantab, MBA): While managing partner of a medium-sized Devon law firm, Simon took the MBA in Legal Practice Management at Nottingham Law School between 1996 and 1998. He was elected to the executive of the Law Management Section (LMS) of the Law Society in 1999, and in 2001 was elected by LMS members to the Society's Council as their representative, subsequently becoming a member of the Standards Board, and the Rules and Ethics Committee. He is now a freelance author, consultant and trainer, and has written the *New Partners' Guide to Management*, published by the Law Society.

1 Firmwide policies

1.0 Introduction

The purpose of this manual is twofold. First, it is a clear statement of the aims and beliefs which govern the firm's operations. Secondly, it is a source of reference for all aspects of those operations, at all levels. As such, it is equally applicable to all personnel throughout the firm, whatever their post or seniority. It is therefore a document which will feature in the induction of all staff to the firm, and will then be available for them to consult at any time during their careers within the firm. Consequently, in order to offer ease of access, copies are available not only in printed form, a copy being [issued to each person *or* held within each department *or as the case may be*] but also on the firm's computer network, within the [*name of folder or programme, etc.*].

The manual will be reviewed not less than annually, and will be kept up to date by [*insert name or title*]. (For ease of reference (s)he is referred to throughout [*this section of*] this manual as the quality partner.) Only (s)he has the authority to make any changes to the manual, although consultation will often take place before any final changes are decided upon. Suggestions for alterations are always welcome at any time. In order to ensure that only one version is in circulation at any time, a record will be kept of all amendments which may be issued, and individual holders of copies will be asked to initial an amendment sheet to confirm that they have received the new version.

[*Where firms have a computer system accessible to all confining the manual to the firm's intranet has obvious advantages in this regard*]

1.1 The legal status of the firm

The firm is constituted as a [partnership *or* limited liability partnership *or* limited company]. [Its administration is undertaken from *or* Its Registered Office is at] [*insert address*]. The owners of the firm are the [partners *or* members *or* shareholders]. They have chosen to regulate the governance of the firm by a [partnership *or* shareholders'] agreement, but that is naturally confidential to them, and does not form part of this manual.

or

Throughout this manual, the term 'the firm' is used to refer to the department known as [*insert name*] which forms part of the overall organisation ('the Organisation') which is known as [*insert name*]. That Organisation is a [local authority *or* limited company *or as the case may be*]. The way in which the firm is controlled, within the context of the Organisation, is set out in [*specify briefly relevant legislative provisions or internal documentation as appropriate*]. References throughout this manual to 'clients' should accordingly be read as references to the other constituent parts of the Organisation to whom the services of the firm are provided.

In order to comply with the requirements of Lexcel the firm will need to be able to demonstrate that the practice has covered the following points:

- management and voting rights;
- the authorisation of individual partners, etc. to bind the firm by contract;
- rights to share in profits;
- how capital contributions and rights to interest will be dealt with;
- how capital will be repaid;
- entry to and expulsions and retirements from the firm;
- the rights of partners, etc. to elect for part-time working patterns, and provision for parental leave, including maternity provisions;
- the situation in case of long-term illness or incapacity;
- how succession will be achieved if appropriate;
- continuity of the practice in the event of death or incapacity (for sole practitioners or small practices).

1.2 Reviewing the business structure

As part of the responsibility of the firm's management, the partners will keep under periodic review the question of whether the current legal status of the firm remains the optimum legal structure for its operation. Included within this consideration will be the question of whether it is appropriate, desirable and possible to limit the personal liability of the owners of the firm, through a change in the legal status of the firm. (This may be viewed in the light of the ability of the firm effectively to limit its overall liability by agreement with its clients.) This process of review will be an inherent part of the review of the firm's strategic and business plans as described in section 2.

1.3 The firm's commitment to quality

The firm exists to provide legal services. Section 2, dealing with strategic and business planning, indicates the ways in which particular types or areas of services are to be selected as those which the firm will from time to time offer to clients. Whatever the type of legal service, however, the emphasis should be on the 'service' element, and the requirements of the client should be accorded priority accordingly.

The firm is committed to the concept that all aspects of its operations should be of the highest quality. As part of this commitment, it [has achieved and is determined to retain *or* is committed to attaining and then retaining] the following externally certified quality mark[s]:

- Lexcel – confirmation of compliance with the Law Society's Practice Management Standards;
- [Investors in People];
- [the Legal Services Commission's Specialist Quality Mark].

Such external accreditation is, however, only a part of the firm's quality programme, and it is important for all personnel to understand the principles which underlie this commitment to quality. The legal profession is no different from any other service provider, in that it only exists so long as that service is valued by those who are the consumers of the service. As a result of growing public awareness of this simple fact, the expectations of consumers generally have increased considerably over recent years, and continue to increase. The fact that substandard service is unacceptable is also marked by the poor complaints record of the profession, and by increasing insistence from various governmental or quasi-governmental agencies on higher standards being met.

It is therefore not only in order to comply with the beliefs of the firm's management that the provision of a quality service is required, but also as a matter of professional and commercial necessity. The damage which can be done to the firm where substandard service is provided can be much greater than might be expected, whether it be in terms of the reputational damage which can be inflicted by a dissatisfied client broadcasting their concerns, or by the time of senior management and others which is inevitably taken up by the handling of any complaint. On the other hand, the commercial advantages which can accrue from the firm's attracting a reputation for provision of a high quality service are manifold.

The consequence of this is that all personnel within the firm must judge their actions from the client's viewpoint, and be aware that in addition to the provision of the highest levels of technical legal expertise, clients have a right to expect that their lawyers will be:

- available
- approachable
- comprehensible
- prompt
- courteous.

For details of the firm's client care policy and procedures see section 7.

It is in many ways the manner in which the service is received and perceived by the client which will be the key, rather than the outcome of a matter in purely legal terms. Thus the issue of communications with the client is a crucial one. Such professional requirements as Practice Rule 15, and the Solicitors' Costs Information and Client Care Code are thus vital, and it is the individual responsibility of each lawyer within the firm to be fully aware of the latest version of them. Nonetheless, they should be regarded only as a starting point, within the context of a policy of full, prompt and clear communication to clients.

This manual, by setting out the policies and procedures which should be followed by everyone throughout the firm, aims in general terms to provide a framework within which all will be able to work in a way which will offer the best chance of providing a consistent, safe, level of excellent service. There are good reasons for referring to this as a quality 'assurance' system. One effect of these procedures is to provide those within the firm with the best chance of performing their individual roles in the most effective manner, to the benefit of their own professional standing and careers.

1.4 Responsibility for maintenance of the quality assurance system

As mentioned above, the ultimate responsibility for the maintenance of the quality assurance system is placed at a very senior level, i.e. with the [quality partner/managing partner]. (S)he reports regularly to the management of the firm on the performance of the system, and any concerns which arise in respect of it. (S)he is also responsible for ensuring that the overall performance of the system is reviewed by the firm's senior management not less than annually.

Certain aspects of the operational maintenance of the system have been delegated by him/her, with the approval of the firm's management. It is important that everyone is aware of who has which responsibilities in this connection.

Details are as follows [*set out devolved responsibilities*]:

- **Quality partner**
  - plan, control and direct quality policies within the firm and maintain relationships with any external accrediting bodies;
  - determine changes to the firm's quality system and manual;
  - supervise the quality assistant;
  - liaise with departmental quality representatives.

- **Quality assistant**
  - prepare revisions of the manual and distribute them;
  - maintain lists of holders of manuals and a record of all authorised revisions;
  - host any external inspections against quality standards.

or

Details are set out in an organisational chart which [appears as an appendix to this manual *or* will from time to time be distributed to all personnel].

1.5 The process of review of the quality assurance system

The quality partner will be considerably assisted in his/her role by receiving suggestions as to ways on which the quality system may be improved. Such suggestions may either be made directly to him/her or be channelled through the appropriate line manager. [To facilitate such suggestions, a folder has been created within the firm's word processing network entitled 'Suggestions Box', and all personnel are encouraged to enter ideas for improvement in this way. Others may comment on such suggestions, within the same facility. Anyone using this facility is encouraged to indicate their name, and the date upon which the suggestion or comment is made, in order that the quality partner may discuss this further with them; but such disclosure is not essential.] [Another way in which suggestions for improvement may be raised is through the Staff Liaison Committee meetings.]

Any potential changes to the system, whether they arise in the context of an annual review, or as a result of the quality partner's own observations, or as a result of staff suggestions, will be viewed in relation to the overall commitment to quality on behalf of the firm, and also in relation to the strategy of the firm as determined in accordance with section 2. In other words, any change, in order to be implemented, will have to be one which will enhance both the firm's service provision levels and its attainment of its business goals. Changes to the system are not to be made lightly, and hence the effect of any such change will be viewed over a time frame of at least a year.

1.6 Non-discrimination with regard to services

Applicable prohibitions

All personnel must be aware of prohibitions which exist against discrimination in two areas. The first, dealt with in this section, relates to discrimination in the context of:

- accepting instructions from clients;
- using experts and counsel;
- the provision of services to clients.

The second, in relation to discrimination within the context of personnel matters, is dealt with in section 1.7 below.

In connection with both aspects, it is the case that all personnel must comply not only with the Law Society's professional requirements but also with the law of the land. The former can be found in the Society's publication *The Guide to the Professional Conduct of Solicitors 1999*, but when using this reference should also be made to the Society's website, in order to avoid the use of outdated versions (**www.guide-on-line.lawsociety.org.uk**). The provisions currently consist of three elements, namely,

- the Solicitors' Anti-Discrimination Rule 1995 (as amended);
- the Solicitors' Anti-Discrimination Code;
- a model anti-discrimination policy.

With regard to the latter, everyone should be aware that the legislation relating to discrimination generally is developing rapidly. The firm's management is responsible for disseminating information as to such developments, and for providing such training as is necessary for all personnel in these issues. Legislative changes or prospective changes which all should be particularly aware of at the present time are:

- The Disability Discrimination Act 1995 (Amendment) Regulations 2003 (SI 2003 No. 1673), which (amongst other things) extend certain provisions of the Disability Discrimination Act 1995 to partnerships (as from 1 October 2004).
- The Employment Equality (Religion or Belief) Regulations 2003 (SI 2003 No. 1660) which brought religion into the field of statutory anti-discrimination law as from 2 December 2003.
- The 'age strand' of the European Employment Directive 2000/78/EC, which will be implemented by regulations by the Government by October 2006 at the latest, and which will prevent discrimination in the employment context on the grounds of a person's age.

(When these changes come into force, references in the model code set out below, and particularly those in paragraph C(4), should be read as including references to them as well as to those provisions currently listed.)

The model code

The firm has determined to adopt the Law Society's model anti-discrimination policy. (In the event of any alterations to the model code, the firm shall be deemed to have adopted those changes from the time they come into force, and any references in this manual shall be read as references to the code as so altered.) In relation to the issues which are the subject of this section, the relevant provisions of that code are currently as follows:

B. Clients

The firm is generally free to decide whether to accept instructions from any particular client, but any refusal to act will not be based upon the race, colour, ethnic or national origins, sex, creed, disability or sexual orientation of the prospective client.

C. Barristers

(1) Barristers should be instructed on the basis of their skills, experience and ability. The firm will not, on the grounds of race, colour, ethnic or national origins, sex, or sexual orientation, or unfairly or unreasonably on the grounds of disability, avoid briefing a barrister and will not request barristers' clerks to do so.

(2) Clients' requests for a named barrister should be complied with, subject to the firm's duty to discuss with the client the suitability of the barrister and to advise appropriately.

(3) The firm has a duty to discuss with the client any request by the client that only a barrister of a particular racial group or sex be instructed. The firm will endeavour to persuade the client to modify instructions which appear to be given on discriminatory grounds. Should the client refuse to modify such instructions, the firm will cease to act.

(4) In relation to the instruction of counsel, the firm will be mindful of the provisions of section 26A(3) of the Race Relations Act 1976 as inserted by section 64(2) of the Courts and Legal Services Act 1990 and section 35A(3) of the Sex Discrimination Act 1975 as inserted by section 64(1) of the Courts and Legal Services Act 1990 (provisions regarding discrimination in relation to the giving, withholding or acceptance of instructions to a barrister).

D. All dealings

The firm will deal with all persons with the same attention, courtesy and consideration regardless of race, colour, ethnic or national origins, sex, creed, disability or sexual orientation.

Compliance with the code

The firm will take any breach of this code extremely seriously. The firm's staff policies are set out in full in section 5 of this manual. In determining those policies and procedures, the firm's management has again considered carefully whether they comply with the above provisions, and will also take these into account when examining any changes in such policies and procedures.

Similarly, the risks attaching to any breach of these provisions are extremely serious, and the same comments with regard to compliance with the code above, in relation to the disciplinary position, will apply in the same fashion to these aspects of the prevention of discrimination.

The firm will also comply with the law and the code in relation to its partners or prospective partners. Thus the existing partners will not discriminate, on any of the grounds which are from time to time prohibited, in the arrangements they make for the purpose of determining to whom they should offer a partnership; the terms on which any partnership is offered; or by refusing to offer, or deliberately not offering, a partnership to anyone. Nor shall partners discriminate in any way in relation to the provision of benefits to any partner; or in relation to any matter relating to the expulsion of any partner or any detriment to be suffered by him/her. No person who is or who has applied to be a partner shall be subjected to any harassment in relation to the position of partner.

Everyone should be aware that any such breach is a potential major risk to the practice. The firm does not carry insurance against the consequences of any illegal breach, and any claims in this regard are likely to involve the firm in very significant commitments of managerial time. Further, a breach may be a serious professional offence, and liability may attach not only to the individual(s) concerned, but also the owners of the firm. For that reason any breach will be regarded as a serious disciplinary offence.

If anyone is concerned that a breach of the code may be occurring, or has a complaint that they have been the victim of a breach, they should immediately report this, either through their line manager, or direct to the quality manager.

For its part, the management of the firm has considered all aspects of its operations, as set out in this manual, to ensure their compliance with the code. Any developments of the firm's strategic and business planning, or changes in this manual, will similarly be examined in order to ensure that no inadvertent breach of the code occurs.

1.7 Non-discrimination with regard to personnel

Applicable provisions

The second strand of the provisions relating to the prevention of discrimination are concerned with issues regarding personnel within the firm. This does not only mean the staff employed by the firm, but also those who may be, or be on the threshold of becoming, partners (or equivalent owners) within the firm.

As already stated, the firm has adopted the Law Society's model code in relation to these areas as well as those outlined in section 1.6 above. The relevant parts of the code are set out below. (There is also a schedule which deals with the setting of targets for the employment of ethnic minority fee-earners within firms. These provisions are not set out in full here, but will at all times be observed by those members of the firm responsible for the recruitment of such staff.) The code states:

A. Employees and partners

(1) General statements

The firm is committed to providing equal opportunities in employment. This means that all job applicants, employees and partners will receive equal treatment regardless of race, colour, ethnic or national origins, sex, marital status, sexual orientation or disability.

It is good business sense for the firm to ensure that its most important resource, its staff, is used in a fair and effective way.

(2) Legislation

It is unlawful to discriminate against individuals either directly or indirectly in respect of their race, sex or marital status; or to treat a person who has, or has had, a disability 'less favourably' without reasonable justification. The Race Relations Act 1976, the Sex Discrimination Act 1975 (both of which have been amended by subsequent legislation) and the Disability Discrimination Act 1995 are the relevant Acts. Regard must also be had for the Equal Pay Act 1970.

Codes of practice relating to race and sex discrimination have been produced by the Commission for Racial Equality, the Equal Opportunities Commission and the Law Society and have been used as the basis for this policy. There is also a code of practice for the elimination of discrimination in the field of employment against disabled persons or persons who have had a disability, published by the Department for Education and Employment. The firm is committed to implementing these codes.

(3) Forms of discrimination

The following are the kinds of discrimination which are against the firm's policy:

(a) Direct discrimination, where a person is less favourably treated because of race, colour, ethnic or national origins, sex, pregnancy, marital status, disability or sexual orientation.

(b) Indirect discrimination, where a requirement or condition which cannot be justified is applied equally to all groups but has a disproportionately adverse effect on one particular group.

(c) Victimisation, where someone is treated less favourably than others because he or she has taken action against the firm under one of the relevant Acts, whether or not such victimisation is unlawful.

(4) Positive action

Although it is unlawful positively to discriminate in favour of certain groups on the grounds of race or sex, positive action to enable greater representation of under-represented groups is permitted by law and encouraged by the firm.

(5) Recruitment

The firm will take steps to ensure that applications are attracted from both sexes and all races and from people with disabilities, and regardless of sexual orientation, and will ensure that there are equal opportunities in all stages of the recruitment process.

(6) Targets

The firm is committed to compliance with Law Society policy on targets for the employment of ethnic minorities, as outlined in the Schedule to this policy.

(7) Promotion

Promotion within the firm (including to partnership) is made without regard to race, colour, ethnic or national origins, sex, marital status, sexual orientation or disability and is based solely on merit.

(8) Monitoring and review

This policy will be monitored periodically by the firm to judge its effectiveness. The firm will also appoint a senior person within it to be responsible for the operation of the policy. In particular, the firm will monitor the ethnic and sexual composition of existing staff and of applicants for jobs (including promotion), and the number of people with disabilities within these groups, and will review its equal opportunities policy in accordance with the results shown by the monitoring. If changes are required, the firm will implement them.

(9) Disciplinary and grievance procedures

Acts of discrimination or harassment on grounds of race, colour, ethnic or national origins, sex, marital status, sexual orientation or disability by employees or partners of the firm will result in disciplinary action. Failure to comply with this policy will be treated in a similar fashion. The policy applies to all who are employed in the firm and to partners.

The firm will treat seriously and take action when any employee or partner has a grievance as a result of discrimination or harassment on grounds of race, colour, ethnic or national origins, sex, marital status, sexual orientation or disability.

(10) Maternity policy

The maternity rights available to partners shall be no less favourable than those required by the Employment Protection (Consolidation) Act 1978 (as amended) for employees. In relation to its dealings with job applicants, employees or partners, the firm will be mindful of the provisions of the Sex Discrimination Act 1975, the Equal Pay Act 1970 and subsequent relevant legislation.

Once again, the code must be read in the light of legislative change. Thus, the provisions of those regulations, etc. referred to in section 1.6 above must be taken into account. Also, reference in paragraph (10) of the code should now be to the Employment Act 2000, rather than the 1978 Act.

1.8 Money laundering

The firm has safeguarded against becoming involved in the processing of illegal or improper gains for clients. As a profession which habitually handles substantial sums of money, solicitors are particularly attractive to criminals wishing to convert gains to a respectable status. Recent legislation has very considerably broadened the scope of measures aimed to prevent this.

The main change effected to the law was the extension of the previous need to report on money laundering activity beyond drugs trafficking, terrorism and serious criminal conduct to all criminal conduct leading to the acquisition of criminal property. The provisions of the Proceeds of Crime Act (POCA) 2002 are very wide and include tax evasion.

The net effect may be that there are more occasions when firms need to report suspicions in this regard. Further, there are some instances where the legal obligations which follow a suspicion, e.g. an inability to process a transaction until NCIS clearance has been given, coupled with a prohibition against 'tipping-off' the client by telling him/her the reasons for the delay may lead to serious operational difficulties. In order to minimise the very real risks to personnel it is essential that prompt and proper action be taken when any suspicions arise: **failure to do so promptly could result in your being convicted of a criminal offence**.

The Money Laundering Reporting Officer (nominated officer) and reports

The recent changes to the law have extended the need to comply with the provisions of the Money Laundering Regulations 2003. The firm has decided that the safest way to ensure compliance with these rules is to apply them to all areas of work undertaken by the practice even though it would seem that certain areas of litigation in particular may be exempt from them.

> Firms will need to be certain that they are outside the areas covered by the Money Laundering Regulations 2003 (SI 2003/3075) if they do not implement the required procedures throughout the firm, since an error on this point could lead to a conviction. If the firm feels that any or all of its services are outside the regulated sector, the latest Law Society Guidance should be consulted. Where this is the case, it would relieve the firm of the legal duty to comply with the Regulations, but the firm will still be subject to the general offences in the Proceeds of Crime Act 2002 and the Terrorism Act 2000, and in most cases it would be wise to implement such procedures in any event. Some firms may wish, however, to restrict identification checking to those areas where it is necessary.

The [quality partner/compliance partner/other] has been appointed as the firm's MLRO (nominated officer). (In the absence of the MLRO, [*name*] is authorised to deputise for him/her.) His/her duties in this regard are to:

- ensure that satisfactory internal procedures are maintained;
- arrange for periodic training for all relevant personnel within the firm;
- receive reports of suspicious circumstances;
- report such circumstances, if appropriate, to NCIS on behalf of the firm;
- direct colleagues as to what action (if any) to take when suspicion arises and a report is made;
- report annually to the partners on the operation of the anti-money laundering policy and procedures.

Training and guidance for the firm's personnel

As a matter of law, all personnel involved in certain areas of work must receive training in relation to the prevention of money laundering. For safety's sake, the firm has decided that all personnel within the firm will receive such training. It should be emphasised that staff at all levels and in all types of job may find themselves involved in circumstances which relate to attempts at money laundering. For that reason, it is a requirement that everyone shall attend such training when required to do so.

From time to time guidance may also be issued in written form, whether this emanates from the Law Society or from any other source approved by the firm's management. When this is issued, it should be kept carefully, so that it is easily and immediately available as an aid when any problems arise.

Obtaining evidence of identity

Advisers must obtain evidence of identity for all clients from whom instructions are received, unless such a check has already been undertaken, as indicated on the central register [summarised on the client master section of the firm's database *or* maintained by the MLRO]. This applies both to individual and commercial/institutional clients; and applies to existing clients as well as new ones. The firm often acts for staff members, friends and family members or partners and staff: there are no exceptions – the full identification check must be conducted in all cases. Where we already hold evidence of identity, the current address should always be checked in relation to any future instructions. Exceptions to this requirement can only be sanctioned by the MLRO. The evidence of identity check must be undertaken by completion of form ML1 – see appendix 1A. One copy of that form, together with copies of the evidence of identity produced by the client, must appear on the first matter file, for the client in question, which is opened after the check is undertaken. Another copy, with a note of the reference number of the file just referred to, must go to the [chief cashier/MLRO] for the purpose of compiling the central register.

The object of the check is to obtain evidence which is reasonably capable of establishing that the client or prospective client is the person they claim to be, and does in fact satisfy the person conducting the check/MLRO that the person is who he purports to be. This identity check must be done as soon as is reasonably practicable after the first contact is made, and unless and until it is obtained the firm must not undertake any work for the client in question. In instances where this may be felt to cause difficulties, the MLRO should immediately be consulted.

Every attempt should be made to meet the client in person to verify the evidence provided. A client should not send valuable documents through the post: even sending such documents by registered post or recorded delivery could result in them being stolen and therefore used to perpetrate fraud. If the firm is unable to meet the client, the client's identity should be checked by a person qualified to do so such as a solicitor, accountant or doctor, and certified copies should be provided to the firm.

Where the client purports to act on behalf of a third party the adviser must obtain evidence of both identities. We will not act for undisclosed principals.

The position is more complex for commercial clients than for individuals. In such cases the check needs to establish not only that the organisation in question exists and is what it purports to be; but also that the individuals who appear to control the organisation are first who they claim to be, and second are genuinely those in control. This will mean that a mix of types of evidence is likely to be needed. As to the first limb of the test, suitable documents might include:

- For companies, their certificate of incorporation, a list of directors, a list of shareholders and the registered address to identify the company itself. In addition, where reasonably practicable, the firm should obtain evidence in relation to the identity of one of the directors or shareholders.
- For partnerships, evidence of identity in respect of the partner who is instructing the firm, and one other partner, together with satisfactory evidence of the trading address. The same would apply in relation to limited liability partnerships.
- For trusts, the trust deed or other instrument. The trustees' identity needs to be established in accordance with the usual procedure for individuals or companies.
- For charities, their Charity Commission registration details, and the constitution or other founding document.

As to the second limb, checks as for individual clients then need to be instituted with regard to the individuals from whom the instructions are received on behalf of the organisation, i.e. the directors/members/partners/trustees with whom the firm is actually dealing. (See the more detailed instructions that accompany form ML1.)

Special care must be taken with regard to any client coming from an overseas jurisdiction, and the MLRO should be consulted in any such case.

The partners recognise that many clients may resist the request for evidence of identity, but clients should be reassured that this is now standard practice for any financial or professional concern and that there is no choice over it, unless the adviser wishes to risk prosecution. Our client care letter now reflects the need for identity to be checked and this wording may also assist to reassure clients that our actions are not taken because we mistrust them.

Suspicious transactions

The legislation requires that a report must be made if anyone knows or suspects, or has reasonable grounds for knowing or suspecting, that another person is engaged in money laundering, i.e. dealing with the proceeds of any crime. It should be noted that that applies to any third party, not just to a client. As an illustration, if a family lawyer becomes aware of a possible offence on the part of the other side's client, (s)he should report it.

The report should be made as soon as there is suspicion or knowledge of money laundering and consent sought from NCIS before accepting the funds.

Danger signs

The signs to watch for include:

- **Unusual settlement requests.** Settlement by cash of any large transaction involving the purchase of property or other investment should give rise to caution. Payment by way of third party cheque or money transfer where there is a variation between the account holder, the signatory and a prospective investor should give rise to additional enquiries.
- **Unusual instructions.** Care should always be taken when dealing with a client who has no discernible reason for using the firm's services, e.g. clients with distant addresses who could find the same service nearer their home base; or clients whose requirements do not fit into the normal pattern of the firm's business and could be more easily serviced elsewhere.
- **Large sums of money.** Always be cautious when requested to hold large sums of money in the client account, for which there is no apparent immediate need, either pending further instructions from the client or for no other purpose than for onward transmission to a third party.
- **The secretive client.** A personal client who is reluctant to provide details of his or her identity. Be particularly cautious about the client you do not meet in person. If a client or prospective client is not prepared to offer the information and evidence requested of them, the likelihood is that the firm will need to decline to accept instructions from them. This even applies to existing clients.
- **Suspect territory or business.** Caution should be exercised whenever a client is introduced by an overseas bank, other investor or third party based in countries where

production of drugs or drug trafficking, or terrorist activity, or widespread crime of any sort, may be prevalent. A non-exhaustive list of such countries includes the Cook Islands; Egypt; Guatemala; Indonesia; Myanmar (Burma); Philippines; Ukraine; Nigeria; and Nauru. Similarly, certain businesses are more prone to money laundering attempts than others, by virtue of the amount of cash transactions they undertake. These include amusement arcades; bars; builders; launderettes; nightclubs; restaurants; and taxis.
- **Tax evasion.** This is a criminal offence.

Reporting to the MLRO

It is the duty of all personnel within the practice to:

- report without delay all circumstances which could give rise to suspicion that the firm is being involved in some element of the money laundering process for a client;
- follow the directions of the MLRO when a report has been made, bearing in mind the personal risk to the adviser of 'tipping-off' the client (see POCA 2002, s.333 on tipping-off and s.342 on the offence of prejudicing an investigation).

A report of suspicious circumstances is made by use of form ML2 (see appendix 1B). On receipt of a duly completed ML2 the MLRO will:

- consider the form and make such further enquiries as are necessary to form a view on whether a report to the authorities is needed;
- ensure that nothing done by the firm could alert the client in question that a report and an investigation could ensue unless it is one of the situations where the firm considers telling the client may be justified in terms of law and good practice (see Law Society guidance);
- make a report, if appropriate, making full notes of the reasons for doing so;
- make diary notes in the firm's key dates system of when the firm may continue to act (see the seven days note in the firm's training package and the moratorium provisions) and direct the adviser further as appropriate;
- co-operate with any enquiries made by the proper authorities;
- maintain all records of disclosures and reports for at least five years.

Once the individual has made a report to the MLRO, his/her statutory responsibilities in relation to making a report are discharged. It is then the task of the MLRO to deal with reporting to NCIS. The individual is still likely to be involved however, as outlined in the rest of section 1.8, and should continue to liaise with the MLRO. In cases where legal professional privilege might apply there will need to be liaison between the adviser and the MLRO for a view to be taken on whether legal professional privilege applies and thus whether a reasonable excuse is available to the reporting obligation. The law on this issue remains complex and it should be noted that legal professional privilege is not a defence to the primary offences of concealing (s.327), arrangement (s.328) and acquisition and use (s.329).

Obtaining consent for transactions

Once a report has been made, the firm must not in any way deal with the money or property which is suspect, without the prior consent of NCIS or another authorised body. Even if the client issues clear instructions for a transaction to be effected before such consent is given, the firm must not do so.

Tipping-off

The reason that the last mentioned prohibition in particular may cause problems to the firm, and potential considerable professional embarrassment, is that no action may be taken which might lead to the firm 'tipping-off' the client that a report has been made. This prohibition will continue to apply even if consent is given by NCIS for a transaction to be effected, i.e. the fact that the authorities choose to take no action at a particular time may not permit the firm to let the client know what they have done, as this may prejudice subsequent action. There are exceptional circumstances when it may be possible to reveal to a client that a disclosure has been or will be made but these depend on legal professional privilege existing. In order to safeguard the position of personnel in such cases, the consent of the MLRO is needed before any intimation can be made to a client of any disclosure. In any event, no mention of a report having been made should ever be entered onto a client's file, lest this be overlooked in the subsequent event of the client exercising their right to call for the file.

The situation might arise, therefore, where the firm holds money ostensibly (and, quite possibly, in reality) belonging to the client, which the client wishes to be applied for a particular purpose; but the firm is able neither to use the money nor to tell the client why it cannot do so. A clear example would be if a purchase is to be completed on behalf of the client, but the money has come from a suspect source and a report has been made. There are express procedures which should help in such circumstances, but it is acknowledged that the firm's statutory obligations in this regard may mean it has no choice but to breach its normal obligations to its client. Although the firm will have a defence to any charge of professional misconduct, it may nonetheless leave the firm open to a negligence claim, and in those circumstances the MLRO should liaise with both NCIS and the firm's insurers.

Maintaining records

The firm is obliged to maintain records of:

- evidence of identity (the completed form ML1 in most cases);
- what has been done for the client;
- any reports (completed ML2).

The obligation lasts for five years. The difficulty is that, except in the case of a 'one-off transaction' this obligation lasts not simply for five years from the conclusion of a matter, but for five years from the end of the business relationship with that client. If that relationship continues, then the file may not be destroyed after the normal period (see section 8.23 below) unless the relevant paperwork is removed from it for separate storage. This may also be relevant if the file is to be handed over to the client at any time. Any file which has any such documentation upon it must therefore be marked clearly on the outside 'Identity documentation included – remove before destruction or handover'.

Cash receipts

There is more to money laundering than cash being introduced to the banking system, but cash receipts do carry added risk. The firm has therefore decided that [*state policy*]. See section 3.6 for the firm's procedures on cash receipts.

1.9 Mortgage fraud prevention

[*This provision may be omitted if the firm does not undertake conveyancing work*]

Another aspect of the criminal law which affects the firm is in relation to the prevention of fraud, especially in connection with mortgages. There have, regrettably, been many instances where firms' clients have been involved in such frauds, and the firms have been unwitting participants in the arrangements which have allowed such frauds to succeed. In such instances, the firms often pay a heavy price, since lenders will often be able to make the firms responsible for repayment of monies lost. In order to avoid this, it is essential that all procedures, as determined from time to time by the head of the conveyancing department, are followed. Further, the provisions of the *CML Lenders' Handbook* should be strictly observed at all times to the extent that there is no contradiction with money laundering provisions or Law Society guidance.

Acting for buyer and lender

Close attention needs to be paid to the duty of confidentiality, if the firm is acting contemporaneously for a buyer and a lender. The position must be considered very carefully if there is any change in the purchase price, or if the firm becomes aware of any other information which the lender might reasonably be expected to think important in deciding whether, or on what terms, it would make the mortgage advance available. In such circumstances the duty to act in the best interests of the lender requires the firm to pass on such information to the lender with the consent of the buyer. If the buyer will not agree to the information being given to the lender, then there will be a conflict between the firm's duty of confidentiality to the buyer and the duty to act in the best interests of the lender. The firm will then have to cease acting for the lender, and to consider carefully whether to cease acting for the buyer.

Solicitors must not withhold information relevant to a transaction from any client. Where the client is a lender, this includes not only straightforward price reductions but may also include other allowances (e.g. for repairs, payment of costs, the inclusion of chattels in the price and incentives of the kind offered by builders such as free holidays and part-subsidisation of mortgage payments) which amount to a price reduction and which would affect the lender's decision to make the advance. It is not for the firm to attempt to arbitrate on whether the price change is material: the lender should be notified. The firm's standard letter of instruction informs the client that it would be regarded as fraud to misrepresent the purchase price, and that the firm is under a duty to inform the lender of the true price being paid for a property, but the client may need to be reminded of this.

Indicators of possible fraud

Some of the measures outlined in section 1.8 above are applicable to this section as well, e.g. the requirements for the lawyer to establish his/her client's identity properly. Additional guidance has, however, been issued by the Law Society, and the following are warning signs which have been identified in that guidance:

- **Verify the identity and bona fides of your client and solicitors' firms you do not know.** The requirements for getting to know the client appear in section 1.8 above. Check also that the solicitor's firm and office address appear in the *Directory of Solicitors and Barristers* or *Solicitors Online* (a part of the Law Society's website). The same applies to any third parties of whom you may be suspicious.
- **Question unusual instructions.** If you receive unusual instructions from your client discuss them with your client fully. Examples of these might be:
    - a client with current mortgages on two or more properties;
    - a client buying several properties from the same person or two or more persons using the same solicitor;
    - a client re-selling property at a substantial profit, for which no explanation has been provided;
    - instructions from a seller to remit the proceeds of sale to someone other than him/herself.
- **Discuss with your client any aspects of the transaction which worry you.** If, for example, you have any suspicion that your client may have submitted a false mortgage application or references, or if the lender's valuation exceeds the actual price paid, discuss this with your client. If you believe that the client intends to proceed with a fraudulent application, you must refuse to continue to act for the buyer and the lender.
- **Check that the true price is shown in all documentation.** Check that the actual price paid is stated in the contract, transfer, mortgage instructions and report on title. Ensure also that you have a satisfactory explanation for any part of the price (e.g. a deposit) being paid direct to the seller. Where you are also acting for a lender, tell your client that you will have to cease acting unless the client permits you to report to the lender all adjustments in the price, and all allowances and incentives. The department's standard letter of confirmation of instructions already informs the client that this is the case, but you may need to reinforce the provision.
- **Do not witness pre-signed documentation.** No document should be witnessed by anyone within the firm unless the person signing does so in the presence of the witness. If the document is pre-signed, ensure that it is re-signed in the presence of a witness.
- **Verify signatures.** Consider whether signatures on all documents connected with a transaction should be examined and compared with signatures on any other available documentation.

- **Make a company search.** Where a private company is the seller, or the seller has purchased from a private company in the recent past, and you suspect that the sale may not be on proper arm's length terms, you should make a search in the Companies Register to ascertain the names and addresses of the officers and shareholders, which can then be compared with the names of those connected with the transaction and the seller and buyer.

Reporting and acting upon suspicion of fraud

Where a suspicion of fraud arises, it should immediately be reported in one of two ways. The wide provisions of the money laundering legislation mean that a report should always be made to the MLRO. The apparent fraud should also be reported to the head of conveyancing. The fee-earner concerned, acting together with the head of department (and, if appropriate, the MLRO), will then take the action which is advised to him/her as being necessary.

1.10 Data protection

The firm is required to comply in a number of ways with the Data Protection Act 1998 ('the Act'). The first of these is registration under the Act. It is the responsibility of the quality manager to ensure that:

- the firm is registered for all necessary activities under the Act;
- there is a process of continual review to determine whether any changes in the firm's registration are required as a result of changes in the nature of the business;
- the details of the firm as registered are kept up to date.

Data protection principles

The second aspect of compliance is the observance of the principles which underlie the Act, namely that all data which is covered by the Act (which includes not only computer data but also personal data held within a filing system) is:

- fairly and lawfully processed;
- processed for limited purposes;
- adequate, relevant and not excessive;
- accurate;
- not kept longer than necessary;
- processed in accordance with the data subject's rights;
- secure;
- not transferred to countries without adequate protection.

Codes of practice

A further layer of compliance is that there are a number of codes of practice provided under the Act, which the firm will observe. These may be altered or added to by the

Information Commissioner, who is responsible for the administration of the Act. At present, applicable codes apply to:

- use by the firm of CCTV cameras;
- various aspects of employment practice, including
    - recruitment and selection
    - records management
    - monitoring at work
    - medical information.

The application of these codes of practice which relate to employment matters are dealt with in section 5.

Subject access requests

Any individual whose data is held by the firm may make what is called a 'subject access request', i.e. a request to see what data is actually held about them. All such requests should be addressed in writing to the quality partner, and (s)he will arrange for the firm to comply promptly with the request.

Security of data

One of the aspects which the firm is keen to observe is with regard to the security of data. This may mean electronic or physical security, or, as with a laptop computer, both. All personnel must comply with such policies as are from time to time notified to them in respect of the firm's computer system, and in particular must observe secrecy in respect of any password or user name. Access to any part of the firm's network must not be given to any unauthorised person. This may be a matter for particular concern where someone is teleworking, or carrying out the firm's work on a computer at home. Measures must then be agreed with the firm's [quality manager *or* IT manager] for storage of the firm's data within a secure and protected area of the home computer's memory.

CCTV cameras

The firm's management has concluded that it is necessary, for the security of the firm's personnel, premises and property, for CCTV cameras to cover all points of entry to the premises and reception areas. No other methods were felt to offer sufficient protection. The [quality partner/office manager] has responsibility for the operation of the system, and for ensuring its compliance with the appropriate code of practice. For that purpose (s)he will check weekly that the system and the information it automatically records, are working correctly and accurately. These checks, and all maintenance of the system, will be logged by him/her.

The cameras and any recordings taken will not be used for any purpose other than as above. Suitably sized warning signs will inform the firm's personnel and visitors when they are entering an area likely to be covered by the cameras, which will state the purpose of the scheme, the person responsible for it, and whom to contact in respect of it. The cameras do not have a sound recording facility. Any recordings will be kept for no longer than [*31*] days, unless they are required for evidential purposes in any legal proceedings. After that they will be erased.

Recordings may only be watched in a restricted area, under the supervision of the [quality manager/office manager]. Any request for access to or disclosure of recordings should be made to him/her, and will be logged by him/her. Third party access will only be granted in accordance with the code of practice. Subject access requests will also be dealt with as described in the code.

1.11 Health and safety

The firm is concerned to ensure the safety of all its personnel (whether at the office or working elsewhere) and all visitors to the firm's premises. To that end the firm has appointed [*name*] ('the Health and Safety Manager') to take particular responsibility for health and safety issues. (S)he will report to the firm's management on such matters as and when they arise, and in any event at least [half] yearly, when a review of the firm's health and safety position will be undertaken. In the absence of the Health and Safety Manager [*name*] will deputise for him/her. Also, (s)he may from time to time delegate certain health and safety matters to others. In that event all potentially affected personnel will be notified in writing of the details of such delegation.

Detailed procedures on health and safety are contained in part IV of section 4 of the manual.

APPENDIX 1A

MONEY LAUNDERING REGULATIONS: CLIENT IDENTITY CHECK (ML1)

(Keep a photocopy of all documentation on file: black and white copies only)

	Tick:

Exemption?
 	
  Client is an authorised business under Money Laundering Regulations
 	
  Referring firm has provided evidence of identity	

Private individuals
 	
One of: Full passport
     Full UK / EU driving licence
     Other evidence of identity (specify)
 	
One of: Utility bill
     Recent bank statement
     Other evidence of address (specify)	

Quoted company
 	
  Copy certificate of incorporation
 	
  Companies search
 	
  Evidence of authority of representative	

Other businesses
 	
  Personal checks on two officers as per private individuals
 	
  Copy certificate of incorporation, if relevant
 	
  Evidence of authority of representatives	

If none of the above, client accepted because:	
Notes (e.g. check of certifying professional where client not met)	

NOTES FOR COMPLETION OF FORM ML1

This form must be filled in on all new matters unless otherwise stated by the MLRO.

For individuals you meet: one item of identity and one item of address. In the case of joint clients, the check must be conducted on all of them unless the MLRO sanctions otherwise.

For individuals in UK you do not meet: as above, but do not ask clients to send items such as passports through the post. You could instead accept the certification of identity and address by a local solicitor or other professional, in which case certify that you have checked on the identity of the certifying person in an up-to-date or on-line directory.

For individuals outside the UK: as above, but suggest local checking by local lawyer with a check on their status if you do not meet them. An identity card may be available.

For trustees/executors/administrators or other such legal representatives: complete as above, but perform for two such individuals wherever possible.

For disadvantaged clients who do not hold passport, bank details, driving licence, etc.: consider any official correspondence or evidence of benefits received.

For students: choose term-time address or home address. If term-time, consider correspondence from landlord or institution in relation to address.

For mentally incapacitated clients: consider evidence from health authorities, doctor, care-worker or institution.

For partnership: conduct personal checks as above on two partners and check trading address from notepaper and directory.

For quoted companies: conduct companies search.

For other businesses: conduct companies search and personal check on two individuals. Are you sure that they are entitled to represent the company?

In all cases: all copies must be black and white only, to avoid any confusion with originals.

In the event of doubt, consult the MLRO and see Law Society's guidance at www.lawsociety.org.uk.

APPENDIX 1B

MONEY LAUNDERING REGULATIONS: FORM ML2

STRICTLY CONFIDENTIAL

Great care must be taken to ensure that this form is not seen by the client at any time. A copy of this form must be forwarded to the MLRO who will also retain a copy in his/her records

Client
(Mr) (Mrs) (Miss) (Ms) (   ) Forenames _____
Surname _____   Any alias? _____
Phone (day) _____ (evening) _____
Address _____

_____

e-mail (if any) _____
Date and place of birth, if known _____

Source of client _____

Introducer (if any) _____

Nature of instructions

Reason for report (attach confidential memo if necessary)

Professional privilege apply?   Should client be advised?

Signed _____ (Adviser)

MLRO Date received _____ Report to NCIS? _____

Reasons for not reporting _____

_____

I consent to client being informed that we will be reporting/have reported to NCIS on grounds of legal professional privilege

(Only sign if consent is granted) _____

Date of consent _____

Date of report to client (attach copy letter or attendance note) _____

APPENDIX 1C

MONEY LAUNDERING REGULATIONS: REPORT FORM (ML3)

HIGHLY CONFIDENTIAL

Client name	Matter number and fee-earner	Date of receipt of ML2	Report to NCIS? Reasons	Consent to inform client?	Date of report to NCIS	Date permission to proceed received	7 days expiry	Moratorium period expiry date

2 Planning

Introduction

The section in Lexcel on planning requires for the most part a business plan and a related marketing plan. Law firms are prone to very much more turbulence in their practices than used to be the case, making all elements of business planning increasingly important.

Firms applying for Lexcel accreditation may need no procedures at all for this section and it is therefore primarily by way of guidance. Of needs be the format and contents of business plans will vary so much between different firms that it would be questionable to set out a model format for one in this book.

This section therefore deals with the planning which is undertaken by the firm in the interlinked fields of the strategy and direction chosen for the firm's business. The selection of services and marketing methods which will carry that strategy into practical effect also need consideration. The ways in which those plans are to be brought into being, reduced into writing, and subsequently reviewed, are also covered.

In general terms, it is essential that such plans, although they will naturally express the aspirations of those within the firm, are practical and set reasonably achievable goals. It is also important that all personnel within the firm are not only aware of the plans (so that communication of them is vital) but also supportive of them. To that end the ways in which all may play a part in the planning process will be set out.

The plans will be considered in three stages. First, the formation of an overall business plan. Secondly, the selection of the services which are to be offered by the firm in order to achieve the goals set in the business plan. Thirdly, the choice of the marketing techniques which are to be used to promote those services to the firm's existing and prospective clientele. As an overall consideration, the ways in which all those levels of plan are to be reviewed will then be set out.

In most partnerships it will be for the managing partner to take responsibility for the conduct of the process whereby these plans are to be formulated, documented, disseminated and reviewed.

2.1 Developing and maintaining the business plan

The object of any such plan, whether in its original format or as revised from time to time, is to articulate clearly:

- the key objectives of the firm over the next year at least;
- additional objectives for at least the two years following the initial year;
- the features which will chart progress towards achievement of those objectives;
- the financial implications of the above.

In broad terms the purpose of the plan is to show where the firm wishes to go, and to allow the management of the firm to assess how successful the firm is being in getting there.

The first task in connection with the preparation of the plan is to assemble the raw data as to the firm's position which can then be analysed. That data may relate to the internal circumstances of the firm, or to the external market and other forces which may affect the environment in which the firm is to practise. The former might include such matters as the geographic spread of the firm's existing client base; the levels of capital available for investment; the nature of the expertise held within the firm; and the known financial performance of the firm. Examples of the latter would include predicted economic trends; forthcoming legislation impacting upon the legal profession; plans determined by applicable local government bodies; changes in the competitive environment within which the firm is operating; or alterations in the profession's rules and structure.

In either case the range of factors which may affect the firm is so diverse that it is desirable to obtain the views of as many people as possible on the subject. To that end, the managing partner will therefore select, on each occasion when a plan is to be formulated or reviewed, one or more of the techniques which may be available for consulting personnel throughout the firm. It is likely that the methods selected will deliberately be varied from time to time. Examples of these methods include:

- questionnaires or similar surveys;
- meetings of personnel;
- focus groups;
- 'brainstorming' sessions;
- individual interviews;
- 'away days';
- intranet forums.

Each of these methods may be used for the whole firm, or for groups selected according to any chosen criteria.

The managing partner may choose to use one of a number of analytical techniques for the assessment of the data to be collected as above. Depending on the model chosen, that may involve incorporating it as part of the collection process itself, so that it serves as a framework for the assembly of the data. An example of a technique which can be used in both these ways is a 'SWOT' analysis, whereby data on a subject is grouped into four categories, namely,

- **S**trengths
- **W**eaknesses
- **O**pportunities
- **T**hreats.

The managing partner may determine that it is appropriate for plans to be formulated not just at the level of the firm as a whole, but in respect of any department or other selected business unit. In that event (s)he may either conduct the collation and analytical work referred to above him/herself, or delegate that to a suitable person such as a head of department. In the latter event, it will be the managing partner's responsibility, acting in conjunction with the delegatee in question, to oversee the way in which the subordinate plan shall be fitted into the main plan.

Throughout these processes, whether at firmwide or subsidiary level, due regard shall be had at all stages to the financial implications of the matters under discussion. Thus the managing partner will be responsible for ensuring that sufficient internal management accounting information and advice is available, and that any external support from the firm's accountants is obtained. Some of this information may of course be confidential, and hence not appropriate for disclosure to all personnel.

Setting key objectives for the next year

After having assembled and analysed the data relating to the firm's position, the managing partner will lead the discussions within the firm's management as to the direction which the firm should take. This should result in the setting of a number of key objectives which are believed to be capable, given sufficient effort and resources, of being achieved within the next year. Such objectives will reflect the wishes of the firm's owners as to what they seek to achieve, but should avoid being too vague or merely aspirational. Where possible, they should be framed in such a way as to enable them to be tested against the 'SMART' criteria, i.e. that they are:

- **S**pecific
- **M**easurable
- **A**chievable
- **R**ealistic
- **T**ime-limited.

This test, and the requirement as above for financial data to be considered at all stages, should ensure that any reader of the plan can establish easily what the firm actually hopes to succeed in doing over the year in question, and what means can be used for assessing how the firm is managing the progress towards those objectives.

Not all objectives will be purely financial. Some will be targeted at the overall positioning of the firm. Where this is the case some form of measurement should be included as part of the target setting. Examples of different forms of objective, and metrics which are appropriate to them, might therefore be:

- Single-issue achievements, e.g. the opening of a new office.
- Absolute financial measures, e.g. a 10% increase in net profits per equity partner.
- Ratios, e.g. a reduction in costs as a percentage of gross fees.
- Growth, e.g. recruitment of a specific number of new lawyers and attraction of the work for them.
- Market share, e.g. an increase of instructions in a specific work area measured as a percentage of the existing level.
- IT development, e.g. a project to put a PC on the desk of every person within the firm, or to create an interactive website.
- Service improvement, e.g. an improvement in telephone response times, as measured by telephonic monitoring equipment; or client satisfaction, as measured by client satisfaction surveys or other appropriate market research techniques.
- Reputational prominence, e.g. as assessed by the number of mentions in local media over a defined period.

Some objectives may relate only to specific departments or other business units within the firm, and naturally this will be so in respect of any sub-plans.

Setting objectives for subsequent years

The plan should not be restricted to just the one year. It should go on to consider the next two years at least, and set further objectives for that period. Many of the same points as above will apply to the choice and framing of such objectives, but it is accepted that the longer-term ones are less likely to be detailed, and may be more susceptible to change on subsequent review. The purpose of this part of the exercise is to ensure that the management is not merely planning for one year in isolation. As above, these objectives may be firm-wide, or related only to specific areas of the firm.

Tying in the financial aspects of plans

As mentioned above, financial considerations must form a significant part of the planning process. The implications for the firm's finances, in terms of such matters as resources required for the implementation of plans; the cash flow consequences of chosen steps; and the anticipated profit yield of the measures to be taken, should be carefully considered, and should be stated either on the face of the plan itself, or in a separate but cross-referred document. (This will involve an element of budgeting, but this will be distinct from the detailed budgeting exercise described in section 3 below.) Where possible, the financial element of the planning process should include a sensitivity analysis, i.e. an assessment of what the consequences will be if the attainment of any particular objective either exceeds or falls short of expectation.

Selecting the format for plans

The managing partner will be responsible for determining the format in which the plan(s) appear. Where there are subordinate plans, these may be in a different format from the main plan. It may be decided that the plan should be one single document, or a number of interlinking documents. Some parts of the plan may be developed in more detail than others, e.g. by the addition of lower tiers of sub-objectives and operational plans.

Further, the managing partner may decide that it is appropriate for there to be different versions of the plan (containing, for instance, different amounts of confidential information) for different audiences. Thus some readers might be given a version of the plan from which certain financial information has been omitted, whereas the management and certain external stakeholders such as the firm's bankers would see the complete plan. If this course of action is taken, however, all versions must be entirely consistent.

Disseminating the plan

The managing partner will arrange for the plan to be published in such a way or ways as the management may think fit. Options include giving all personnel a suitable copy of the plan; posting the plan on the firm's intranet; or holding meetings of personnel at which the plan is presented. Whatever method is chosen, all personnel must be made aware at least of the core parts of the plan and (unless confidential in nature) of the measures by which success is to be judged. Where appropriate, during the lifetime of the plan, all personnel should be given sufficient information for them to assess whether the desired goals are being achieved.

2.2 Documenting the services the firm is to offer

An essential part of the business planning process above is the selection of the services which the firm wishes to offer to the public (and, as a corollary, those services which it is not offering, e.g. because it does not have the expertise or resources to do so, or because it does not believe it can do so profitably). The services selected may be those which the firm is offering already, and/or others which it wishes to incorporate, either by development of existing service lines, or by acquiring fresh expertise and resources in order to enable it to do so. It is the responsibility of the managing partner to ensure that the choice of the selected services is fully documented, whether as part of the business plan or separately.

An inherent part of the choice of services to be offered will, in many instances, be the selection of the groups of clients to whom they are to be offered. Such groupings may differ according to the particular service in question. They may be defined in a number of ways, e.g. geographically; by social need; by business size or type; or in any other way which does not entail breach of the anti-discrimination provisions referred to in section 1.6 above. These choices should be documented.

The methods of service delivery

In respect of each selected service, and each selected client grouping, the firm will also consider whether there are any special needs attaching to the particular choice, in terms of the means by which the service is to be delivered to the client. Such matters may include:

- the provision of out-of-hours or emergency contact details;
- the availability of facilities for disabled clients;
- a willingness to visit clients at their own premises;
- means of electronic communication and data transfer which may be available to clients;
- an ability to deal in languages other than English (either routinely or by arrangement);
- the possibility of assisting with financial concerns, e.g. by funding disbursements during a case, or by fee arrangements.

Once again, these methods should be documented.

Publicly funded work

[It is not the policy of the firm to undertake publicly funded work. *or* It is the policy of the firm to undertake publicly funded work. The firm currently has contracts in the following categories [*specify*]]

[Work will be undertaken in these categories, and in any others for which the firm may subsequently obtain a contract. Work will not be undertaken on a publicly funded basis:

- in any category for which a contract is not held, or
- at any time after the firm has reached any limit imposed upon its acceptance of instructions by the Legal Services Commission, whether by way of limits on matter starts or otherwise.

The firm will maintain documented procedures for ensuring that any prospective client, whose instructions have to be declined by reason of this provision, receives all necessary information and assistance to enable them to seek the appropriate legal advice and services from another firm or agency]

[The firm's policy on accepting legal help matter starts is [*specify*]]

Varieties of documentation on services planning

The purposes for which the services planning processes referred to above need to be documented will be diverse. The firm's management will need to have the documentation available to it, in order to enable it to treat this as part of the business planning process, and to measure actual performance against the plan accordingly. All personnel within the firm will need to have the information available to them in order for them to deal with the public, and existing or prospective clients in particular. (This information will be particularly important for personnel at the induction stage.) Some external stakeholders (e.g. the firm's bank, IT suppliers, etc.) will have an interest in the information. Perhaps most of all, existing and prospective clients will need to know the range, methods and conditions of the firm's service offerings. In each such case, the nature and format of the means of communication of this information may differ. It is the responsibility of the managing partner, or of those to whom (s)he may delegate specific tasks, to ensure that appropriate means of communication are chosen. These are likely to include, for the benefit of all those outside the firm, statements in any brochure, website or similar materials.

Services to be provided internally, etc.

[The nature of the firm means that its services will, to some extent, be offered either internally to other departments of the organisation of which the firm is a part; or to sister organisations in accordance with contractual arrangements made at the level of the organisation generally. In such instances the documentation referred to above may consist of, or include, service level agreements or like documents]

2.3 Producing a marketing plan

Either as part of the business planning process referred to above, or as an adjunct to it, the firm will consider its approach to the marketing of its chosen services. That approach will be such as will best serve the overall strategy of the firm. Without limiting the scope of that consideration, the firm will consider the following.

- Whether, in respect of either all or any specific aspects of its services, it wishes to:
    - reduce or maintain its current level of activity, so that active marketing may be inappropriate, or
    - increase its current level of activity, so that active marketing is required.
- What specific marketing methods (see section below) will be appropriate for either:
    - each specific area where active marketing is required, or
    - the overall profile and market positioning of the firm.
- What it will seek to achieve by each of the chosen marketing methods, and how those aims will tie into the firm's strategy.
- How the effectiveness of any chosen marketing method may be assessed and evaluated.
- What resources will be needed for any marketing activity, and whether they are proportionate to the anticipated benefits which may be derived from them.
- Whether the chosen methods will comply with the Solicitors' Publicity Code.

Available marketing methods

The firm will not need to be limited in the marketing and promotional methods which it adopts, and indeed will seek to be innovative in its methods. Among the 'tools' upon which it may draw, however, will be:

- surveys, questionnaires, and other market research methods capable of informing the firm about its actual or prospective clients and their needs;
- hospitality and entertaining;

- gifts at Christmas or on other suitable occasions;
- seminars, whether general or specifically for selected groups, or in-house to a client's personnel;
- newsletters or other means of communicating changes in the legal environment related to clients;
- staff exchanges or secondments;
- discounts for personal legal services offered to institutional clients' personnel;
- advertising in various media;
- brochures and leaflets;
- websites;
- engagement of marketing agents (provided that all professional regulations are complied with).

In the case of hospitality, entertaining and gifts, the firm will need to be especially sensitive to any restrictions on the ability of an intended recipient to accept what is offered. Those in the public sector, in particular, are subject to stringent limitations in this regard.

The level of documentation of marketing planning

The management of the firm may from time to time determine the level at which its marketing plans are to be documented. Thus they may form part of the general business plan (provided the above issues are addressed fully), or they may be devolved to the level of any department or other recognisable business unit within the firm. (In the latter case, the business plan must indicate where the subordinate plans may be found; by what means they may be identified; and who is to have the authority to create and subsequently amend them.) It is the responsibility of the managing partner to ensure that, whatever pattern of documentation is adopted, it does actually cover all areas of the firm and all aspects of the marketing consideration and planning directed as above. Amongst the matters which will be considered when deciding the level at which the plan(s) should be prepared is the extent to which staff can be involved in the planning process, and what benefits will be derived from their involvement.

In all instances it is incumbent upon those producing the marketing plan, or any constituent part of it, to ensure that they include in their documentation:

- the aim of the activity, in relation to the strategy of the firm or the appropriate unit within it;
- the financial implications, in terms both of the cost of the exercise and the anticipated yield from it;
- the identity of the person(s) who will be responsible for implementing it;
- the means by which the success or failure of the initiative may be measured;
- the timing of the effort;
- any risks attached to the activity.

Communicating the marketing plans

Whatever level the marketing plan(s) apply to, they will need to be communicated effectively to all affected personnel. Further, even personnel not directly involved in a specific activity should be made aware at least of the existence of the initiative, to such a degree as will enable them to make any third party aware of the effort for the overall benefit of the firm. Those formulating the plan(s) should consider what means of conveying this information would be appropriate, e.g. training sessions, written communications, newsletters, staff liaison committee meetings, etc.

2.4 Reviewing the firm's plans

All those plans which have been prepared in accordance with any of the requirements of this section (i.e. the overall business/strategic plan; the services plan; and the marketing plan) must be reviewed by the firm's management on a regular basis. It is the responsibility of the managing partner to ensure that this review process is effected. (In determining the level(s) at which plans are to be prepared, the managing partner will take into consideration the additional administrative complexity of ensuring that a multiplicity of plans at diverse levels is actually reviewed with the necessary frequency and thoroughness.)

2.5 The process of review

The firm's management is responsible for determining the ways in which each constituent part of the planning documentation is to be reviewed. In all cases those issues which are outlined in this section as being appropriate for the preparation of an initial plan are just as applicable to any review. The consideration will need to include:

- by whom the review is to be undertaken;
- how the results of the review are to be communicated to those responsible for co-ordinating the planning exercise;
- when the review is to occur;
- what criteria are to be applied in the course of the review, to evaluate the success or failure of the initial plan;
- what authority may be delegated to change the plan;
- how any changes are to be communicated to
    - personnel within the firm
    - third party stakeholders
    - clients;
- what effects any change in a subordinate plan may have upon a higher-level plan;
- what the financial implications of the review may be;
- what period (being not less than a year) the review may apply for;
- what method of evidencing the fact of the review having occurred, and the outcome of the review, is appropriate (e.g. minutes of appropriate meetings, revised written plans, strategy papers forming part of the review process, etc.).

3 Financial management

Introduction

The accounting and time recording systems used by practices can vary considerably in sophistication but are now almost invariably computerised. The choice of system will influence the precise financial procedures in use. The following procedures must therefore be seen in this context.

For the most part, accounting in a solicitors' practice does not require in-depth accountancy skills. What does make financial management more difficult is that the accounting (and time recording) functions are fragmented by being divided across the number of individual fee-earners employed and the range of legal work undertaken. Multi-office practices provide another factor. Complexity is often the issue.

What is essential therefore is that the accounting procedures are clearly documented, understood and implemented, and are then monitored closely on a continuous basis. An assumption that all is well is an invitation to problems.

3.1 Responsibility for financial management

Whilst all partners have a responsibility for financial management, [*name*] as managing partner, has the direct responsibility to the partnership for overseeing and managing financial affairs. In this task (s)he is supported by other partners with more specific responsibilities such as a branch office partner or departmental partner. On a daily basis much of the control and supervision is delegated to the [practice manager/accountant] through to the accounts department staff.

Individual fee-earners are responsible for the financial management of their client matters especially as required by the Solicitors' Accounts Rules and the detailed instructions that follow.

If anyone has cause to be concerned about any aspect of financial management, especially as related to client monies, they should refer their concern to the managing partner or other partner at once.

3.2 Computer system

The firm has a centralised accounting and time recording system and all personnel have direct access to much of the system and the data through the computer network. The software is provided by [*name*]. Immediate control is exercised by [practice manager/office manager/accountant/senior cashier] and any difficulties concerning the system should be directed to him/her.

Generally, all personnel have enquiry access to all client accounting and time recording data together with related printouts. In addition partners have access to the nominal ledger and some of the management reporting facilities. Apart from time recording entries (see section 3.21), only the accounts department personnel have password-protected access to the various posting programs.

Fee-earners and secretaries are encouraged to use fully the accounting information available to support their client work but should refer to the accounts personnel if specific help is required.

3.3 Management reports

The accounting system is capable of producing a very large range of management reports both in respect of client matters and on the firm's accounting performance. The following main reports are produced each month by the accounts department. The managing partner, with the [practice manager/accountant], has specific responsibility for reviewing such reports.

[*The distribution of such reports will vary considerably between different firms*]

- Profit and Loss Account
- Balance Sheet
- Budget Variance Report
- Client Debtor Report
- Work in Progress
- New Matters Reports
- Fee-earner Performance Report
- Fee Income Report by Work Type
- Client Ledger Balance Report
- Cash Flow Report.

Other reports can be produced on request to the accounts department.

3.4 Income and expenditure budgets

Annual income and expenditure budgets are prepared at practice and branch office levels and these are used in the monitoring of the firm's financial performance. Each month the managing partner and [practice manager/accountant] and the branch office partners, review budget variance reports.

3.5 Cash flow

Based largely upon the income and expenditure budgets and any known or anticipated cycles in either, a cash flow forecast for the forthcoming year is prepared by [practice manager/accountant]. The cash flow forecast is kept under continual review and forms part of the [*monthly management review*].

Whilst cash flow is largely managed at firm level, it is important that all fee-earners remain alert to the need for them to manage their own client matters carefully by ensuring that where possible money on account is obtained; chargeable time is fully recorded; that interim bills are raised when a matter allows; that final bills are raised promptly; and that the fee-earner remains involved in any credit control action [see section 3.18].

3.6 Receipts of cash and cheques

A policy of refusing all cash receipts would reduce the risk of exposure to the most obvious form of money laundering – 'placing' – where criminal proceeds are introduced to the banking system. Most firms are likely to find this unwieldy, however, and will consider a cash receipt limit. It should be noted that the Proceeds of Crime Act has no *de minimis* provisions on this subject and funds are treated as criminal property if they arise from criminal conduct or represent such a benefit 'in whole or part' (POCA 2002, section 340(3)).

Another difficulty with substantial cash receipts are arrangements for staff to bank them safely.

Many firms require all cash to be counted by two persons to minimise the danger of later allegations of loss or dishonesty.

It is advisable to include details of the firm's policy on cash handling in any terms of business or client care letter.

Most money is received by cheque through the post but payment of cash is often offered. The firm's policy on cash receipts is influenced by its responsibilities under money laundering legislation (see section 1.8 above).

[Set out policy, stating limit, if any, and responsibility for checking total amount]

Cash is never to be left unattended, for example on a desk.

Cheques received in the morning post must be sent direct to the accounts department without delay in order that they can be safeguarded, identified and banked on the same day. Cheques received later in the day or direct by a fee-earner, are also to be sent to the accounts department without delay even if they cannot be banked on that day.

Any cash or cheques held by the accounts department overnight are to be secured in the strong-room.

3.7 Receipts for cheques and cash

Only personnel of the accounts department are authorised to issue formal receipts for cheques or cash. *[If any exceptions, please state]*

3.8 Cheque requisitions

If a fee-earner requires a cheque to be drawn on Client General Account, Client Trustee Account or Office Account, the fee-earner is to complete a cheque requisition form in duplicate as shown below. The client name, matter number, bank account on which the cheque is to be drawn, payee, amount and brief details of the reason for the cheque, are to be fully completed. The top copy of the requisition form is to be sent to the accounts department and the second copy retained on the client matter file. The accounts copy serves also as the posting form.

[Alternatively, describe the procedure if cheque requisitions can be made to the accounts department direct from a fee-earner's personal computer]

Cheques are printed daily through the accounting system. The printing run will take place at [*3 pm*] after which the cheques will be distributed to the fee-earners in time for them to be sent out in the afternoon post. If required urgently, a handwritten cheque can be prepared by the accounts department but this should remain the exception to the rule.

The accounts department will make the assumption that cheques will be issued on that day and will effect the ledger posting accordingly. If the issue of the cheque is to be delayed, then the fee-earner must make this clear and liaise with the accounts department.

[*Include here a copy of cheque requisition form*]

3.9 Transfers

A transfer form [*as shown below*] is to be used for authorising transfers of client and office monies. It is also to be used for authorising telegraphic transfers. Two copies of the form should be raised, the top copy to be sent to the accounts department for action and the duplicate retained on the client matter file. On occasions it may be necessary to support the transfer form with a note of explanation.

The proper transferring of monies is directly the responsibility of fee-earners and verbal instructions will not be accepted by the accounts department.

[*Include here a copy of the transfer form*]

3.10 Payment out of client monies

Payment out of client monies by cheque or transfer, irrespective of the amount, can be authorised only by a partner.

3.11 Write-offs

The write-off of any balance in respect of costs or disbursements can be authorised only by a partner and if the amount is [*£100*] or greater, the authority is first to be obtained from the managing partner.

In exceptional occasions it may be desirable to write off a balance of client monies where, despite all endeavours, it has not been possible to trace the client. In such circumstances and on the authority of the managing partner, the balance may be paid to the Solicitors' Benevolent Association. The SBA will undertake to repay the money to the firm if the client is subsequently traced.

3.12 Petty cash

With one exception, all petty cash transactions are controlled by the accounts department. If petty cash is required, a petty cash form as shown below is to be fully completed and taken to the accounts department for their action. The form must clearly identify whether the expenditure is in respect of a client matter and is therefore recoverable, or is a charge to the firm itself.

A small petty cash float is held by the receptionist for the receipt of insurance premiums only.

[*Include here a copy of the petty cash form*]

3.13 Issue of bills and cheques

Occasionally there may be a reason for a fee-earner not to immediately send out to a client a costs bill or cheque that has been processed through the accounts department. However, the accounts department will not be aware of the delay and will therefore have posted the appropriate accounting transaction. In respect of a costs bill this could lead to debt collection action being taken for the non-payment of the bill when action should not have been taken. In respect of a delayed cheque, this could cause problems when reconciling the bank account.

Whenever there is delay in issuing cost bills or cheques, the accounts department is to be informed at once. If a bill or cheque is to be cancelled altogether, then it must be returned to the accounts department for proper cancellation.

3.14 Amendments to cheques

No cheque, whether drawn on Client Account or Office Account, is to be amended in any way without reference to a partner and the accounts department. If the amount of a cheque is to be altered, then it must be returned to the accounts department so that the related posting transaction can be altered. Normally the faulty cheque will be cancelled and a new cheque issued.

3.15 Receipts from third parties

> Firms should consider their approach to receipts from third parties in the light of the anti-money laundering regime now in place and follow any Law Society guidance on the point. One possible approach is to photocopy any third party cheque and require it to be stored on the matter file.

3.16 Client Ledger Balances Report

On [*the 15th day of each month*] or nearest working day, the accounts department will issue a list from the Client Ledger Balances Report to each fee-earner. The report will show:

- client name, matter number, work type;
- balances on client and office accounts;
- balance of unbilled disbursements;

- balance of outstanding debts;
- balance of work in progress;
- lapsed months since last accounting or time recording activity.

Each fee-earner is to review the report against his/her client files within [*three*] days of receipt of the report, and to update the matter files by:

- updating the client on costs information including estimates, and matter activity;
- raising any outstanding client to office transfers (partner authority required);
- raising an interim bill where due;
- hastening any client debts in liaison with the accounts department;
- clearing any remaining small balances on completed matters;
- archiving files that are fully completed.

Through taking such action, client matters will be kept up to date which should be seen as a significant part of client care procedures.

3.17 Investigation and clearance of ledger queries

Inevitably from time to time fee-earners will have queries on their client matter ledgers such as those that give rise to small uncleared balances. Whilst the accounts department will afford all reasonable help, it is the direct responsibility of the fee-earner to first carry out the investigation to clear the query. Fee-earners have the advantage of having the client matter file to help identify transactions and are able to review the ledgers from their own personal computers.

If a problem persists, please raise it with the accounts department as soon as possible.

3.18 Credit control

Credit control is a matter of some professional responsibility and whoever is responsible for it should be conversant with chapter 14 of the *Guide to the Professional Conduct of Solicitors*. The main rules are that:

- Bills should be rendered within a reasonable time of concluding the matter (14.06).
- The bill should be sufficiently detailed for the client to be able to identify what it relates to (14.07).
- Under section 69 of the Solicitors Act 1974 a solicitor may only commence proceedings for non-payment of an invoice before the expiry of one month from the delivery of the bill with court leave; the same provision deals with the need for a signature of a partner or principal on the bill.
- A client may only be sued for recovery of unpaid invoices if they have been served with the requisite notice for either contentious or non-contentious business, as the case may be.
- Firms should consider their policy on interim bills: either the bill could be driven by time or amount of time expended, or both.

The firm's credit control procedures are based upon the following main principles:

- Wherever possible money on account from the client is to be obtained in respect of fees and disbursement.
- Wherever possible interim bills are to be raised at least [monthly/every two months]. Agreement to this must be obtained from the client. Smaller regular bills are less likely to be subject to non-payment and where this does arise, consideration may need to be given as to whether to continue to act for the client.
- Fee-earners remain closely involved in the credit control process notwithstanding any action taken by others such as the accounts department staff. A matter is not completed until the bill has been paid. Early intervention by the fee-earner is more likely to generate payment than hastening correspondence from the accounts department.
- There will be a hastening process of escalating severity finalising in court proceedings being taken against the client.
- The credit control procedures will automatically be activated for all client debts unless under exceptional circumstances a partner intervenes to prevent some or all of the procedures from taking place.
- Except under exceptional circumstances, court proceedings will be taken if necessary irrespective of the client.
- The credit control procedures will be actioned as a priority task by whoever has the responsibility. [*Name*] has been appointed as the credit control partner and [*name*] is the credit controller within the accounts department.

The procedure

> Note that some accounting systems now have an automated credit control facility which would inevitably vary the following procedure. However, the principles should be the same.

Once private client bills have been posted onto the ledger, they will be filed in the accounts department in date order on a lever arch binder [with a separate binder being used for each branch office]. Within the binder(s) there will be further weekly sub-divisions. When a bill has been paid, it will be transferred to a paid binder with the bills filed in alphabetical/bill number order.

This method of filing will greatly assist with the credit control procedures as it will immediately identify those unpaid bills that require hastening action at whatever stage. In particular, as bills are paid and removed, there will be a residue of bills remaining that justify special attention. Any bill that remains unpaid for three months is regarded as being a potential problem.

Publicly funded bills are filed in the accounts department in separate binders.

Once a bill enters the credit control process, the credit controller will record what action has been taken plus any instruction or information about the debt received from the fee-earner or other person concerned. It is most important that fee-earners liaise closely with the credit controller to ensure that proper action is taken.

The escalating procedure for private client debts is as follows.

- **Step 1.** Bill sent to client with copy retained on the client file, and a copy passed to the accounts department for posting action and for filing in the unpaid bills binder. This copy is the VAT invoice. Details of the client's rights to a certificate under the Solicitors' (Non-Contentious Business) Remuneration Order 1994 are included on the reverse of the bill.
- **Step 2.** After four weeks the credit controller sends a statement to the client.
- **Step 3.** After six weeks the credit controller asks the fee-earner to contact the client about the non-payment. There may be understandable reasons from the client's point of view and a process for settlement could be agreed.
- **Step 4.** After eight weeks, following further liaison with the fee-earner, the credit controller sends the client a letter threatening court proceedings if payment is not forthcoming. This letter is always to be signed by a partner.
- **Step 5.** After ten weeks from the date of the issue of the bill, if payment has not been made or alternative payment arrangements have been agreed with the client, a final letter will be sent to the client stating that court proceedings will be taken unless payment is made immediately. This letter will be signed by the credit control partner who first will have necessarily liaised with the appropriate supervising partner.
- **Step 6.** When proceedings are to be taken a new debt matter will be opened but the outstanding debt will remain on the fee-earner's printout records for analysis and records purposes.

The credit control partner will carefully monitor these procedures and will liaise with other partners when necessary.

Debt Management Report

An aged debt report will be [*produced at the end of each month*] and after perusal by the credit control partner with the credit controller, it will be distributed to the individual fee-earners. All fee-earners will therefore be fully aware of their personal client debtor position and should liaise as necessary with the credit controller on any action that can be taken.

3.19 Reserving and write-off of debts

At the end of each financial year [*date*], all debts that have been outstanding for 12 months or more will be automatically reserved in the firm's accounts. This will have the effect of reducing the profits for that year by the amount of the reserved debts but it will enable the firm to recover any output VAT. The reserved debts will remain on the individual client ledger account and can continue to be hastened for payment. If payment or part payment is received then the profit costs will be reinstated as if it was a new bill. Both the credit controller and the fee-earner must liaise closely when this occurs.

Any remaining reserved debts from the previous financial year will normally be written off on the authority of the credit control partner after discussion with the relevant supervising partners. Such write-offs will have no effect on the profits as the reduction will have taken place at the reserving stage.

There will be times when a bill should be written off without the need to be first reserved, e.g. following bankruptcy. Again write-off can only be authorised by a partner.

3.20 Billing guides or draft bills

Billing guides or the preparation of automated draft bills may be part of the accounting and time recording system. If so, the related procedure should be fully described. A copy of the documentation should be included if practicable.

3.21 Time recording

Time recording is used to support the billing process and also provides essential management information.

The firm's time recording system is directly linked to the accounting system. When a new client matter is entered onto the system, the time ledger is automatically opened. Time recording information on every matter can be obtained direct from individual personal computers, either on screen or by a printed report.

Time is recorded in six-minute units with each unit being costed:

1. For private client work at the charge rate applicable to the fee-earner concerned. For private non-contentious work it is not necessary to differentiate between activities such as attendance on client, letters, telephone, etc. Simply record as Standard Time. For litigation matters activity is to be differentiated to support the billing process.
2. For publicly funded work, at the appropriate public funding rate allowed for each activity which must be recorded.

The computer time record will show individual time postings per fee-earner and a running total on unbilled time shown in terms of hours and minutes, value and activity. All time spent on a client matter must be supported by relevant evidence on the client file such as a copy letter or attendance note.

When a bill is posted onto the matter ledger, the amount of unbilled work-in-progress is either reduced to nil, or it can be reduced by a set amount as indicated by the fee-earner. This may often be the case when an interim bill is prepared.

Time postings

Time postings can be made in one of two ways, or a combination. Entries can be made by the fee-earner direct from his/her PC keyboard, usually contemporaneously with the activity. Alternatively, fee-earners can maintain a daily handwritten time sheet which will then require the time entries to be separately input onto the time ledgers by [*state by whom and how*]. A combination of the two methods may be appropriate.

The objective is to ensure that all genuine chargeable time is captured both for billing and management purposes. [*Include details here of any daily, weekly or annual targets or guidelines*]

Non-chargeable time must also be recorded and should be differentiated, e.g. holiday, training, sickness, administration, etc. A particularly useful non-chargeable activity is 'non-chargeable client time' where brief client work is undertaken, e.g. a phone call after the matter has been finished, and the fee-earner is clear that the time will not be charged out.

4 Facilities and information technology

Introduction

This is the most general of the sections in the Lexcel standard, covering all the office facilities and services that solicitors need to function effectively. Within this book there is some overlap with section 1, which deals with firmwide policies. The firm's management policy on health and safety, for example, appears in the section dealing with policies, while the more detailed procedures are set out here. It is a matter of style as to whether policy and procedures should appear together or be separated in this way.

Most readers will need to give particular attention to the new provisions in the Lexcel standard on Information Technology. Computer use is a growing issue and will become critical to the success of most practices in the next few years, particularly with the advent of e-conveyancing and e-litigation. Meanwhile, there is a bewildering array of regulations affecting most aspects of office computer use, coupled to disturbing evidence that most practices are non-compliant in many regards. The risks of fines, convictions, claims and the resultant publicity for firms should be taken seriously by every practice.

For ease of reference the requirements of this section have been set out in groups of procedures.

I RECEPTION AND TELEPHONE FACILITIES

4.1 Premises

The standard of repair and decoration of the firm's premises, both internal and external, will be maintained through a budgeted rolling [*five*] year programme prepared by the practice manager and approved by the managing partner. The reception area, including the main office door and the adjacent windows, and the interview rooms, may require more frequent attention.

The extensive window area at street level and the reception area itself provide important opportunities to display marketing materials about the firm. This must be kept up to date and changed regularly. Professional help in the design of materials is provided by [*name of company*].

An untidy office does not create a good impression. Whilst accepting that files being worked upon and paper in general cannot be hidden, every endeavour is to be made to keep the office tidy during the day and in the evening. In particular, fee-earners should tidy their own offices before a client appointment if they are not to use one of the designated interview rooms.

4.2 The client appointment procedure

For a potential new client, the enquiry for an initial appointment will normally be made by telephone or through visiting the reception in person.

If by telephone, the first impression the client gains of the firm is by the manner in which the call is answered. Invariably the name of the firm should be clearly given [*state preference: 'Good morning, Bloggs & Co' or 'Bloggs & Co, may I help you?', etc.*]. If the call is taken by anyone other than the telephonist, it is good practice to give a name ('Mrs Biggins speaking'). The tone should be friendly, interested and professional.

The telephonist will need to ascertain what the client enquiry is about and then transfer the call to the appropriate department where the enquiry can be dealt with more fully. Please bear in mind that until the telephonist has transferred the call (s)he is prevented from dealing with any other incoming calls.

It is understood that for many reasons fee-earners are not always immediately available to speak to new clients. Therefore each department is to designate a secretary or a fee-earner on a [daily/weekly] rota basis to be available for dealing initially with all new client enquiries. The telephonist and receptionist are to be informed. Outline information about the client's concerns is to be obtained for it then to be passed to a designated fee-earner. If at all possible an appointment should be agreed then or it may be necessary for the fee-earner to agree it later. The objective is to show the client that something is being done without delay and in a professional manner, and to secure a new client matter.

If a new client has called in person to reception, then similarly the receptionist is to ascertain what the client wants and then pass the enquiry to the relevant department for processing. All personnel should avoid a conversation about possible services occurring in the reception area: see section 7.3 below.

Conveyancing quotation

Some enquiries will be specifically for obtaining a conveyancing quotation. These enquiries are to be directed immediately to [*name* or *name*] in the property department who [has/have] responsibility for this task. It may be possible to arrange an appointment at once but often the caller will not make a commitment there and then. In either circumstance, the quotation is to be confirmed in writing that day and is to include a copy of the firm's [*Client Services*] leaflet.

Confirmation of an appointment

If time permits, an appointment is to be confirmed in writing supported by the firm's [*Client Services*] leaflet which includes a location map of the office and details of parking facilities.

Parking

There are [four parking bays for clients in the car park at [*location*]: these are strictly not for use by the firm's personnel]. Parking reservations are to be made through the receptionist. [Alternative public parking is nearby at [*location*]]

FACILITIES AND INFORMATION TECHNOLOGY   45

Interview rooms

[There are three small interview rooms (one for disabled persons) and a conference room suitable for meetings of up to 12 persons, located on the ground floor adjacent to reception. If these are to be used, a reservation should be made with the receptionist.]

Appointment notification to receptionist

All appointments in the office are to be notified to the receptionist who will maintain an appointments diary for the office. It creates a good impression if it can be seen that a client is expected.

4.3 Telephone calls

The firm's objective is to ensure that incoming calls are answered promptly. At peak times, when the volume of incoming calls may be too much for the telephonist to deal with without delays, a proportion of the calls will be cascaded to designated secretaries to act as temporary telephonists.

The procedures for telephone answering are as follows.

Telephone switchboard

The telephonist will give the name of the firm and 'good morning' or 'good afternoon'. The telephonist will ascertain the identity of the caller and the person they wish to speak to (see section 4.2 above for appointment/new work enquiries).

The call will be put through to the relevant person as required by the caller, and announced. If that person is not at his or her desk then he or she should have redirected the telephone to whoever is delegated to take the calls.

[*or*: The call will be put through to the relevant fee-earner's secretary. The switchboard should announce who is calling and the person the caller wishes to speak to. The secretary should greet the caller by name and say who (s)he is and his/her role.]

When the caller requires to speak to someone who is not on the firm's premises the caller will be told that the person is 'out of the office' or 'at a meeting'. It is important that the client is not given the impression that someone else's business is more important than theirs. The telephonist should indicate when the person is expected back before asking if the caller would wish to leave a message with the relevant secretary.

Individuals' extensions

Any person answering a telephone, whether the call is internal or external, is to answer with his/her name. It may be appropriate on external calls to explain role, e.g. 'secretary to X' as well.

Any fee-earner who leaves his or her desk for longer than a few minutes is required to divert his or her telephone to a secretary, or another member of the firm, for message-taking purposes. It is not necessary to notify the switchboard, only the person to whom the telephone has been diverted. [*In most firms automatic divert procedures will have been arranged and these might be explained here*]

Group 'pick-up' systems apply to teams of secretaries. Answer another phone in the group by picking up your own phone and pressing [*specify*].

Fee-earners should notify their secretary of the period in the day when they will return any calls which come in when the fee-earner is unavailable. This:

- gives a client a time when (s)he will call back;
- prevents the client from calling again before the stated times;
- gives a businesslike and efficient impression to the client.

Personal calls

Short, local personal telephone calls are allowed. You may also receive incoming personal calls, but please be sure to keep these calls to a reasonable period of time. All other calls should be made with partner consent.

[*Include as much information as possible on the features of the firm's telephone system, e.g. how to transfer calls; how to divert calls; how to 'camp on'; stored telephone numbers; short codes; group-call facilities. Alternatively many such details can be referred to on a separate telephone instruction list*]

Direct lines

[*If direct telephone lines are provided to key fee-earners, include guidelines on how they are to be used. A clear benefit will be that they reduce any volume pressures on the main switchboard, but if a fee-earner widely gives out his or her direct line number, this is automatically inviting interruptions for the fee-earner. Selective issuing of direct lines numbers is often more sensible*]

Voice mail

[*If voice mail facilities are in use, state whether they will become active before a call transfers from a fee-earner's extension to a secretary, i.e. are calls routed to the voicemail first or to a secretary first?*]

It is the fee-earner's responsibility to check incoming voice mail messages and to respond to them promptly or arrange for a message to be given to callers. If you are out of the office for longer periods of time, please record a specific voice mail message. For example, 'It is Wednesday 19th November and I shall be in court all morning. Please leave any message and I will return your call this afternoon.' It is essential that any dated message is brought up to date without delay.

Mobile phones

[*The use of mobile phones is now commonplace and for many solicitors is no more than another office facility. However, a firm may well want to issue guidelines on the use of mobiles, such as whether the giving out of individual numbers should be restricted in any way rather than wholesale, private use, etc. It should also be remembered that the cost of mobile telephone calls, both received and sent, can be substantially more than calls on a conventional land line. It would be advisable to warn staff of the risks of using mobile telephones while driving unless they have a legally effective hands-free facility*]

4.4 Facsimile (fax)

Although e-mail correspondence has to a large extent reduced the volume of messages by fax, it still remains an important means of communication with the firm's clients and professional contacts. Fax machines are located as follows:

[*location*]	[*number*]
[*location*]	[*number*]
[*location*]	[*number*]

Whilst there is no restriction on using fax for transmitting correspondence or documents, the facility should be used with common sense and not just because it is available. The general rules are:

- If there is no urgency to get the document to the addressee on the same day, use the DX or normal mail, first or second class (see section 4.6 below).
- If you need to be sure that the document is received by the addressee first thing the following morning, send the document at close of work using the automatic transmission facility timed for after 6 pm when transmission costs are substantially cheaper.
- Unless essential do not follow up a fax transmission by sending the original copy by mail.
- Remember that whilst an outgoing message is being transmitted, the fax machine cannot receive an incoming message which may be genuinely urgent.
- For outgoing messages, the standard fax transmission sheet is to be used. This is stored as a standard precedent document.
- Secretaries are responsible for sending their own fax messages including the re-transmission of messages that have become corrupted.

[*In many firms there may be further departmental fax machines where numbers are not given out to clients. Elaborate here if necessary*]

II POST AND COMMUNICATIONS

4.5 Incoming mail

All incoming post is to be opened in the presence of a partner or, if a partner is not available, in the presence of [*name and appointment*]. This forms an important component of the overall supervision structure of the firm.

Morning post

The opening of the main morning post is supervised by a partner, organised on a rota basis. The post opening will commence at 8.15 am in order to ensure that the post is distributed by 9 am. Often substantial amounts of monies are received by cheques and these are to be controlled and passed to the accounts department without delay.

Later post

Other post can be received throughout the day, usually delivered to reception. It is important that such post is processed properly and expeditiously. The receptionist will inform receipt to the office junior who is to take the post for it to be opened in the presence of a partner, or the practice manager if a partner is not available, and for it then to be distributed to the relevant department. Hand deliveries can often be marked urgent and the receptionist is then to ensure that the delivery is passed direct to the departmental partner or other partner without delay.

Post is not to be left on reception desks or anywhere else un-actioned.

Unidentifiable mail

Where it is not possible to identify the intended recipient of an incoming letter, for example, because there is no reference, it should be placed in the Daily Folder and taken to the [*office manager*]. The [*office manager*] is first to endeavour to identify the recipient through searching the client database and if this fails, the office junior is to be instructed to take the letter around the firm to identify the recipient. In exceptional circumstances it may be necessary, if possible, to telephone the sender.

4.6 Outgoing mail

Secretaries are responsible for delivering outgoing mail to the general office by no later than [*time*] daily. Post Office mail and Document Exchange mail is to be separated. The juniors will frank the post and take it by hand to the Post Office [*or specify other arrangement*]. It is greatly appreciated by all concerned if batches of post can be with the general office as early as possible to avoid the daily last minute rush.

Document Exchange

The firm is a member of the Document Exchange (DX) system – a privately operated postal system to which most solicitors belong, together with banks, building societies and barristers chambers. All secretaries have access to the DX Directory of Members. The DX system is cheaper for a firm to use and is often more reliable. It is to be used in preference to the Post Office whenever possible. The DX address and city/town is to be clearly shown on the envelope and the firm's sticker [*or stamp*] must be put in the top left-hand corner of the envelope by the secretary.

Class of mail

All mail to be sent by the Royal Mail is sent first class unless second class is stipulated by the originator.

Business reply service

On occasions, clients may be asked to return documents, etc. to the firm. A supply of first class business reply labels is available for this purpose.

Courier service

Also, there will be occasions when it is necessary to send mail or documents by means of a courier service when normal postal services will be insufficient. When this is required, the fee-earner concerned is to make the necessary arrangement though the [*general office*].

III INFORMATION TECHNOLOGY

The Lexcel standard makes the requirement at 4.4 for a 'policy on the use of IT facilities within the practice and any planned changes'. Areas that should be covered are stated to include:

(a) responsibility for IT purchasing, installation, maintenance, support and training;
(b) the current and planned applications within the practice of IT;
(c) a data protection compliance statement in relation to staff, clients and others and registration with the Information Commissioner;
(d) compliance with all appropriate regulations and requirements;[1]
(e) user safety;
(f) appropriate use of e-mail and attachments, both externally and internally, including storage of messages and the implications of not observing such procedures;
(g) computer data and system back-up, to the extent not covered in any disaster recovery plan.

Clearly, the policy for IT use within any given firm will need considerable thought to ensure that it is appropriate to that practice.

The first consideration is responsibility. This could be delegated to one of the partners, an IT administrator or a manager. His or her remit will be to manage the practice's technology to:

- assess application needs and desired uses;
- ensure integration with client technology;

---

[1] The full list – still growing – looks rather daunting and should include Electronic Communications Act 2000; Data Protection Act 1998; Regulation of Investigatory Powers Act 2000; Telecommunications (Lawful Business Practice) (Interception of Communications) Regulations 2000; Human Rights Act 1998; Consumer Protection (Distance Selling) Regulations 2000; E-commerce (EC Directive) Regulations 2002; Electronic Signatures Regulations 2002; Brussels Regulation (44/2001); Information Commissioner's Code of Practice on Employment 2003 (particularly Part 3: Monitoring in the workplace); Defamation Act 1996; Obscene Publications Act 1959; Sex Discrimination Act 1976; Race Relations Act 1976; Copyright and Trademarks (Offences and Enforcement Act 2002; European Copyright Directive (2001/29/EC); Privacy and Electronic Communications (EC Directive) Regulations 2003; and the Disability Discrimination Act 1995.

- assess the financial implications;
- introduce systems that are 'user-friendly' for personnel in the practice;
- identify training need;
- overcome resistance to IT.

Whoever has the role will need a working knowledge of:

- the legal services provided by the practice;
- solutions most appropriate for the practice;
- competing software solutions and costs;
- installation procedures and costs;
- maintenance and support procedures and costs;
- training requirements and costs.

So far as the current and planned IT applications are concerned, the main steps are to start with a view of the firm's likely needs. At the outset, the practice should ask three questions of its overall business plan:

- Where is the practice now in terms of the services it is offering?
- Where does the practice want to be in terms of its profile?
- What steps are needed in terms of IT to enable the practice to get there?

Properly analysed answers to these questions will enable the practice to identify practice areas where:

- no IT investment is required; or
- some basic IT investment is required; or
- significant IT investment is required.

The IT introduced will then be relevant to its practice areas and investment can be considered by direct reference to the services that are, or are to be, provided. Driven by the business plan, the strategy will represent the shared views of the partnership and its proper planning will enable the practice to forecast its expenditure, assess any risks and draw up an action plan with assigned responsibilities.

Examples of technologies are now available for numerous legal and office functions including accounts, accounting reporting, time recording, legal aid compliance, databases, diary/scheduling and case management systems. Technologies that are becoming more commonplace include speech recognition and digital dictation.

4.7 Management of the firm's IT system

Firms are increasingly reliant on computer technology for the preparation and delivery of services to clients. The firm has invested in case management software to improve certain of its services and an increasing proportion of clients expect to deal with the firm via e-mail as opposed to the more traditional postal system. This increases the significance of effective computer management systems within the practice. There are also important rules and procedures in relation to e-mail protocols and the use of the Internet.

The person with overall responsibility for the management of the IT system is [*name*]. (S)he is assisted in this role by [*name*], the IT administrator [*and any others*].

The [*IT partner*] has responsibilities to review the firm's IT requirements in the light of the business plan and to advise the firm on purchases and developments that seem to be appropriate. (S)he is also responsible for organising ongoing training on IT use for all personnel in the practice.

Computer back-up is the responsibility of [*chief cashier*] who will back up daily and store the disk off-site [*expand on arrangements*].

4.8 E-mail

It will be necessary for the firm to establish its policy on the use of its e-mail system in the course of business. Given the sensitivity over issues such as monitoring of personal messages, the e-mail policy should also be regarded as a condition of employment; similar considerations apply to the use of the Internet. It will apply to all staff including temporary and contract staff. The objective is to ensure that the firm and employees gain maximum benefit and avoid exposure of the firm and its employees to any legal liability.

The matters below should be considered for inclusion in the policy.

Sending and receiving e-mail

- the use of automatic messaging systems;
- the checking of attachments;
- opening other employees' e-mail;
- replying to e-mail;
- the use of lengthy attachments;
- the forwarding of e-mail;
- practice information to be included in an e-mail.

E-mail protocol

- the content of e-mail;
- the style of e-mail;
- prohibited uses (e.g. defamatory or obscene e-mail);
- permitted personal uses of e-mail;
- forbidden personal uses of e-mail.

Legal issues

- avoidance of negligent or misleading statements;
- the conclusion of contracts by e-mail;
- the giving of undertakings by e-mail;
- the issue and acceptance of proceedings by e-mail;
- compliance of Law Society requirements on stationery use vis-à-vis e-mail.

Security

- the employment of encryption and digital signatures;
- the employment of virus scanning software;
- the employment of firewalls.

E-mail notices

- Confidentiality
- Disclaimers
- Copyright
- Virus protection
- Contracting by e-mail.

The position on monitoring both of e-mails and Internet use is particularly complex. The firm will need to comply with the provisions of the Telecommunications (Lawful Business Practice) (Interception of Communications) Regulations 2000 and the Code of Practice of the Information Commissioner relating to monitoring. This is achieved by ensuring:

- compliant monitoring processes and procedures
- compliant software installed on the firm's network to track network activity;
- compliant treatment of collected data;
- disciplinary proceedings if appropriate as a result of any breach.

The policy should be read, understood and accepted and the employee should thereby agree to the firm monitoring e-mail messages transmitted and received in the course of work.

Increasingly, e-mail messages are now used as the routine method of correspondence. This facility, together with access to the Internet, is available to all personnel through the firm's computer network. [*Or include what access there is within the firm. For example, there may be a single designated access point for the firm or perhaps access points for each specialist department, both for incoming and outgoing messages*]

The following guidance is given to ensure that the facility is properly used and not abused. If there is any doubt or concern, reference should be made to [*head of IT*].

The overriding principle is that e-mail messages are to be controlled and processed to the same standards as for normal correspondence. Because e-mails, both received and sent, are processed on an individual personal computer, in the majority of instances without the knowledge of a supervising partner, there must inevitably be a high degree of trust from everyone in the use of e-mails. [*If all e-mails are processed on a designated computer(s), describe the control procedure*]

Incoming messages

- All incoming messages related to client work must be printed out and a hard copy placed on the appropriate client file.
- As appropriate, the fee-earner is to refer any message of substance to the supervising partner, either by direct discussion or by forwarding an additional copy of the message to the partner.
- Any suspicious or offensive messages received are immediately to be referred to a supervising partner.
- No undertaking may be accepted by e-mail – a signed letter must be received.
- If a fee-earner is away from his/her desk for half a day or more, the auto-office message should be set and the relevant secretary is to check for any e-mails received and should refer messages to the supervising partner.

Outgoing messages

- As appropriate, outgoing messages of substance must first be approved by the supervising partner before being transmitted. [*Where the firm operates checking of outgoing post it will need to consider what arrangements apply with e-mails*]
- A printed copy of outgoing messages is to be placed on the relevant client file.
- Undertakings are not to be given by an e-mail message. On approval of undertakings in general, see section 8.19.
- No potentially offensive messages are to be sent. Defamation, harassment and breaches of the firm's discrimination policy are all potential risks. Please also be wary of the temptation to send off a hasty message that, on reflection, would seem unwise. A good rule is to reply later or the next day if annoyed or offended by action taken or a communication received: allowing yourself a 'cooling off period' can avoid putting yourself in the wrong.
- The following e-mail distribution lists are stored in the address book:

    - all personnel
    - all partners
    - all fee-earners etc.

- All e-mails are to be restricted to the firm's professional work. [*Or state arrangements for personal e-mails*]
- Always check the state of attachments to see that you are sending the correct draft. Be particularly wary of a draft that might have been amended without your knowledge by someone outside the firm – client, opponent or other. Where this is a risk you should attach the document as a PDF which cannot be amended (see IT trainer/IT administrator if you do not know how to do this).

Deletion of e-mails

It is the responsibility of the individual regularly to review all stored messages and delete those that are no longer required. Please be aware that all incoming and outgoing messages on client matters must be regarded as being normal correspondence and are therefore subject to the normal retention periods (see section 8.23). Fee-earners are in any event asked to ensure that printed copies of messages, including draft documents, have been placed on the client file before deletion of messages [*where the firm operates data files please elaborate on arrangements*]. Please remember that deleted e-mails are still actually stored on the system and could be accessed in future: legal actions have been brought on the basis of incriminating, 'deleted' e-mails (see *Western Provident Assurance v. Norwich Union*, 17 July 1997, QBD).

Virus protection

The firm's e-mail facility is protected by [*name the system*] and regular protection updates will be received and must be actioned on each individual personal computer. The updates will initially be received on the central computer server [*or describe how*] and the IT supervisor [*name*] will then direct a copy of the update to each PC and will advise individuals by an e-mail message that an anti-virus update needs to be actioned. This is done by opening the anti-virus program on the PC desktop screen and clicking 'Action' [*describe procedure*]. All anti-virus updates are to be processed without delay.

Nobody may introduce to their PC any disk without the permission of [*IT supervisor*]. Failure to seek his/her permission before doing so will be treated as a disciplinary offence.

If a suspicious e-mail message is received, for example from an unidentifiable sender, especially with attachments, it should not be opened. Particular caution is needed where the message is from a familiar source but there is no text in the message. In such circumstances please telephone the sender before opening that attachment to see if they have indeed sent a bona fide message to you. Alternatively, please refer the issue to the IT supervisor or the supervising partner. Where there is still doubt, the message should be deleted without being opened.

4.9 Internet use

The Internet can be a powerful business tool for research on anything of concern to the practising lawyer, including the law itself, or it can be a highly disturbing waste of staff time. Worse still, the Internet permits access to pornography and other forms of offensive material. The observation has been made that everyone with access to the Net is just three clicks away from criminal behaviour in the event of certain downloads. All firms will be concerned to know that the facility is being properly and appropriately used and that core policies on areas such as anti-discrimination are not being breached by offensive viewings or downloads.

Firms should therefore consider setting out their approach on:

- typical permitted uses in the course of the firm's business;
- the need to ensure accuracy of information downloaded;
- acceptable personal use;
- prohibited uses, including copyright issues.

Issues of security also require attention, in particular:

- the need to observe security requirements;
- security procedures in place, e.g. passwords;
- the type of security installed;
- breaches of security requirements and disciplinary proceedings.

Access to the Internet is possible from [*specify*]. Acceptable uses of the Internet include:

- legal research [*specify any sites or services that the firm subscribes to*];
- client or practice research.

Common uses of the Internet within the firm include: [*provide list of sites where formal links are established – e.g. Land Registry, Research agencies, etc.*]

Any other personal or social use of Internet facilities must be kept to a minimum and in no circumstances should any individual within the firm visit sites that could reasonably be regarded as pornographic or offensive, unless it is necessary to do so in pursuance of client instructions.

Users must also be wary of breach of copyright from inappropriate downloads.

4.10 Electronic delivery of legal services

The trend for practices to offer services electronically to clients is likely to develop, especially with the imminent arrival of e-conveyancing and e-litigation. In such cases it is sensible to have a policy governing how services are supplied and any payment methods involved. The policy should specify:

- the key legal, regulatory, professional and codified provisions to be observed;
- the procedures to be observed for online contracting;
- the method of handling of electronic payments.

More particular considerations include:

- compliance
    - the services delivered electronically [*insert list*];
    - ensuring compliance with all legal, regulatory and professional provisions;
    - providing education and training.

- notice
    - the applicable law and jurisdiction for posted information or advice posted;
    - the law and jurisdiction to apply in the event of legal issues arising.

- online transactions
    - authorities required for:
        (a) concluding contacts electronically;
        (b) giving undertakings electronically;
        (c) serving and receiving proceedings electronically;
    - encryption of electronic documents when delivering legal services;
    - verification of the identity of clients and others involved;
    - any limitation of liability for ancillary services from a linked site.

- electronic payments
    - technology employed for the receipt of electronic payments;
    - provision of suitable education and training;
    - consultation with clients on administration and reassurance on issues of privacy and security.

IV HEALTH AND SAFETY

4.11 Introduction

The firm's main policy on health and safety is set out in section 1. A number of more detailed procedures are set out in this section of the manual.

The Workplace (Health, Safety and Welfare) Regulations 1992 complete a series of six sets of health and safety regulations implementing EC Directives, and have replaced a number of old and often excessively detailed laws. They cover a wide range of basic health, safety and welfare issues and apply to most workplaces, including offices.

Employers have a general duty to ensure, so far as is reasonably practical, the health, safety and welfare of their employees and towards people who are not their employees but use their premises.

Whilst working in an office is likely to be far less risky than working in a factory, nevertheless accidents do happen and therefore health, safety and welfare measures need to be matched to the levels of risk. There is a wide range of extremely helpful publications, many of them free, on health and safety topics that affect office working which are available from the Health and Safety Executive (HSE). Further free advice can be obtained from the Health and Safety Inspector at your local council, usually located in the Environmental Health Department, or from the HSE itself.

The following is a list of some of the relevant publications current as at September 2003 which can be obtained from:

HSE Books, PO Box 1999, Sudbury, Suffolk CO10 2WA
Telephone: 01787 881165   Fax: 01787 313995
E-mail: **hsebooks@prolog.uk.com** or online at: **www.hsebooks.co.uk**

HSE Books Catalogue – reference CAT34/03/01
Workplace Health, Safety and Welfare: A short guide for managers – leaflet INDG244
Manual Handling – leaflet INDG143(rev1) 04/02
COSHH: A brief guide to the regulations – leaflet INDG136(rev2) 04/03
Working with VDUs – leaflet INDG36(rev2) 06/03
Maintaining Portable Electrical Equipment in Offices – INDG236
First Aid at Work: Your questions answered – INDG214
Passive Smoking at Work – INDG63
Tackling Work-related Stress – INDG341

Health and safety at work

The firm is required to inform you of its general policy to look after your health and safety while at work in its offices, and the organisation and arrangements for carrying it out.

The firm's general policy is to make sure, so far as it is able, that everyone in the firm's offices has a safe and comfortable environment in which to work. The firm is not aware of any unusual hazards to your health and safety and provided reasonable care and common sense is used in carrying out your work, there should be nothing more dangerous encountered here than you would encounter in your own home.

[*Name*] has been appointed health and safety manager for the firm and has responsibility for advising the partners on health and safety issues and for monitoring standards and for carrying out the annual review of health and safety risks. If you have any concerns about possible health and safety issues, please raise them at once with [him/her].

4.12 Legislative background

In undertaking his/her duties the health and safety manager will take all necessary steps to acquaint him/herself with relevant legislation and its development. There are many legislative provisions which potentially apply to the firm, but particular attention will need to be paid to:

- the Health and Safety at Work etc. Act 1974;
- the Health and Safety (Display Screen Equipment) Regulations 1992;
- the Workplace (Health, Safety and Welfare) Regulations 1992;
- the Provisions and Use of Work Equipment Regulations 1998;
- the Management of Health and Safety at Work Regulations 1999;
- the Control of Substances Hazardous to Health Regulations 1999.`

4.13 External advice

The health and safety manager (or others to whom (s)he may have delegated responsibilities in this field) may from time to time need to seek external expert advice on health and safety matters. In such cases, amongst the agencies and businesses they may contact are [*list those whom the firm may use*].

4.14 The role of personnel in health and safety issues

A prime source of assistance for the maintenance of proper working conditions is the help of all personnel throughout the firm. This may take any of the following forms:

- Personnel exercising their own judgement in taking suitable precautions to ensure not only their own health and safety, but also that of all those who may be affected by what they do, or leave undone.
- Participation in consultation exercises that may be arranged with regard to health and safety matters [whether through the Staff Liaison Committee or otherwise].
- Actively supporting the firm's health and safety programme by complying with such procedures as may from time to time be laid down.
- Participating in such training as the firm may arrange.
- Reporting to the health and safety manager any relevant concerns they may have.

4.15 Risk assessments

The firm will take all such steps as are reasonably necessary to ensure proper working conditions for everybody. In order to enable that to be done, the health and safety manager will undertake suitable and sufficient risk assessments, whether by him/her or by anyone to whom (s)he delegates the task. Any such assessor will need to be trained in the task, and have sufficient knowledge of both current health and safety legislation and standards, and the work processes operated by the firm. Assessments will be repeated as often as circumstances (including in particular any changes to the firm's work, premises or equipment) may require. The health and safety manager will retain records of all such assessments.

The purpose of such assessments is to spot any potential problems before any damage or accidents occur, in order to identify any measures which can be taken to remove or reduce risk. Whilst not seeking to limit the scope of such assessments, they will at least cover the following matters, which are commonly recognised as potential risk areas within an office environment:

- floors
- waste disposal facilities
- furniture
- electrical equipment, including
  - VDUs
  - printers
  - photocopiers
- lighting
- ventilation
- heating
- fire precautions
- water and sanitary facilities.

In undertaking assessments, account will be taken of any particular vulnerabilities, e.g. for young persons; for those who are pregnant or nursing; or for those who are known to have any illness or disability.

All assessments will be reported on by or to the health and safety manager. Such reports must include details of any problems discovered. It is then the responsibility of the health and safety manager to:

- Take such steps as may be needed immediately to ensure safety.
- Undertake such consultations, e.g. with the assessor and personnel in the affected area, as may be appropriate to identify suitable remedial measures.
- Take such remedial steps, if that lies within his/her authority, or
- Report the matter to the firm's management, to agree what steps are to be taken, and then implement them.
- Monitor subsequently the effectiveness of the steps taken.

4.16 Circulating information

The health and safety manager will take all such steps as may be reasonably practicable to inform all personnel of health and safety issues which may affect them, by any or all of the following methods:

- training
- written information
- warning signs and notices.

In exercising this responsibility the health and safety manager will pay particular regard to the matters which concern visitors to the firm's premises, as well as to the firm's own personnel.

4.17 First aid

The firm will at all times maintain no less than an adequate number of suitably trained first aiders at its premises. Those first aiders will have been trained in accordance with the requirements of the Health and Safety Executive. The firm will consider providing such training, at its cost, to any personnel who may wish to volunteer for it, and they should contact the health and safety manager to discuss this. First aid boxes will be kept at [*location*] and/or such other places as may be notified to personnel. The health and safety manager will be responsible for ensuring that they are replenished as and when needed.

4.18 Accident book

A book is kept by the health and safety manager in which are recorded details of all accidents which happen to personnel, whether on the firm's premises or elsewhere when on the firm's business. It is essential that details of such accidents are fully and properly reported.

4.19 Central heating

The heating in the offices is by means of [*heating type*]. The system is regularly checked and if necessary overhauled. If anyone has any reason to suppose that any system is not working properly or if, for instance, there should be a smell of gas, (s)he should inform [*name of health and safety manager*] or a partner immediately.

4.20 Working on VDUs

It is important that any user of a VDU helps the firm to ensure his or her safe working conditions by taking adequate precautions to ensure that (s)he is using the VDU in a safe manner. These include:

- Making adjustments to the user's positioning so that they are comfortable when using the VDU and can look at it with their head in a natural and relaxed manner.
- Taking short breaks from the VDU, to do other tasks, at least once an hour.
- Avoiding eye-strain or glare.

If any of the above prove difficult, the user should contact [health and safety manager/IT partner]. (S)he will investigate whether the firm ought reasonably to make any adjustments and, if so, will arrange for them to be made. If any operator is concerned that the use of a VDU may be affecting their eyesight then the firm will, at its expense, provide an eye test by a qualified optician of its choice.

4.21 Smoking

No smoking is permitted anywhere on the firm's premises. Clients and other visitors who are not aware of this should have the policy politely pointed out to them. Warning signs are visible in all public parts of the premises. [Staff are not permitted to take 'smoking breaks' outside the firm's premises, as this is considered to place an unfair burden on non-smoking colleagues. *Or* By way of exception [*room*] has been set aside for use at break times for smokers.] (Research has suggested that employees who take smoking breaks outside the building can lose as much as half a working day per week, placing more strain on their non-smoking or more self-controlled colleagues.)

4.22 Control of Substances Hazardous to Health (COSHH)

There is legislation covering COSHH. Fortunately, in an office environment there are relatively few substances that might be hazardous to health but there are some, such as photocopier toner, typing-correction fluids and kitchen cleaning materials. Where appropriate, the firm has endeavoured to store the main supplies of these substances separately and safely.

4.23 Teleworkers

Some personnel within the firm may from time to time make arrangements, with the approval of the firm, to work from home or from another remote location. The firm is responsible for their health and safety when undertaking work in such circumstances. The following points arise:

- The worker should discuss any health and safety problems with the health and safety manager.
- The health and safety manager or his/her delegatee will need to undertake a risk assessment in respect of the place from which the person is working. If that is the worker's home, then access is subject to the worker's agreement, and should be by prior agreement. The assessment may only be carried out by the worker him/herself if (s)he has been trained in respect of risk assessments. The assessment will apply to both the workplace itself, and the equipment to be used in it.
- A first aid box should be available.
- Accidents whilst working at home should be reported to the health and safety manager.
- The same principles with regard to manual handling apply as to office-based personnel.
- Similarly, the use of VDUs is subject to the same provisions as with office-based personnel.

4.24 Personal security arrangements

The firm is concerned to ensure the personal safety and security of all personnel, whether in the office, or elsewhere on the firm's business. All personnel should comply with such security precautions as the firm has provided, such as locking and access control arrangements, and burglar alarms.

A panic button is installed in the firm's reception area. If used, it emits a [*continuous ringing tone*]. If that is heard, all available personnel are asked to go to reception to render assistance.

The safety of personnel going to meetings out of the office is also a concern. If anyone is going to a meeting with someone they have not previously met, and they are not going to be accompanied, they should ensure that reception knows exactly where they are going, who they are meeting, and what time they are expected to return. If there is subsequently any change in those arrangements, they should inform reception by telephone as soon as possible.

4.25 Security of premises and property

The firm's premises are protected by a burglar alarm system. Details of the operation of this, and of the access control system, will be given to those who need to know about them.

When leaving the premises, all personnel should check that all windows in their area are closed, and that all electrical equipment is switched off (unless notices indicate that particular machines should be left on).

All personnel are responsible for the security of their own property. They should be aware that this might not be covered by the firm's insurance.

The legislation dealing with VDU users covers the equipment itself, lighting, noise, provision of information and training, eye tests and ergonomics. All persons concerned will be given a thorough briefing by [*name*]. Should anyone have any queries or concern about working with VDUs (s)he should speak direct to [*name*] or to [*partner*].

4.26 Electrical equipment

Everyone in the firm uses electrical equipment as part of their daily work. Everyone must use common sense and caution when dealing with electrical equipment as they would in their own homes. If anyone suspects that equipment, plugs or the supply may be faulty (s)he must report it at once to [*name of health and safety manager*] or a partner.

Maintenance checks will be carried out periodically.

4.27 Fire instructions

> The Fire Precautions Act 1971 (as amended) requires that there must be a fire certificate for offices if either:

- more than 20 people are employed at any one time; or
- more than 10 people are employed at any one time on floors other than the ground floor.

The responsibility for applying for a certificate rests with the occupier unless the premises are in multiple occupation, in which case the owner is responsible.

If a fire certificate is required, there must be adequate:

- means of escape;
- 'supporting provisions' for means of escape (such as escape lighting and fire safety signs);
- means for raising the alarm (fire alarm system);
- means for fighting fire (fire extinguishers, etc.).

Once issued, the fire certificate normally imposes specific requirements relating to:

- testing and maintenance of fire equipment, and other managerial duties;
- fire drills;
- fire instructions and training;
- records.

Where there is a fire certificate in force, any proposals to carry out material alterations to the means of escape, etc. or to make material alterations to the layout of the premises, must be submitted to the fire authority for approval.

Further detailed provisions are contained in the Fire Precautions (Workplace) Regulations 1997 (As Amended).

Immediate action to be taken

If you discover a fire:

- raise the alarm;
- attempt to put the fire out if possible with the appliances provided but without taking personal risks;
- once the alarm has been raised:
  - call the Fire Brigade immediately;
  - evacuate the premises. All staff are to assemble at [*location*]. Do not stop to collect personal belongings. Do not re-enter the building.

Detailed Fire Instructions are in appendix 4A below. [*These will vary for multi-office firms*]

Fire alarm

The office is fitted with a fire alarm system. Glass breakage points are located at each exit.

As normal procedure, the fire alarm system is tested at about [*day and time*]. Staff will be notified if other tests or maintenance are carried out on the alarm system.

From time to time fire drills will be carried out and no warning will be given.

Fire protection in the strong-room

A fire protection system is fitted in the strong-room. The system will automatically be activated if a fire starts in the strong-room.

Fire extinguishers

Fire extinguishers are provided throughout the office buildings and extinguishers for use on electrical equipment are provided where required. A maintenance inspection of extinguishers is carried out annually.

Fire wardens

The following persons have been designated as fire wardens with the prime responsibility for ensuring that the building(s) is/are evacuated quickly and safely and for carrying out a roll call at the assembly point.

[*list of names*]

V OFFICE FACILITIES

4.28 Photocopying

Each area of the office is supported by modern photocopiers with [*automatic feed and double-sided print features*]. The copiers are rented from [*name of company*]. In addition to the basic rental charge, a separate copy charge is levied based upon the volume of copies. The cost of the copiers and copy paper is substantial and all personnel should be aware of using them responsibly and not waste copies unnecessarily.

The cost of all but one of the copiers is absorbed as part of the firm's general overheads. The copier that is located in the [*general office*] is especially designated for large copying tasks undertaken by the office junior. This copier is connected into the accounting system so that copies required for client work can be costed and charged direct to the related client matter as a disbursement. The present copy charge is [X*p per copy*].

The rental charges include an element for the routine maintenance of the copier. Service call-outs are to be made in accordance with the instruction given in paragraph [*X*].

[*Some firms include provisions on personal photocopying by staff, imposing similar restrictions of reasonable use as for telephones. If this seems advisable, include here*]

4.29 Office equipment

The firm has made a substantial investment in office equipment, computers, copiers, scanners, telephones, facsimile, etc., by which it provides support to its clients. It is the firm's policy to have service maintenance contracts for all main equipment. The [*practice manager*] is responsible for arranging maintenance contracts and for keeping the supporting documentation.

Most service contracts include a minimum call-out time in the event of unserviceability and this will vary dependent upon the importance of the item of equipment. [For example, the call-out period for the main computer server is within four hours but for an individual personal computer it is eight hours. Usually the response is well within the contracted times.]

Ordinarily, all unserviceabilty call-outs are to be made by the following who also have the responsibility for maintaining a record of call-outs, response and details of the faults:

- computer equipment (servers, scanners, modems, PCs) – IT supervisor;
- computer software problems – practice manager/IT supervisor;
- copiers – office manager;
- telephones and facsimile – telephonist.

4.30 Business continuity

Section 4.3 of the Lexcel standard requires that there should be a business continuity plan that envisages a catastrophic event that would seriously harm the practice in its ability to deliver client services, and the contingency plans that should be put into effect should they become necessary.

The requirement for a business continuity plan is not a mandatory requirement of Lexcel. However, if the firm does have a plan, then the responsibility for it, how it is reviewed and a summary of the main contents should be included in the Office Manual.

Even if there is no formal plan, contingency insurance should always be included as part of the main office insurance policy. The following considerations should be made in determining the extent of cover required:

- Loss of income. A disaster such as the destruction of the office premises by a fire could occur near the end of the insurance year. As cover for the loss of income would relate to the income that would likely have been earned during the 12 months following the date of the disaster, at the time of renewing the office policy it will be necessary to extrapolate income for almost two years ahead. What income would be lost?
- Consider the consequences on professional indemnity insurance.
- Alternative office accommodation. If the premises are severely or completely destroyed, is there an alternative office such as a branch office, to which personnel and functions could be temporarily relocated? If not, alternative accommodation will be necessary. Consider the cost, including:
    - the fitting out of the temporary office – office services such as fitting out, telephones, technology, furnishings, rent, rates, etc., relocation of staff;
    - the continuing costs of the destroyed office such as rent and rates;
    - the cost of rebuilding and fitting out of the destroyed office;
    - staff costs. Will it be necessary to take on additional staff or perhaps make some staff redundant?
    - professional costs such as those for an architect, site/project manager and accountants;
    - the cost of reconstituting client and practice records including electronic records.

Clearly, contingency cover will vary firm by firm and the extent of cover required will equally vary dependent on the circumstances. The worst situation scenario should determine the cover to be taken and best advice should be obtained from your insurers.

VI LIBRARY

4.31 Library

The firm maintains a legal reference library which is sufficient to meet most of the needs of fee-earners. [*Name*] has been appointed as library partner and his/her responsibilities include the following:

- to ensure that the library material is regularly and promptly updated;
- in consultation with other partners and fee-earners, to purchase new books, and control directly expenditure within the library budget;
- to ensure that the library index is kept up to date;
- to ensure that potentially dangerous out-of-date material is removed from the library;
- to review law journals and [*The Times*] for changes in the law and other relevant legal information, and for the prompt circulation of such information to all concerned fee-earners.

Circulation lists for certain journals are in use. Please ensure that journals are passed on within a reasonable time limit. Daily law reports from [*source*] are placed at [*location*].

[*Name*] assists the library partner with much of the administrative support work of the library.

All fee-earners are expected to contribute towards the maintenance of the firm's library by advising the library partner when consideration should be given to the acquisition of new books or the removal of out-of-date material.

Internet library searches

Internet searches can be conducted as follows [*specify procedures*].

APPENDIX 4A

DETAILED FIRE INSTRUCTIONS (sample)

IF YOU DISCOVER A FIRE:

1. **RAISE THE ALARM** by shouting 'Fire'.

2. **INFORM AT LEAST ONE OF THE DESIGNATED WARDENS** who should immediately assume overall control of the fire drill.

3. **PUT OUT THE FIRE IF POSSIBLE.** The fire extinguishers are located:

    (a) [*give location and stipulate whether they are for electrical fires*]
    (b) [*location*]
    (c) [*location*]
    (d) [*location*]
    (e) [*location*]
    (f) [*location*]
    (g) [*location*]
    (h) [*location*]

4. **INSTRUCT THE TELEPHONIST** to take the following action:

    (a) **RING FOR THE FIRE BRIGADE** giving any necessary information
    (b) [*Advise other external organisations as necessary, e.g. premises next door*]

5. **VERBALLY INFORM OCCUPANTS OF OTHER PREMISES ADJACENT.**

6. **SWITCH OFF MAIN POWER SWITCH** in [*location*]. Do not use water if the current has not been switched off.

7. **CLOSE ALL DOORS AND WINDOWS.**

8. **ATTEMPT TO PUT AWAY ANY IMPORTANT DOCUMENTS** into the strong-room if time permits, and close strong-room door.

9. **MAKE YOUR WAY CALMLY TO THE FIRE ESCAPES**

    (a) [*detail separately each of the fire escape routes*]
    (b) [*route*]
    (c) [*route*]
    (d) [*route*]

    UNDER NO CIRCUMSTANCES IS THE LIFT TO BE USED.

10. **A CHECK IS TO BE MADE OF THE OFFICE TO ENSURE THAT ALL STAFF AND MEMBERS OF THE PUBLIC HAVE LEFT THE BUILDING.**

11. **STAFF ARE TO ASSEMBLE IN THE STREET AT** [*location*] and a roll call is to be made by the person supervising the fire drill.

12. A copy of this instruction is to be displayed at all exit doors in the office.

5 People management

Introduction

The section in Lexcel dealing with the area of people management requires a number of personnel management devices to be in place. There is some overlap with the section on policies and, as elsewhere, it is a matter of choice for firms whether they have all their policies here or in the section headed 'Firmwide policies'. A further alternative is to have the bare policy in section 1 and the more detailed procedures here.

5.1 Personnel plan

The requirement for a personnel plan is a new feature of the Lexcel standard – previously it was an optional element of the standard. There are bound to be substantial differences between large and small practices on this point. In larger firms the personnel plan will be a substantial exercise in its own right, drawn up by the partners or employed personnel professionals in line with the firm's main strategic plan. In smaller firms it is likely to be little more than one section of a general business plan and in many firms it might simply form one element of the departmental plans.

In all firms the personnel costs are likely to represent the principal single cost of providing the service to clients. It makes sense, therefore, to keep some form of control over this item as part of the planning process. There are three elements mentioned in section 5.1 of the Lexcel standard: resourcing, development and welfare/entitlements.

Resourcing

The usual process of quantifying recruitment needs is to question:

- What is the current establishment – i.e. how many people does the firm have at what level and in what areas of the firm?
- Projecting forward – how many of them are still going to be here in the next three years, i.e. potential retirements, estimated leavers, maternity/paternity leave plans where known and other changes?
- What changes will be needed as a result of the current plans for the practice?

The other elements of the strategy will then need to be addressed. If growth or contraction is planned this will adjust the likely personnel needs. Ideally it should then be possible to state a forecast of likely recruitment needs as:

$$\text{Recruitment needs} = (\text{Current resources} \pm \text{adjustments}) \pm (\text{Practice growth or retraction})$$

From this it should be possible to review how the firm will identify and fill vacancies and over what timescale (see section 5.3 on recruitment).

Development

The second part of the exercise is to assess development and training needs. This may well be a separate training plan, but could form part of the overall personnel plan. Either way, the steps are to:

- Assess current skills, usually following annual appraisals.
- Consider developments in the work of the firm, the way that it will be organised and any development of roles.
- Consider the needs of those joining the firm.
- Draw conclusions on the training programme required and the most appropriate arrangements to achieve it.

Welfare and entitlements

Firms may need, for example, to explore their pension provision or whether a bonus or other incentive scheme should be developed.

For a model of how to assess recruitment needs see appendix 5A.

The firm considers its recruitment and training needs as part of the annual business planning process. This forms part of [the main strategic review/office plans/the departmental plans/other]. [*Name of firm*] recognises the vital role that all personnel play in the development of the practice and is committed to providing rewarding careers for partners and staff alike.

5.2 Job descriptions

Job descriptions are a useful tool to clarify roles and responsibilities. They help to establish relationships within a practice and should ensure that everyone understands what is expected of them.

There is sometimes the concern that job descriptions can be limiting for the organisation. To overcome this a 'sweep-up' clause is often added to any list of responsibilities along the lines of 'and do whatever else the partners require', which could be seen to devalue the specific nature of the other duties. The main aim of the job description, however, is to clarify for all concerned what is expected of this person.

A job description should include:

- a job title;
- a short description of the major objectives of the role;
- how the role fits in to the practice, i.e. its positioning and reporting lines;
- a list of the major tasks.

Some firms take the basic list of responsibilities further by including an analysis of the expected time spent in each of the primary areas (see appendix 5E).

Job descriptions are particularly useful to those undergoing some form of development (e.g. secretary becoming a para-legal) or for new starters in the practice to help them understand their role and contribution.

In relation to recruitment a job description should make it easier to describe the profile of the jobholder. This in turn is achieved through the person specification.

A person specification should include:

- the required skills;
- the required knowledge;
- the possible experience most likely to help with successful performance in the job.

There is increasing use of competency frameworks within firms. A competency is a set of behaviours that an individual needs to bring to a job in order to perform that job with competence. Competencies are therefore concerned with people's behaviour and should thus link the individual with the job and explain how the person should apply their knowledge, skill and experience to achieve their objectives. A well-developed competency framework can form an alternative to job descriptions and this would be possible under the Lexcel requirements.

Finally, the job documentation will need to be reviewed regularly in order to meet the changing requirements of a successful practice. It is therefore a good idea to review job descriptions during appraisals and any other personal reviews.

See appendices 5B–5K for sample job descriptions.

It is the policy of the firm that all personnel have agreed job descriptions. These are based on one of the job descriptions shown in appendices 5B–5K, if possible. Other more individual roles are specifically agreed with the partners.

At each appraisal interview members of staff will be invited to comment on the appropriateness of their job description and to suggest any amendments. Such discussions will be considered by the partners and, if appropriate, an amended job description will then be placed on the individual's personal file.

5.3 Recruitment

There are four phases of recruitment:

- identifying and describing vacancies;
- attracting candidates;
- selection;
- pre-joining checks and contact.

Section 5.3 in Lexcel deals with the first three of these stages in particular.

Identification of vacancies

In many firms different people may share responsibilities: there may well be different partners or managers in charge of fee-earner recruitment and trainees as opposed to secretarial and administrative appointments. If planning is in place (see section 5.1) a practice's recruitment requirements will be defined in advance as far as is possible and the case for taking on new staff will be evident. An unexpected resignation can be seen as an opportunity to review the best arrangements in that area: a 'knee-jerk' reaction of finding an immediate replacement might be unwise. When a resignation is tendered the following questions should be asked:

- Is the job still there? For example what is the volume of work this person is doing at present and can it be done any other way, e.g. has IT taken some of the administrative burden from the job or could it? Have the job boundaries changed? Can the work be done elsewhere by other means?

- Is the role a 'whole' or 'part' workload?
- Is this a development opportunity for anyone else in the practice offering some promotion potential?

If it is evident from such analysis that the job still exists then the recruitment process can proceed.

The job description

It is always a good idea to review the job description, taking into account any changes to do with the position and how it fits into its overall situation. This is more likely to lead to a more appropriate advertisement and will provide better details on the role for candidates. It is vital at this stage to take into account the legislation around recruitment and the firm's policies (see section 1, especially 1.7).

Methods of attracting candidates can include:

- professional magazines
- recruitment agencies
- local press
- internal advertisements
- selection and search consultancies
- careers fairs
- university visits.

A practice should take into consideration the cost and appropriateness of the methods used. Where possible it is advisable to look to a number of avenues to ensure the job vacancy is placed in front of as wide and diverse a range of prospective candidates as possible.

Selection methods

It is easy to overlook the fact that selection is a two-way process: the firm will wish to select the right candidate, but the candidate will also be assessing whether they will wish to accept a job offer. This suggests that the greater the professionalism of conducting the selection process, the greater the prospect of the firm appointing the desired candidate. Clarity around the selection process will help to ensure those recruiting find a suitable candidate as efficiently as possible. There is a range of methods used in recruitment such as:

- panel interview
- one-to-one interviews
- assessment centre interviews – which use a variety of selection techniques such as tests and activity based assessment to give a full picture of an individual.

A view will have to be taken on the appropriateness of each method for the vacancy in question – many larger firms are now using assessment centres for the recruitment of groups of people such as trainees, but in most firms a simple interview is all that the process entails. For senior staff, different stages of interviews over a period of time allows exposure to a broader range of decision-makers.

A panel interview will allow a number of people to have input into the selection process and would be more commonplace with senior management positions.

Conducting interviews

In any interview process it is vital to ensure consistency between candidates to be sure of fair treatment – it is extremely unwise to ask female applicants about childcare arrangements, for example, unless the same question is addressed to male applicants. If a panel interview is used it is advisable to appoint a chair who has responsibility for the process. It is sensible to agree the main questions in advance and have a clear structure for who will deal with what.

It is imperative that the decision-making process is recorded both at the shortlisting stage and at the selection stage. Candidates can ask to see the notes, so care has to be taken to avoid any suspicion of unfair treatment. Notes from any selection process must be stored pending any feedback queries for a period of 12 months.

Managing the post-interview discussion

It may be helpful to identify answers to the following questions to aid clarity in the decision-making process:

- Did the applicant demonstrate the skills level required for the position?
- Did the candidate have the required qualifications?
- Did the candidate give actual examples which were directly demonstrative of the job requirements?
- Is the candidate's experience commensurate with the levels expected for the position?

Feedback

Any candidate may request feedback from an interview process. It is now a requirement to provide information (section 5.3(f) in Lexcel: see also D1.4 in SQM), as well as an established and recommended way of individuals being satisfied that the decision was fair. It also helps them as part of their personal development to learn and prepare for future interview processes. Those involved in recruitment must identify clear reasons for selection at each stage of the process. A designated person should be appointed to give feedback when requested and therefore post-interview or post-shortlisting notes must be clear and demonstrate links between the individual and the post. The individual should be aware of the need to be factual in communicating the decision-making process and observations at interview. A written post-interview record is helpful to guide this process (see appendix 5O).

Pre-selection/appointment information

It is good practice to ask for references in support of the candidate's application and, increasingly, a requirement of insurers. Any information provided must be actual and true – judgements and opinions are dangerous. As a result references are now primarily to confirm dates of appointment in a job and such factual information as job titles, sickness records, records of 'unspent' disciplinary records and so on. Sight of academic certificates, permissions to work in the UK, national insurance details and other relevant documentation – even including photographs – may be necessary to contribute to the verification of the individual's identity. If a medical examination is a part of the required process, notification and detail of the process must be provided in advance.

Job confirmation

Following a decision, prompt communication of a job offer by telephone and followed by details in writing should be made so that candidates have clear confirmation.

Pre-joining communication

Where some time elapses between appointment and start date (as, most obviously, with trainee solicitors) keeping in touch with the future employee will start to develop an effective relationship and will reassure the individual about their choice of employer.

An opening for a fee-earner, whether through the departure of an existing member of any department or through growth, requires partnership approval. It is the responsibility for the [managing partner/other] to draft the job description and a person specification. The job description and person specification is in the format contained in these procedures at [*appendices 5B–BL*].

It is for the [managing partner/other] to determine the appropriate strategy for developing a suitable field of candidates. Methods employed include personal contacts from within the firm, firm's own advertisement and recruitment agents. Consideration is always given to internal promotion once the job description and person specification have been determined.

Selection methods are confined to interviews. A first interview will be conducted by [*name*]. A second interview is normally held and will involve two interviewers, including a representative of the department in question.

Following a decision to employ an individual, and with their consent, telephone references are taken.

Appointments of support staff are in line with the above procedures save that:

- First interviews are generally held by the administrative manager alone.
- Keyboard skills are subject to appropriate testing as part of the selection procedures.
- A second interview is less likely, but if it does occur a fee-earner will probably be required to assist.

Forms for use in selection of staff appear in the appendices [*see 5N–5P*].

The firm will often be asked to provide references on personnel who are leaving the firm or who have previously worked for it. References must be made or copied to [managing partner/personnel manager] and must be accompanied by the following disclaimer. 'This reference should not be relied upon in any decision which the recipient is considering. We accept no liability for any decisions taken or not taken as a consequence of information provided in this reference, whether direct or indirect.'

[Set out here any separate arrangements for trainee appointments]

5.4 Contracts of employment

A written contract of employment as agreed between the partners and an individual employee will be issued to all employees and will become effective from the first day of employment. (Guidance on contracts of employment is contained at appendix 5M.)

5.5 Induction

The induction process should ensure that the individual feels comfortable in his/her new role as soon as possible and is also therefore productive for the firm. Risk management is also a consideration: the firm is clearly exposed to greater risk of errors while the process of adjustment continues. An effective induction process will lessen this adjustment period. Lexcel requires that the induction process should occur within a reasonable time, while the SQM stipulates a period of no more than two months (see D.2.1). Both standards require or suggest that the induction process should extend to those transferring roles within the firm (in SQM see Guidance to D.1.5; in Lexcel 5.5).

When people join the firm, it is important that they learn its practices and procedures as quickly as possible, so that they integrate within the firm in the shortest possible time. Induction is the responsibility of [*state who is responsible for all inductions, or the different arrangements for different roles within the firm*].

The induction process will cover the issues contained in the induction training checklist (see appendix 5Q).

Induction training commences on the first day on any appointment with a meeting with [*office manager*] on fundamental aspects of the firm and its main policies. The full process may continue later. Certain aspects may be relevant when existing personnel transfer roles within the firm.

The full induction programme for staff (other than trainee solicitors) is carried out at least monthly and is the responsibility of [*specify*].

5.6 Objective setting and performance appraisal

There will need to be a process of setting performance objectives for all personnel within the practice – partners included – and some form of accompanying review at a later stage. This is not to say that it needs to be the same process for all personnel and it may well be in smaller firms that very much less detailed paperwork may be appropriate for partner reviews than would be the case for employees.

The underlying philosophy of this system of performance management is that all personnel are likely to do better when they have a clear idea of how their contribution to the firm is viewed and also how it should be improved or developed. Ideally the objectives should be informed by the overall strategy of the firm: the appraisal meeting should shape the individual's contribution to its achievement.

Performance appraisals work well where:

- the appraiser has prepared well for the meeting and has raised difficult issues in advance;

- there is an opportunity for genuine two-way discussion;
- there is time to explore views;
- the atmosphere is not intimidating or oppressive, but the appraiser is in control of the process nonetheless;
- any criticism is specific and fair examples can be provided;
- both appraiser and appraisee are looking to concentrate on future improvements, not allocate blame for what might have gone wrong in the past;
- clear, specific objectives can be agreed for the [year] ahead;
- a clear action plan, be it training activity or other, is agreed;
- there is monitoring during the year, if the firm operates an annual process, so that the discussion is not simply forgotten until appraisal time next year.

Most firms prefer to conduct all appraisals in a batch. This enables the firm to plan its training for the period ahead with a better overall view of training needs.

The first appraisal schemes in law firms date from the 1980s when individual performance related pay was at its height. Most early systems were therefore ratings based, with scores of A–E or 1–10 for each assessment. Many firms have now abandoned ratings in preference for a comments-only form. The advantages of requiring a comment instead of a mark are:

- it can be too easy to apply a mark and discussion may not be encouraged;
- middle banding often occurs in ratings based systems – as long as the shape of marks looks acceptable the process seems to have been properly conducted;
- inconsistencies between different appraisers can lead to appraisee resentment.

The precedents provided below do still include a ratings based system, but they are not now recommended.

The objectives which come out of the meeting should conform to the oft-quoted mnemonic of being 'SMART':

> **S**pecific
> **M**easurable
> **A**chievable
> **R**ealistic
> **T**ime-limited.

This can be more straightforward for financial targets than others: e.g. to bill £100,000 with a recovery rate of no less than 95%. The value of appraisals is generally seen as being more to do with the 'soft' elements of performance, however, in areas such as:

- personal efficiency
- motivation
- client manner
- internal working relationships
- new skills and responsibilities.

There are different considerations in relation to partner appraisal schemes. In larger firms differential profit-sharing arrangements are becoming more commonplace, but these can be divisive and need great care. A well functioning partner review scheme will certainly help with any such developments.

Finally, appraisals always should have been confidential, but there are now greater concerns in relation to the rights of the appraisee as to who should be able to have access to the forms or data that emerge from the process. In pursuance of data protection principles it should be stated who has access to the data. This in turn should be no more than necessary for the effective operation of the scheme. It also follows that the jobholder should have access to his/her own appraisal record.

The firm operates a performance review system (appraisals) for all members of staff. There is a similar procedure at partner level. The system involves an annual discussion which includes the setting of objectives for the year ahead.

The appraisal scheme is an opportunity to discuss the following:

- **Potential:** the appraisal provides feedback for the firm and individuals to ensure that each individual is meeting his or her potential.
- **Motivation:** appraisal allows each individual to know where he or she stands and to suggest what the firm can do to improve working conditions.
- **Development:** a means of assessing individual development. The appraisal will provide the opportunity for the firm and the individual together to assess skills, how those skills may be developed, how new skills may be acquired and what training and assistance from the firm is needed and can be given.
- **Views:** the appraisal provides an opportunity for individuals to air their views on the firm and its procedures, particularly if they feel that improvements can be made.

The characteristics of the appraisal scheme are that it is:

- **Open:** full guidance on the system is given in the *Office Procedures Manual* so that everyone understands how it works. The appraiser and the appraisee can be frank and open in the interview. Nothing recorded by the appraiser will be kept secret from the appraisee. Both parties will sign the appraisal form.
- **Confidential:** only the appraisee, the appraiser, [*the departmental head and the managing partner*] will see the appraisal.
- **Consistent:** the main procedures will apply to all staff (although there will be different appraisal forms for fee-earners and for support staff). The managing partner will also review and monitor all appraisal reports to ensure fairness and consistency of treatment.
- **Objective:** the appraisal will focus on actual conduct, performance and personal attributes, and not on generalisations or personalities.
- **Self-assessed:** appraisees will be encouraged to contribute fully to the comments, problem-solving, objective-setting and conclusions that will come from the appraisal.
- **Forward-looking:** a major value of reviewing past performance is to identify successes which can be built upon, problems that can be tackled both by the firm and the individual, training needs and new opportunities. Objectives for future action can be agreed.

Appraisal procedures

With two exceptions, all staff will be appraised annually as follows:

- fee-earners: October;
- support staff: November.

Trainee solicitors will be appraised six-monthly to coincide with their change of work area disciplines.

Because it is expected that their career development and experience will increase rapidly in the initial years after admission, assistant solicitors who have been admitted for less than three years will be appraised six-monthly.

Appraisers

The immediate [*supervising partner*] will be the appraiser. Administrative support staff will be appraised by [partnership secretary/office manager/accountant/chief cashier].

Responsibility

The [*managing partner*] will have overall responsibility for administering the appraisal procedures. (S)he will be assisted by the [personnel clerk/office manager] in the preparation and co-ordination of the appraisal documentation.

Documentation

The appraisal documentation will comprise:

- The appraisee's job description. Individuals will already have their own copy but a copy will also be provided to the appraiser.
- A copy of the previous year's appraisal which will be provided to both the appraisee and appraiser.
- A pre-appraisal questionnaire for completion by the appraisee which will be discussed with the appraiser.
- An appraisal form.

Completion timetable

The written objectives, pre-appraisal questionnaire and the appraisal form will be prepared and issued to the relevant appraiser at least two weeks before the date of the appraisal.

The appraiser will then arrange an interview time with the appraisee making sure that sufficient time is given for the appraisee to consider and prepare for the appraisal interview and for completion of the pre-appraisal questionnaire which the individual will keep.

The appraiser will ensure that sufficient time is reserved for the appraisal interview to be carried out thoroughly. The appraisee will keep the pre-appraisal questionnaire and will be given a copy of the agreed objectives.

At least an hour should be allowed for the appraisal. Avoid set appointments immediately following the time allocated for the appraisal.

Following the interview the appraiser must ensure that the appraisal report is fully completed and signed by both parties so that the report can be forwarded to [*name*] within two weeks of the appraisal date. Although the form should be completed during the meeting, the appraisee should have the opportunity to read the appraisal form and sign it subsequently if (s)he wishes.

The appraisal report will be put in the appraisee's confidential personal file and a copy will be provided to the appraisee.

Objectives

A very important part of the appraisal procedure is that objectives are agreed with the appraisee which will provide the framework for the coming year's work, including the continued development of the individual as a valued member of staff. Often objectives will set a higher standard for performance than before, perhaps designate additional responsibility, or assign a new project.

Follow-up action

It will be the immediate responsibility of the appraiser to follow up any action that was agreed as part of the appraisal. This may necessitate discussion with, for example, the departmental partner or the training partner. The appraisee should be kept informed of action being taken.

It is also possible that the appraisee will be required to take some form of agreed action. In such circumstances, responsibility will rest with the appraisee as well as with the appraiser to ensure that action is taken.

Where necessary the appraiser should arrange an interim follow-up interview and not leave matters until the next annual appraisal.

5.7 Training

Training should ideally be more than simply collecting continuing professional development (CPD) hours – important though this may be as a matter of compliance. The Lexcel standard requires all personnel to have their training needs assessed. The firm should be concerned to ensure that all training is relevant, appropriate and effective. Many firms have found in recent years that better management of training can lead to substantial savings on budgets. The most likely way to achieve this is to evaluate training requests more carefully than might have been the case in the past and explore the prospects of conducting more training in-house or closer to the office.

For details of how to obtain an in-house CPD authorisation agreement allowing the firm to apply CPD hours to its own training meetings, or for up-to-date information on the training requirements, contact the Training Department of the Law Society at Redditch.

It is the policy of the firm to maximise the job satisfaction and performance levels of all personnel through the provision of appropriate training.

Training needs are identified in appraisal interviews. All partners and staff should discuss any training needs which arise at any other time of the year with [*staff partner*], who also maintains details of external training courses.

The firm regards the training and development of all members of staff as being vital to its future and to achieving its overall objectives. It is the policy of the firm to ensure that all personnel are competent to perform all tasks that they are responsible for and are developed in a manner which is appropriate for a forward-looking professional practice.

[*Name*] has been appointed as training partner for the firm with the responsibility for planning, co-ordinating and overseeing the firm's training needs and implementation.

All staff share responsibility for the planning, implementing and evaluating of their own training needs. Training will, therefore, be a particularly important subject for discussion at each person's annual appraisal.

The practice subscribes to the [*training organisation*] subscription scheme and therefore qualifies for [*percentage*] discount on all training courses. External courses should generally be [*training organisation*] courses unless there is a course of particular significance organised by another provider.

Any fee-earner attending an external course will be required to offer a lunchtime talk to explain the contents of the course.

Computer training for all personnel is conducted by [*name*].

Any further training needs should be raised with [*training partner*].

The training plan is determined each year by the [*training partner*].

[*Describe here any special training methods, e.g. video updating services such as LNTV and arrangements for viewings*]

There are now a substantial number of providers of legal training and frequently they market their course details direct to individual solicitors or other staff as well as to the firm itself. All staff are therefore encouraged to look out for appropriate courses to develop their professional skills and knowledge, especially if such courses relate to the training needs identified at the time of the annual appraisal.

An application to attend a training course is to be made to the training partner [*name*] using the training form which follows [*see appendix 5Z(1)*].

A training record for all personnel, partners and staff will be maintained as part of the individual personnel records.

Solicitors who are subject to CPD requirements are issued with a training record booklet by the Law Society. The booklets must be maintained by the individuals. Fellows of the Institute of Legal Executives must also maintain their records as required by the Institute.

In order to maintain the central records, individuals must evaluate all external courses attended using the training evaluation form [*appendix 5Z(2)*]. This also confirms attendance.

The partners are prepared to consider day or part-day release courses on merit from any member of staff. Applications should be made through the departmental partner to the training partner. The current policy on legal executive training is available from the training partner.

APPENDIX 5A

PERSONNEL PLAN OUTLINE (5 years)

	Year 1	Year 2	Year 3	Year 4	Year 5
DEMAND **1. Staff numbers required now** Partners Solicitors Legal executives Trainees Para-legals Secretaries					
2. Business need changes to requirements during the year ahead Partners Solicitors Legal executives Trainees Para-legals Secretaries	e.g. successful tender requiring extra resource	e.g. opening new office	e.g. legislative changes requiring new category (advocate)		
3. Total (1+2) Partners, etc.					
SUPPLY **4. Numbers available, i.e. existing staff numbers** Partners, etc.					
5. Gains, e.g. trainee qualifiers, intake from new merger, promotions to partnership, PQE development from junior to senior solicitor Partners, etc.					
6. Losses (a) Retirements (b) Turnover* (c) Promotions out of category Partners, etc.					
7. Total available (4 + 5 – 6) Partners, etc.					
REQUIREMENT Deficit (3 – 7) = Additional numbers required Partners, etc.					

* Turnover calculation:

$$\frac{\text{Number of leavers in a specified period (usually 1 year)}}{\text{Average number of employees during the same period}} \times 100 = \text{Turnover}$$

APPENDIX 5B

JOB DESCRIPTION: PARTNER

Title: Partner

Reports to: The Partnership

Reported to by: [names]

Main purposes of role

1. Undertake and supervise fee-earning work in [category] and deputise in the supervision of [any other area].
2. Ensure the successful development of the firm in line with the strategy identified in the business plan.

Key tasks (not an exhaustive list)

3. Conduct of matters on behalf of clients.
4. Supervision of fee-earning work (including acting as designated supervisor and liaison manager with the LSC).
5. Management of all fee-earning and support staff within the department.
6. Financial control with particular regard to cash flow control through collection of monies on account and billing procedures.
7. Undertake regular reviews of business development, to include reviews of the forward and services plan for franchise compliance.
8. Promoting the firm and organisation of marketing activity undertaken by the firm.
9. Ensuring compliance with quality control procedures for all matters within his/her control.
10. Deputising during absences of other partners, in particular [specify].

Skills and experience

11. Admitted as a solicitor with [number] years post-qualification experience.
12. Competent in computer use for fee-earners.
13. As supervisor of all franchise categories within the office it is necessary to undertake all necessary CPD training.

APPENDIX 5C

JOB DESCRIPTION: PARTNER – longer format

Name:

Department:

Responsible to:

Date:

1. Qualifications

1.1. Admission to the Solicitors Roll.

2. Role

2.1. An equity partner has three major roles within the partnership:
   (a) to be an owner/shareholder of the firm and thereby entitled to a share in the declared profits;
   (b) to be a senior manager of the firm's affairs;
   (c) to be a prime fee-earner.

The commitment of a partner is beyond that expected of an employee. Such commitment is not limited to office hours. A partner is expected to devote such hours as are required to carry out the full role of a partner including the duties summarised in this document. [*Modify if appropriate for part-time partners.*]

Main duties

3. Management and administration

3.1. To undertake compliance with and to be fully aware of all aspects of requirements imposed on a partner by the Solicitors Act, Solicitors' Accounts Rules and Trust Account Rules, and all other Statutory and Law Society Rules and Regulations from time to time in force for the conduct of the business of a solicitor.

3.2. To comply faithfully in all respects with the impositions of the partnership deed and all resolutions, directions or request from any body or group exercising delegated authority of the partners.

3.3. To encourage and promote the image and ethos of the firm.

3.4. To actively seek ways to contribute to the continuing evolution and development of the firm.

3.5. To have special regard for the needs and interests of any member of staff within an area of responsibility delegated to the partner.

3.6. To advise and supervise any member of staff and especially within an area of responsibility delegated to the partner.

3.7. To contribute towards training both in respect of staff and own self-development.

3.8. To undertake both staff and partner appraisals.

3.9. To communicate the needs of the partnership especially to all members of the staff within an area of responsibility delegated to the partner.

3.10. To undertake any specified management responsibility. [*Consider specific financial responsibilities re billing, cash collection and monitoring of reports and other data*]

3.11. To be familiar with and comply with the requirements of the firm's *Office Manual* and quality standards procedures.

4. Fee-earning

4.1. To ensure the confidentiality and security of all firm and client documentation and information.
4.2. To maintain high standards in the processing of client work, both in respect of professional standards and client care.
4.3. To maintain good professional working relationships with external institutions and organisations.
4.4. To adhere to agreed practice procedure as determined from time to time, especially as related to quality standards.
4.5. To achieve agreed financial targets, both in respect of fee income and the recording of chargeable hours.
4.6. To provide advice and guidance and thorough supervision to other subordinate fee-earners and support staff within an area of responsibility delegated to the partner.
4.7. To develop leadership skills and the ability to optimise team performance.
4.8. Through training and other means, to keep fully up to date with relevant legislation and practice.
4.9. To monitor and help develop systems and procedures within the partner's work area, including the use of technology.
4.10. To market the firm's client services.
4.11. To assist in the development of new products and service opportunities.

Special duties

[*Record here any specific duties, responsibilities or appointments of the partner*]

APPENDIX 5D

JOB DESCRIPTION: FEE-EARNER

Job Description: Fee-earner

Reports to: Head of department

Reported to by: Secretary

Main purposes

1. To undertake fee-earning work and provide a profitable contribution to the work of the department.
2. To ensure the successful development of the firm in line with the business plan.

Key tasks (not an exhaustive list)

3. Conduct of matters on behalf of clients.
4. Supervision of fee-earning work undertaken by colleagues.
5. Management of support services for which (s)he is responsible, including supervision of own secretary.
6. Participation in marketing activities whether on a firmwide, departmental or office basis.
7. Financial control with particular regard to cash flow control through collection of monies on account and billing procedures.

APPENDIX 5E

JOB DESCRIPTION: PARTNER – showing breakdown of office time

Job title	Solicitor

Main responsibility	1. Client management
	2. Business development
	3. Legal advice (specialist area – commercial property)
	4. Management of systems – financial and quality
	5. Firm responsibilities for management of people and relationships
	   (a) management of secretarial and administration support
	   (b) supervision of trainees

Time allocation guidance to be reviewed annually	It is expected that the responsibilities within this role divide into the following proportions: **Job description – time guide** Pie chart legend: ■ Client contact ■ Legal advice □ Billing and time recording □ File management ■ Management and supervision
Detail of tasks	**Client management and development** 1. To manage all client work allocated by [*specify*]. 2. To ensure client communication and contact is regular, timely and sufficient for the client's requirements. 3. To participate as a member of the firm in client development activity and to promote the firm. 4. To produce work to the required standard of professionals to encourage referrals and repeat business. **Legal advice** 1. To keep up to date with developments in the law, taking responsibility for self-development and ensuring CPD is observed. 2. To apply the law effectively to client problems. 3. To meet with all requirements of the Law Society regulations for professional conduct and comply with the Solicitors' Accounts Rules. **Billing and time recording** 1. To ensure firm's procedures are followed when recording time and managing the billing process. 2. To meet set targets. **File management** 1. To manage work in accordance with the firm's set procedures and quality standards. 2. To ensure confidentiality and security of all documentation. 3. To progress work efficiently and effectively. **Management and supervision** 1. To manage and supervise secretarial and administration staff to produce the best service for the client. 2. To develop less experienced staff to achieve their full potential. 3. To supervise trainees within the Law Society's definition when required. 4. To manage his/her own relationships within the firm to contribute to a positive working environment for everyone.

APPENDIX 5F

JOB DESCRIPTION: PARA-LEGAL

Title:	Legal administrator/Para-legal
Reports to:	[specify]
Reported to by:	Junior
Member of:	Family Law Team

Main purpose of job

1. To provide cost effective administrative and secretarial support to the partner and other senior fee-earners in the team in the work of the department.

Key tasks include

2. Undertake certain elements of fee-earning work under supervision. In particular:

   - file creation;
   - generation of suitable client care correspondence;
   - completion of client questionnaires;
   - drafting of petition/court documentation;
   - attendance at routine directions/interlocutory hearings.

   The jobholder is not designated as a matter handler for file review purposes and does not therefore have his/her own file caseload.

3. Deal wherever possible with routine client enquiries and communications.
4. Manage the collation of matter start and matter completion data and prepare all claims for costs, referring major matters to costs clerk by agreement with [specify].
5. Deputise for [specify] in his/her absence, passing urgent issues to another senior fee-earner for guidance [if a small team].
6. Co-ordination of the key dates reminder system as outlined in the Office Manual.

Person specification

7. The main qualifications for this position are experience of family work over a [number] year period in the firm.
8. The jobholder must display a pleasant, but assertive manner in dealing with colleagues and clients. Tact and resilience are essential qualities.
9. An effective communicator, both orally and in writing, having a good command of written English [add any other linguistic skills if dealing with high degree of ethnic client group not having English as a first language. Note: a requirement for good written English should be kept under review. If not actually necessary for the job in question it could be seen as discriminatory.]
10. Personally efficient and well organised, with good control of diary systems and competent in the firm's computer facilities.

Likely training requirements

Background to area of law, if not attending legal executive study
Billing/costs/legal aid
IT
Basic advocacy

APPENDIX 5G

JOB DESCRIPTION: LEGAL SECRETARY

Name:	**Appointment:** Legal Secretary
Department:	**Responsible to:**
Date:	

1. Required qualifications, skills and experience

1.1. Trained in secretarial practice.
1.2. High word-processing and audio-typing skills.
1.3. Preferably previous experience as a legal secretary or experience of working in an alternative professional office.

2. Role

The prime role of the legal secretary is to provide direct support to his/her principal to enable the principal to operate at optimum efficiency. This will include but will not be limited to the main responsibilities given below. The legal secretary is expected to use a high degree of self-management and initiative.

3. Main responsibilities

3.1. To prepare correspondence and documents through audio-typing and word processing.
3.2. To administer filing which will include daily filing and the opening, closing, storage and retrieval of client files in accordance with the detailed procedures contained in the Office Manual.
3.3. To prepare mail and enclosures for despatch.
3.4. To arrange for all copying to be done, in person if the office junior is not available to undertake the task.
3.5. To make appointments, arrange meetings and to maintain an up-to-date diary for his/her principal.
3.6. To prepare the Conference Room for meetings as necessary and for the tidying and clearance of the room at the end of the meeting.
3.7. To provide refreshments when asked to do so.
3.8. To provide support to other secretaries as required.
3.9. To provide guidance to junior and temporary secretaries when required to do so.
3.10. To attend clients both in person and on the telephone and to provide such support in a professional and friendly manner in keeping with the firm's standards for client care.
3.11. To undertake any specific training when required to do so and overall to have a responsibility towards self-development.
3.12. To ensure the confidentiality of all the firm's and clients' documentation and information.

4. Specific requirements

[*specify*]

APPENDIX 5H

JOB DESCRIPTION: RECEPTIONIST

Name: **Appointment:** Receptionist

Department: Administration   **Responsible to:**

Date:

1. Required qualifications, skills, experience

1.1. Trained on modern telephone systems and preferably with experience in a professional office. High standard of inter-personal and communication skills, especially in the context of client care.

2. Role

2.1. The prime responsibilities are first to process all incoming telephone calls with no undue delay and in a courteous and helpful manner. Similarly, as receptionist, to receive and process all visitors to the firm, especially clients, in a helpful, friendly and professional manner. In these respects, there is a high degree of responsibility to project the image and ethos of the firm at all times.

3. Main responsibilities

3.1. The effective processing of all incoming telephone calls including the logging of calls and the conveying of messages.
3.2. The provision of telephone support to partners and other staff members as required.
3.3. Dealing with all visitors to the reception area, especially new clients.
3.4. Administration of the facsimile machine.
3.5. To ensure the tidiness of the reception area.
3.6. To undertake other clerical and administrative duties as may reasonably be required from time to time.
3.7. To ensure the confidentiality and security of the firm's and clients' documentation and information.

APPENDIX 5I

JOB DESCRIPTION: LEGAL CASHIER

Name: **Appointment:** Legal Cashier

Department: Accounts **Responsible to:**

Date:

Required qualifications, skills and experience

Trained in the principles of book-keeping and preferably with sound experience in legal cashiering. Computer literacy is desirable/a requirement.

Main responsibilities

1. To undertake daily banking functions including bank reconciliations.
2. The administration and reconciliation of petty cash.
3. The processing of client and office accounting transactions including postings.
4. The preparation of cheques.
5. The processing of bank transfers.
6. The control of designated client deposit accounts.
7. The preparation of credit control advice.
8. The administration of the purchase ledger.
9. Financial management reporting as required.
10. The preparatory work for the annual accounts.
11. PAYE.
12. VAT administration and returns.
13. Administration of the partnership cars, office insurance, practising certificates, professional indemnity insurance.

Specific responsibilities

[specify]

APPENDIX 5J

JOB DESCRIPTION: OFFICE JUNIOR

Name: **Appointment:** Office Junior

Department: Administration   **Responsible to:**

Date:

1. Required qualifications, skills, experience

1.1. Smart in appearance and manner and has a willingness to learn administrative skills in a professional office.

2. Main responsibilities

2.1. Deliver messages to the courts.
2.2. Undertake photocopying tasks.
2.3. Collect and distribute Document Exchange mail.
2.4. Deliver Document Exchange mail to [*specify scheme*].
2.5. Prepare post for despatch.
2.6. Take special deliveries to the Post Office.
2.7. Return library books to [*local law library*].
2.8. Act as relief telephonist/receptionist.
2.9. Provide refreshments when asked to do so.

APPENDIX 5K

JOB DESCRIPTION: TRAINEE SOLICITOR

Name: **Appointment:** Trainee Solicitor

Department: As required **Responsible to:**

Date:

1. **Required qualifications, skills and experience**

1.1. Completion of degree and LPC.
1.2. Preferably computer keyboard skills.

2. **Main responsibilities**

2.1. Carry out client work as allocated by partners and other fee-earners, under their supervision.
2.2. Ensure that all client work is progressed expeditiously.
2.3. At all times to exercise high standards of client care in a professional and pleasant manner.
2.4. Ensure the confidentiality and security of all of the firm's and client documentation and information.
2.5. Comply with the Solicitors' Accounts Rules and the Rules on the Professional Conduct of Solicitors.
2.6. Maintain clear and precise communications with other personnel of the firm.
2.7. Ensuring good working relationships with external institutions and organisations.
2.8. Adhere to the terms of the Training Contract.

3. **Specific responsibilities**

[*specify*]

APPENDIX 5L

PERSON SPECIFICATION: GENERAL

Job title	Senior solicitor
Essential	Years qualified at PQE Experience of [*specialist area*]
Desirable	Level of academic attainment IT skill Experience of [*client sector*]
Special responsibilities	Must demonstrate the ability to handle a high workload, largely unsupervised Must have experience in supervision of trainees and some involvement with managerial responsibility
Required competencies	Effective communication Problem-solving skills Openness to change etc.

APPENDIX 5M

CONTRACT OF EMPLOYMENT FORMAT

Explanatory Notes

The legal relationship between employer and employee is one of contract, based on common law principles. Statutes have established a number of rights of employees arising out of their employment.

A contract of employment exists when an employer and an employee agree upon the terms and conditions of employment. This is often shown by the employee's starting work on the terms offered by the employer. Both are bound by the agreed terms. A contract of employment need not be in writing when formed and can be oral, implied or a mixture of all three. Employees are entitled to receive a written statement of the main particulars of their employment. This statement is not in itself a contract but it may be used to establish what has been agreed in the contract of employment.

ACAS is an excellent source of information and advice on contracts of employment and their variation. A range of publications is also available. For up-to-date information go to **www.acas.org.uk**. There is a publications choice on this website. Another useful source of advice is **www.dti.gov.uk**.

It remains the case that disciplinary procedures as such are not a requirement of Lexcel. Nonetheless, such procedures should be included in any contract of employment. ACAS guidelines are that disciplinary procedures should:

(a) Be in writing.
(b) Specify to whom they apply.
(c) Provide for matters to be dealt with quickly.
(d) Indicate the disciplinary actions which may be taken.
(e) Specify the levels of management which have the authority to take the various forms of disciplinary action, ensuring that immediate superiors do not normally have the power to dismiss without reference to senior management.
(f) Provide for individuals to be informed of the complaints against them and to be given an opportunity to state their case before decisions can be reached.
(g) Give individuals the right to be accompanied by a trade union representative or by a fellow employee of their choice.
(h) Ensure that, except for gross misconduct, no employees are dismissed for the first breach of discipline.
(i) Ensure that disciplinary action is not taken until the case has been carefully investigated.
(j) Ensure that individuals are given an explanation for any penalty imposed.
(k) Provide a right of appeal and specify the procedure to be followed.

As of 2004 there will be compulsory requirements for dispute resolution procedures in relation to disciplinary and grievance procedures.

If a restrictive covenant is included the firm will need to consider if it is proportionate and likely to be upheld.

It is necessary to state if there are any collective agreements that affect the employee – this draft envisages that there are none.

Other issues that firms should consider include:

- parental leave;
- adoption leave;
- paternity leave;
- how requests for flexible working will be dealt with;
- access to stakeholder pension.

Precedent

To:

From:

The following particulars are the terms on which you are employed and are given to you pursuant to the Employment Rights Act 1996 as amended principally by the Employment Relations Act 1999. There are no collective agreements in place within the firm.

1.　Parties

1.1.　Employer

　　　The partners collectively at any particular time practising as [*name*] of [*address*] or their successors (hereinafter called 'the partners')

1.2.　Employee

　　　Surname:

　　　Forenames:

2.　Date of employment

The date when your employment began was [*date*]. Any employment with a previous employer does not count as part of your period of continuous employment with this firm.

3.　Appointment

Your appointment is as an assistant solicitor. It is a condition of employment that you remain on the roll of solicitors.

4.　Hours of work

The normal office hours are [*specify*] Monday to Friday inclusive with a luncheon period from [*specify*], subject to any variation required in the normal course of business or as otherwise agreed with the partners.

5.　Salary

Your current salary is [*amount*] per annum payable monthly in arrears on the [25th day] of each calendar month direct into your private bank account. [Your salary will be reviewed annually as at [1 November] in each year of employment.] [(*for newly admitted solicitors*) Your salary will be reviewed as at [1 November] and [1 May] in each year of your employment or until you have been admitted for three years. Thereafter your salary will be reviewed annually as at 1 November.]

6.　Pension

The firm has contracted into the state pension scheme.

7.　Motor insurance and motoring expenses

7.1.　You are required to have a motor vehicle for your own use on the firm's business and you are to ensure that it is fully insured for such purpose. The cover must include a situation when another member of staff may be carried as a passenger in your private vehicle when being used on the firm's business and that the passenger may be travelling on different firm's business to that of yourself.

7.2. A mileage allowance at a rate to be determined from time to time by the partners will be paid to you for any mileage that you may make on the firm's business.
7.3. [You will be provided with a local authority car park season ticket.]

8. Other expenses

The firm will pay for your [practising certificate, membership of the Law Society, local Law Society, Solicitors Benevolent Association and other professional organisations] as the partners may approve.

9. BUPA

From the [date] the firm will pay for membership of BUPA on an individual basis.

10. Holidays

10.1. During the first five years of employment you are entitled to 20 working days per year.
10.2. Upon completion of five years of employment excluding any time under articles, you are entitled to 25 working days per year.
10.3. In addition to public holidays you will be entitled to additional days holidays at the discretion of the partners.
10.4. The holiday year commences on the [1 May] and subject to agreement by the partners there is no restriction on when holidays may be taken or the number of days taken at any one time.

11. Retirement

The normal retirement age will be 65.

12. Sickness

The provisions of the Social Security Contribution and Benefits Act 1992 relating to the payment of statutory sick pay will apply. In order to maintain the statutory sickness records, you are required to report all periods of sickness to the partners, and for periods of sickness of seven consecutive days or more, a doctor's medical certificate is to be provided. You are required to make application for sickness benefit when eligible in accordance with the statutory provisions for the time being in force. Your full salary, abated in full by any sickness benefit, will be paid to you for the following maximum cumulative periods in any 12-month period terminating on the day to which entitlement to remuneration is being calculated at any time.

12.1. During the first 12 months of employment, [one month].
12.2. Between 12 and 24 months' employment, [two months].
12.3. After 24 months' employment, [six months].

13. Recovery of damages

If at any time whether during or after the termination of your employment with the firm, you recover in damages from any other person or personal injury resulting in absence from work with the firm, you shall, whether demanded of you or not, repay to the partners an amount equivalent to the total of all remuneration paid to you by the firm in respect of the period or periods of any such absence (save that you will not be required to pay under this provision a sum greater than the sum recovered by way of damages which is attributable to the loss of remuneration).

14. Notice of termination of employment by the employee

The following periods of notice of termination of employment are to be given by the employee:

14.1. The minimum period to be given is four weeks.
14.2. After 12 months' completed service, two calendar months.
14.3. After 12 years' completed service, 12 weeks.

15. Notice of termination of employment by employer

The following periods of notice of termination of employment will be given by the employer:

15.1. The minimum period to be given will be four weeks.
15.2. After 12 months' completed service, two calendar months.
15.3. After 12 years' completed service, 12 weeks.

16. Waiver

Employers or employees can waive their rights to notice or to payment in lieu of notice. Either party can terminate the contract of employment without notice if the conduct of the other justifies it.

17. Pay on termination of employment

On termination of your employment, you will be entitled to pay calculated as a proportion of one month's salary equivalent to the same proportion which the number of days worked bear to the number of days for the month in which the employment terminates plus payment for any days holiday accrued but not taken.

18. Discipline and grievance procedure

18.1. A breach of the following rules may result in instant dismissal without warning by any two partners:

18.1.1. improper use of or disclosure of information concerning the partners' practice or the clients of the firm which may come to your knowledge by reason of your employment;
18.1.2. any conduct which in the opinion of the partners may have the effect of bringing the integrity and reputation of the firm into disrepute.

18.2. In the event that any one of the partners being dissatisfied with your work, conduct, time keeping or any other aspect of your employment, any such one or more partners may give you a verbal warning as to the matter causing dissatisfaction.
    If after a reasonable period the partners remain dissatisfied with the matter complained of, you may be given a final written warning and if the partners continue to be dissatisfied with the matter complained of, you may be given the minimum notice of dismissal to which you are entitled by virtue of the length of your employment with the firm.

18.3. If during the course of your employment you receive more than one verbal warning under sub-paragraph 18.2 of this clause for any one or number of matters, then you may be given a final written warning that if any matter subsequently warrants a further verbal warning, you may be dismissed.

18.4. No disciplinary action will be taken until your case has been investigated by at least two partners. If any disciplinary action is taken, you will be given a full explanation by the partners.

18.5. If you are dissatisfied with any disciplinary decision relating to you or have any grievance relating to your employment, you may apply in writing within 14 days of such decision or the occasion of such grievance, to the branch partner or any other partner who is acting branch partner in his or her absence, or to another branch partner. You will be given the opportunity to state your case to him or her before any decision is reached and you may be accompanied by any one employee of your choice from the firm.

18.6. If you wish to appeal against any decision taken by the branch partner relating to your employment this should be made in writing within 14 days to the senior partner present at the time. An appeal will be heard by three partners (including the branch partner when possible) and you may be accompanied by any one employee of your choice from the firm.

18.7. If you wish to raise any issue by way of grievance please do so initially by talking to your head of department. If this does not resolve matters to your satisfaction please address your concerns in writing to the managing partner. In all cases we will take all steps that we are reasonably able to do to address any problem brought to our attention.

19. **Restrictive covenant**

Save with the written consent of the partners you will not:

19.1. during the period of one year after the termination of your employment with the firm canvass, solicit, approach any client of the firm for the purpose of providing or giving legal advice or services to that client;

19.2. during the period of one year after the termination of your employment with the firm either alone or in partnership or as an agent, consultant or employee of any other person or firm practise as a solicitor within a range of [one/two/three] miles from any office from which the partnership practises at the date hereof.

The foregoing restrictions are considered reasonable by the partners and shall be treated as separate obligations and shall be severally enforceable as such.

20. **Unions**

The partners confirm your right to join a union of your choice and to take part in its activities.

21. **Pregnancy**

In the event of your becoming pregnant, the maternity provisions set out in the Employment Rights Act 1996 as amended will apply. These regulations will be explained in detail should the need arise.

22. **Car usage**

It is a requirement of the job that you maintain a driving licence [*consider whether appropriate for office based personnel*].

23. **Money laundering training**

The firm has a responsibility to ensure anti-money laundering training for all personnel and it is a condition of your employment that you undertake such training as instructed.

24. **Compliance with quality system**

The firm is committed to the Lexcel scheme of the Law Society and you must follow the firm's policies and procedures as set out in our quality system.

Signed ....
A partner for and on behalf of [*name*]

Signed ....   Dated................................
Employee

APPENDIX 5N

INTERVIEW ASSESSMENT FORM

[Bear in mind that this form, when completed, will be disclosable under Data Protection principles to the candidate that it relates to. Also ensure that all criteria are objective and necessary for the position in question.]

VACANCY		CANDIDATE				
FACTOR	**COMMENTS**	**RATING**				
		A	B	C	D	E
Qualification and training Experience Knowledge & skills Personality Recommendation						

A = Excellent
B = Good
C = Average
D = Poor
E = Very poor

Comments and Actions

Interviewer/head of panel _____ Date _____

APPENDIX 5O

COMPETENCY BASED INTERVIEW PAPERWORK

1. Competency definition

Job title	Solicitor
Client contact	Demonstrates client management skills
Legal advice	Applies technical know-how in a practical and commercial way
Time recording and billing	Completes and provides time records Meets targets
File management	Presents high quality of work Demonstrates good personal work Management skill and is able to handle high workload
Management and supervision	Uses internal resources effectively

2. Interview assessment form

Name of applicant: Interviewers:		Date of interview:	
Example			
Competence 1	**Problem solving**		**Notes of example**
Question 1	Describe the most complex client issue you have dealt with recently		
			Competence demonstrated: Y/N
Competence definition	• Finds new ways of solving problems • Identifies clear goals and proceeds logically through the decision-making process to achieve the goal • Gathers information from range of sources • Analyses information to identify issues • Considers risk and has alternative strategy for action • Takes a systematic approach • Identifies inconsistencies in information • Considers views of others		
Total score	Problem solving		

Competence 2	Influencing	Notes of example
Question 2	Give an example of an occasion where you have had to advise a client or a partner or a colleague to make a difficult or controversial decision	
		Competence demonstrated: Y/N
Competence definition	<ul><li>Delivers powerful argument</li><li>Sells benefits</li><li>Negotiates to find solutions</li><li>Challenges others when it is in the client's or firm's best interests to do so</li><li>Supports arguments with facts, logic and reason</li><li>Handles objections with skill</li><li>Understands others' position</li><li>Involves others appropriately</li></ul>	
Total score	Influencing	
Etc. per competence		
Total overall score on measured competences		

APPENDIX 5P

REFERENCE REQUEST

Dear Sir/Madam

Re: Reference Request

Mr/Mrs/Miss/Ms [*name*] has applied for the position of [*specify*] in our firm.

Mr/Mrs/Miss/Ms [*name*] has given permission to contact you and any information you provide will be treated in strict confidence. I would be grateful if you could provide us with details of his/her position in your organisation and comment on his/her suitability for the position applied for.

Please provide any additional information which would be relevant to this reference.

Yours faithfully

APPENDIX 5Q

INDUCTION TRAINING FORM

Name:
Job title:
Supervising Partner:
Start date:

Pre-start date

Check work area

Appoint a supportive colleague

Brief other staff

Book any introductory training – IT, telephone?

Book appointments to meet 'key' colleagues/partners

First day lunch arrangements

First day

Welcome

Show the individual his/her personal working area/desk/office

Introduction to key staff

Tour of the building – key areas

Cover key staff/legislative issues – fire drill, security, accident, smoking, breaks, staff exits/entrances outside hours – door codes, etc.

Check receipt of key documents – Staff Handbook/contracts, etc.

Explain structure of team/firm – key names and jobholders

Explain quality procedures

Allow for questions

Book follow-up meeting

Short-form money laundering package provided and explained?

Within 3 weeks

Check health/welfare – risk assessment

Ensure policies and procedures understood

Allow for questions

After 12 weeks

Training needs

Check knowledge and understanding of role and firm

Within 6 months

Initial performance review

Set objectives for period up to formal annual review

APPENDIX 5R

PARTNER REVIEW/APPRAISAL FORM – small firm

1. Job responsibilities: [*add specific responsibilities not reflected in job description*]
2. Professional issues: challenges arising in area of practice
3. Personal objectives for next 12 months
4. Legal training requirements
5. Management training requirements
Reviewer Signed ....Date .... Partner under review Signed ....Date ....

APPENDIX 5S

PARTNER REVIEW/APPRAISAL REPORT FORM
[with optional ratings]

Partner reviewed:	Reviewed by:
Date of review:	

Business performance

Fees billed in year individually _____

Fees billed in year by team _____

Profitability of department or team
(if applicable) _____

Comments

Objectives

Professional responsibilities

Knowledge and expertise

Problem solving

Areas for professional development
(see also later: Training)

[Rating]

Client handling skills and marketing

Client handling skills

Organisation and support for marketing functions and activities

Personal profile in local or client community

[Rating]

Managerial and supervisory quality

Leadership: setting directions and goals for team

Motivation: ability to inspire team

Application of quality system
Co-ordination of team or department (if applicable)
[Rating]
Personal qualities
Sensitivity of personnel welfare
Flexibility
Resilience
Personal motivation and enthusiasm
[Rating]
Overall rating
Business performance
Managerial and supervisory
Professional responsibilities
Personal qualities
Client handling skills and marketing
Overall rating
Personal development objectives
_____ by when? _____
_____ by when? _____
_____ by when? _____
Training to undertake
_____
_____
_____
Signed
Reviewer (1) _____   Date _____
Reviewer (2) _____   Date _____
Appraisee   _____   Date _____

APPENDIX 5T

PRE-APPRAISAL QUESTIONS FOR APPRAISEE

Please reply to the following questions: [*or select from these if you would like a shorter form*]

1. What skills do you believe are necessary to carry out your job?

2. What personal qualities are needed to carry out your job?

3. Which part of the job interests you most?

4. Which part interests you least?

5. How do you feel you have performed in the last six months/year?

6. Which tasks do you think you could have performed more effectively and why?

7. Which tasks do you feel you have performed particularly well?

8. Are there any improvements which could be made to the way in which you work that would make you more efficient?

9. Do you possess skills, knowledge or experience acquired elsewhere of which we do not make full use?

10. Which areas of your job are you unclear about?

11. Does your job description properly describe your duties and responsibilities?

12. Do you feel that you could take on other responsibilities, such as supervision, administrative duties, etc.?

13. Where would you like to be in one year and five years' time?

14. Are there any general matters that you would like to discuss?

This preparation form could either be required to be submitted a day or two before the appraisal meeting or it could be brought to the meeting by the appraisee. Users may consider limiting questions to the more important ones – this is quite a long list.

APPENDIX 5U

ALTERNATIVE PRE-APPRAISAL QUESTIONNAIRE

Name of Appraisee:	Department:
Job title:	Appraiser's name:

In order to prepare for your appraisal meeting, please spend a little time considering the issues raised in this form. You should note your comments so that you will be able to discuss the issues raised. This form will not be taken in by the person conducting your interview and does not form part of the formal record of the interview.

The appraisal meeting is your opportunity to:

(a) discuss your work and how it fits in with the work of the team that you belong to and the firm as a whole;

(b) agree on possible improvements to your role and the means by which improvements will be achieved;

(c) decide what training might be appropriate during the year ahead.

At your appraisal meeting a report form will be filled in. You will see this report and you should sign it only if you agree with the comments contained in it.

1. Job description

You will find attached to this form a copy of your current job description. Is this a fair and correct description of your role or does it need amendment? If so, how?

2. Your work

What do you like best about your job?

And what do you like least about your job?

(Fee-earners and managers only)

If possible, list two tasks which you think you achieved particular success in.

If possible, list two tasks which you did not perform as well as you should have, and the reasons why.

3. Your team

How could your job be reorganised to make it more satisfying for you and/or more effective for the firm?

Would you benefit from changed supervisory arrangements? If so, what changes would you suggest?

4. Your development

Are there any personal goals that you would like to set for yourself over the next year? If so, what are they?

In which areas would you welcome training, if any?

APPENDIX 5V

FEE-EARNER APPRAISAL WITH RATINGS – short form

Name:	Date of review:
Job title	
Main tasks of job **Main purpose(s) of job** 1. 2. 3. 4. 5.	Skills, knowledge, abilities and experience required to undertake these tasks
Aspects of my job that I most enjoy	
Main purpose(s) of job	
Aspects of my job I least enjoy	

Aspects of my job where I could improve
Personal objectives for next 12 months

Training (if any) that will enable me to achieve these objectives	
	By when

Signed ………………………………. Signed ……………………………….
(Appraiser)   (Appraisee)

APPENDIX 5W

APPRAISAL FORM WITHOUT RATINGS

This form is confidential once it has been completed but will be discussed between each of the people in the appraisal meeting. It will then be a formal record of the review meeting. Appraisers should not record comments unless they have been discussed and, preferably, agreed. If agreement is not possible please set out the different views held.

Appraisees are asked to sign the form at the end and put in their own comments if appropriate.

Name of Appraisee:	Department:
Job title:	Appraisors:

1. Job description

Do you consider that the current job description is in need of amendment? If so, please note the required changes here.

2. Technical ability   (Fee-earners)
    Secretarial skills   (Secretaries)
    Job expertise   (Administrators)

Comment:

3. Volume of work and reliability

Comment:

4. Knowledge of the firm

Please comment on knowledge of the firm and compliance with quality procedures:

5. Personal organisation

Please comment on:

Organisation of work

Ability to meet deadlines

Reliability of administration

6. Problem solving and decision making (Fee-earners only)

Comment on ability to inspire confidence in clients in respect of the above:

7. Relationship with colleagues

Comment:

8. Communication

Please comment on communication, both written and verbal, with colleagues, clients and others:

9. Personal objectives

In the light of the above, please try to agree a number of performance objectives. Please be as specific as possible and put a time limit on each.

1.

2.

3.

4.

10. Training

What training might assist in achieving the objectives set out above?

1.

2.

3.

4.

Summary comments by Appraiser

Date

Summary comments by Appraisee

Date

Notes: Managing partner/HOD/Staff partner/Personnel manager

Date

Future action (if any)

APPENDIX 5X

COMPETENCY BASED APPRAISAL FORM

Example – requirements need to be tailored to individual firm requirements

---

Name:

Start date:

Date of qualification:

Review date:

Date of last review:

Objectives of the appraisal/performance review

- To ensure understanding of expected work standards and to give feedback on the achievement of these
- To identify areas of strength and those areas that need further development
- To plan future development and career goals
- To encourage continuous self-assessment of performance
- To assist open communication of the firm's objectives and the role individuals play in their achievement
- To give an opportunity for individuals to feedback to the partners to encourage a two-way flow of information

Policy

- Everyone will have an annual appraisal
- New staff will be reviewed at 6 months and at 1 year after joining
- A post-appraisal discussion is available with a third party if requested
- The supervising partner is responsible for the appraisals process being carried out as agreed by the firm's policy
- Both parties will prepare for the interview
- Objectives for the year will be agreed in line with the firm's business plan
- A record of the discussion and the agreed objectives will be made and kept by the individual and the firm

Main areas of competence required
Solicitor

- Technical ability – legal advice
- Management of people and relationships
- Management of systems – financial and quality
- Client management
- Business development

PEOPLE MANAGEMENT 115

Tasks and Competence	Notes and supporting examples	Achieved level: very competent (V) competent (C) needs development (D)
Technical competence (definitions demonstrate (C) level)		
Demonstrates appropriate level of technical knowledge for years PQE by: • demonstrating confidence with basic procedures for the work type • seeking support at appropriate level • developing self by expanding technical knowledge • identifying accurately areas of development required • applying legal and common sense solutions • carrying out work in a 'commercial' way • presenting a consistent high quality of work		
Management of people and relationships • Uses resource appropriately, i.e. secretarial support, other business support departments • Communicates appropriately • Gives clear instruction • Maintains good working relationships • Develops others		
Management of systems (a) Financial • Provides time records to support management and financial information requirements • Meets targets for WIP, billing and time • Manages realisation rate • Meets billing targets • Manages utilisation to acceptable level (b) Quality systems • Organises client/matter files to meet quality standard requirements • Manages personal workload effectively and efficiently • Meets objectives		
Client management • Manages existing client relationships effectively • Meets client requirements in terms of contact, communication, managing expectations		
Business development • Sees opportunity for cross-selling firm's activities • Takes part in business development activity • Contributes to business development/client database		

Main competencies/behaviours (See role definitions)	Evidence	V C D
Problem solving		
Influencing		
Effective communication		
Resilience		
etc.		

Record of discussion

Objectives for next 12 months

Development areas

Signed Appraisee ....

Appraiser ....

Date ....

APPENDIX 5Y

STAFF APPRAISAL FORM WITH RATINGS

Name:

Department:

Appraiser:

Period covered by appraisal:

Please see separate notes concerning the descriptions

This form is for completion at your appraisal meeting and is the formal record of your discussions. Each criterion should be discussed and a tick entered as appropriate. The appraisee may either sign the form at the meeting or take it away for further consideration.

Individual attributes	Excellent	Good	Satisfactory	Needs improvement
Professional specialist knowledge				
Overall professional effectiveness				
Effective intelligence				
Client relationships				
Managerial competence				
Written expression				
Oral expression				
Teamwork				
Energy				
Presence				
Self-development				

Objectives	**By when**
_____	_____
_____	_____
_____	_____

Training

Specify training which will help with above:

Appraiser comments

Appraisee comments

	Appraiser	Appraisee	HOD
Signed:	_____	_____	_____
Date:	_____	_____	_____

GUIDANCE ON COMPLETION OF ATTRIBUTES

Professional specialist knowledge

In relation to experience, assess professional knowledge both for any specialised work and in the context of wider legal matters.

Overall professional effectiveness

A general view of technical effectiveness.

Effective intelligence

Consider judgement, common sense, imagination, soundness of ideas, ability to identify and resolve problems, perceptiveness, practical reasoning and response to challenge.

Client relationships

Consider manner and attitude towards clients, both in person and in dealing with their affairs.

Managerial competence

Consider ability to delegate effectively, to manage time efficiently and relations with subordinates.

Written expression

Consider ability to inform and convince in writing.

Oral expression

Consider ability to inform and convince by speech.

Teamwork

Consider ability to co-operate and get along with other professional colleagues and with members of support staff.

Energy

Consider drive, appetite for work, work output and staying power.

Presence

Consider impact upon and ability to mix with others, demeanour and appearance.

Self-development

Consider in what manner you have improved, both in insight and achievement, due to your own efforts.

APPENDIX 5Z(1)

TRAINING REQUEST FORM

Name of proposed course:	Date of proposed course:

Course title:

Course provider:

Venue:

CPD hours, if appropriate:

What should the trainee be able to do as a result of the course?

What are the expected benefits to the business? Applicant: _____ (initials) _____ Date:_____

APPENDIX 5Z(2)

EXTERNAL COURSE EVALUATION FORM

Name:_____ Date: _____

Course due to be attended:_____ Date of course:_____

Either

(A) I did not attend this course because:

Or

(B) I attended this course: Please add any comments in any box

1. Relevance to my work/responsibilities

1	2	3	4	5
No relevance				Very relevant

2. Quality of content

1	2	3	4	5
Very poor				Excellent

3. Quality of presentation

1	2	3	4	5
Very poor				Excellent

4. Quality of administration by course provider

1	2	3	4	5
Very poor				Excellent

5. Extent to which my learning objectives were met

1	2	3	4	5
Not at all				Very well

Additional comments (if any):

Signed: _____ Date: _____

APPENDIX 5Z(3)

POST-COURSE REVIEW

Your comments on today's course will be appreciated and acted upon. Thank you for your time and trouble. Please return to the presenter or your training manager as requested.
Please provide an assessment as follows:

1. Less than adequate
2. Satisfactory
3. Good
4. Excellent

Please also add any comments in the box provided. Please continue any comments overleaf if necessary.

	1 Less than adequate	2	3	4 Excellent
Pre-course information				
Contents of the session				
Quality of presentation				
Use of visual aids, if any				
How well my interest was addressed				

Please also comment on:

What I most liked about this session

What I least liked about this session

Overall comment, if any

Your name: .... Date: ....

6 Supervision and risk management

Introduction

This section looks at risk management in the context of operational risk management – the reduction of claims and client complaints. This area may well form the single most persuasive reason for a Lexcel application and the best explanation for the growing popularity of the Lexcel standard.

Lexcel has some specific risk avoidance procedures which have mostly been drawn up in the light of the Turnbull Report on risk management (*Turnbull Report on Internal Control: Guidance for Directors on the Combined Code*, published by the Institute of Chartered Accountants in England and Wales). The starting point, however, should be a thorough review of supervision in the practice. This in turn can be examined in terms of the structures and then the personal interests and skills of those who have a supervisory role.

So far as supervision is concerned Lexcel requires a designated supervisor for each area of the firm's work. There is no requirement that supervisors must be member of panels or have certain specific experience, in marked contrast to the onerous requirements in the SQM. The provisions are that supervisors 'have appropriate experience of the work supervised and are able to guide and assist others'.

Practices should also consult Practice Rule 13 on Office Supervision.

6.1 Supervision

Supervision is achieved through the departmental structure outlined in the organisational chart which appears at appendix 6A. It is important that all fee-earning work is directed to the appropriate department so that it is conducted subject to proper quality control. All individuals should be wary of 'dabbling' in areas that they are not proficient in. In all cases the head of department is the nominated supervisor of all work in his/her department unless otherwise indicated.

The departments are:

[*specify and describe their range of activities*]

The departmental heads with responsibility for the expertise and development of their departments are:

Conveyancing	Head of department	[*name*]
	Other partner	[*name*]
Crime	Head of department	[*name*]
	Other partners	[*name*]

[*include other areas of work as appropriate*]

[An alternative is to list all posts held in a supplement which can be changed regularly, or even as part of the internal phone directory]

It is the responsibility of the supervisor to:

- ensure the maintenance of appropriate professional expertise and standards in the area that (s)he supervises;
- determine if instructions should be accepted. In most instances the signature of any partner on any matter opening form will be acceptable as evidence that the work can and should be handled by the firm. Fee-earners must, however, refer matter opening forms to the supervisor, or a deputy in their absence, if there is any doubt as to the propriety of the instructions (see sections 1.8 and 1.9 on money laundering and mortgage fraud) or the ability of the firm to undertake the work given the expertise required or the resources available;
- allocate work within the [department/section/team] to ensure that matters are dealt with sufficient expertise and under appropriate supervision;
- review the performance and workload of fee-earners who (s)he supervises through monthly 'one-to-one' review meetings at which a computer printout of all matters under the control of the fee-earner will be checked or discussed;
- act as the risk manager for the area of work that (s)he supervises, attend meetings of the risk management committee and assist in the conduct of the annual risk audit within the firm.

The designated supervisors in litigation areas have the responsibility for the specific risk assessment where conditional fee arrangements are being considered. (Some firms have a specific financial review on the opening of such matters, as through the Finance Partner or Managing Partner.)

The signature of a partner is needed on every matter opening form as evidence that the matter should be undertaken by the firm and can be handled by the designated matter handler.

Other important managerial and administrative roles are:

Managing partner	[*name*]
Finance partner	[*name*]
Risk management partner	[*name*]
Chief cashier	[*name*]
Assistant cashier	[*name*]
Health and safety manager	[*name*]
Librarian	[*name*]
Buildings and equipment supervisor	[*name*]
Post room/general office supervisor	[*name*]
Training partner	[*name*]
Information technology partner	[*name*]

6.2 Systems of supervision

> The following procedure is a useful 'mop-up' to cross-refer to the total pattern of supervision throughout the practice. Not all firms will wish to adopt all of the procedures that follow, but it may be useful to consider them.

Supervision is effected by:

- The allocation of all work to the appropriate department and specialists.
- All incoming post, including faxes, being seen by the supervisor or another partner/senior manager (for monitoring of e-mails see section 4.8).
- All fee-earners of up to 2 years' post-qualification experience having to copy letters of substantive advice to their immediate supervisor at the time the letter is created.
- Monthly departmental meetings, when technical problems can always be discussed.
- The monthly printout review by head of department, with particular emphasis on the number of live files, values of work-in-progress, bills outstanding and any apparent inactivity on files.
- Regular file reviews and audits.
- In publicly funded work, reviews of the exercise of any devolved powers.
- Open-door periods for consultation in the day.

6.3 Work allocation

Work is to be allocated by a partner in all cases. The signature of a partner on the matter opening form is evidence that the partner considers that:

- this is the type of matter the firm should accept;
- the matter can be fairly allocated to the person named as matter handler;
- the partner agrees with the risk assessment that will need to be completed before the form is signed by the partner.

Particular care is needed with internal transfers of work. A fee-earner wishing to involve a colleague in another department should always refer to the head of department or another partner in that department and not to an assistant directly.

6.4 Maintaining progress

Fee-earners are under an obligation to ensure that there is no undue delay on the matters that they are handling and this will involve regular checks of all files. This will usually take the form of a regular 'trawl' of the filing cabinet.

or

As a matter of principle all files should be subject to ongoing review at least once a month by the fee-earner responsible for that file. Reviews should consider whether the client's instructions are being adequately met and whether action is needed to implement instructions or if contact is needed with the client to vary the case plan or instructions in any way. Reviews are therefore both technical and procedural. The evidence of this personal check will be the initials of the fee-earner on his/her monthly matters printout. The fee-earner is required to retain the last three printouts which also form the basis of the monthly 'one-to-one' review with the supervisor. The date of this meeting must be noted on the printout in question.

In addition, heads of department will check regularly for inactivity through the monthly matter printout review/receipt of reports on all matters where over three months has elapsed since time was recorded, etc.

6.5 Devolved powers

In publicly funded work it is the responsibility of the designated supervisor or, in their absence, [the deputy supervisor/another litigation partner] to consider and approve all exercises of devolved powers, having regard to the guidelines in force from the LSC. Any consideration of the exercise of devolved powers will be recorded on the form appearing at appendix 6B.

6.6 File reviews

> The need for independent file reviews often seems to be one of the most problematic aspects of a Lexcel programme, but most fee-earners will agree that they do form an essential component of effective supervision. It is important to stress that the firm has control over its file review procedures. It may decide the frequency and, to a degree, the depth of the reviews. There is no reason why file reviews have to happen as a set exercise once a month or quarter: they can be performed progressively as supervisor and fee-earner meet. The overriding aim is to ensure that the traditional autonomy of the fee-earner is challenged. Every file should be seen as a file of the firm and not the individual concerned.
>
> It should be noted that the file review can be procedural only, which would most obviously be appropriate where there is no other specialist in the firm to conduct a substantive review.
>
> All fee-earners need to be subject to a file review process including the supervisor. It is not a requirement that all file reviews are conducted by the supervisor in person, though he or she should have overall control of it.

The firm operates a system of occasional, independent file reviews.

This is a task that will usually be undertaken within the department in order that substantive issues can also be discussed. The selection of files should be generated by the monthly matter printout and it is likely that files with high work in progress value or long periods of inactivity will be selected. Where the fee-earner undertakes a range of different work type matters the selection should be representative of the fee-earner's work spread.

A file review sheet (appendix 6C) will be completed when any such independent file review occurs. Copies will be put onto the matter file and onto a central departmental list of all review sheets to verify that reviews are occurring as planned and that any corrective action identified as being necessary is being taken. When corrective action is specified as being required it is the responsibility of the matter handler to undertake the corrective action specified within the time specified, and in no case will this be longer than 28 days. The reviewer must then verify to his or her reasonable satisfaction that the corrective action has been performed and then sign off the form at the next monthly review.

It is the responsibility of [*the quality partner*] to review all file review data at least annually and include an analysis and recommendations based on the data that emerges from such review into the annual review of the operation of the quality management system.

Files are reviewed as follows [*specify*].

> *Example*
>
> | Partners | 1 file per month/quarter |
> | --- | --- |
> | Assistants and senior executives | 3 files per quarter |
> | Other fee-earners | 5 files per quarter |
>
> The reviewers are [supervisors and/or others]

6.7 Managing risk

Section 6.7 addresses the need for management of risk as set out in section 6.7 of the standard. This in turn embodies most of the Turnbull guidelines on operational risk management. The key recommendation in this report is that there should be one person who has ultimate responsibility for the management of risk. This person should:

- understand the practice;
- have appropriate delegated structures in place;
- understand the nature of the risks that the firm is exposed to;
- ensure that internal controls are established and remain effective;
- establish communication lines to ensure that the partnership or top management is made aware of the risk profile as it develops;
- review plans for future developments to see what implications they may have for the risk profile;
- install warning systems and ensure that appropriate action is taken.

A useful reference source on risk management is the SIF self-assessment audit pack, produced in 2001 and distributed free of charge to all firms in private practice. In line with its recommendations there is no great distinction drawn in this section between complaints and claims – that guide recommends treating both as 'risk events'.

The fees for the firm's annual indemnity insurance represent a considerable item of expenditure for the firm and are geared very heavily to its risk profile, which in turn is judged largely on its claims record. In any event, if the firm is committed to providing the best legal advice possible it needs to consider its responsibilities to clients to avoid the loss and inconvenience that could arise from its negligence and the harm that would be effected to its reputation.

It has to be accepted that the firm cannot possibly operate a 'risk-free' practice. It is important, however, that it takes all reasonable steps to minimise the risk of a claim or a complaint against it. This has to involve all personnel.

The main thrust of the firm's risk management policy is that prevention is better than a cure. The [risk/quality/compliance/senior/managing partner] is responsible for the management of the firm's risk profile. In this respect (s)he will:

- keep under review the firm's policy, procedures and arrangements for the management of risk and submit an annual report on risk management to the partnership;
- call meetings of the risk committee as appropriate, and in any event every six months, to discuss issues of concern. [*Note: a committee would be appropriate in a larger firm but would probably not be needed in most smaller practices, where informal arrangements could be quite as effective*]
- receive risk reports (see appendix 6D) and take such action in respect of them that seems appropriate;
- monitor new aspects of risk that could develop and report accordingly to the partnership/management board;
- negotiate and liaise with the firm's professional indemnity insurers/brokers;
- take whatever action seems appropriate to ensure that risk is identified, anticipated and guarded against, so far as possible;
- arrange training, in conjunction with [*training partner*] on risk issues if appropriate.

The [risk/quality/compliance/senior/managing partner] is helped in these duties by a committee representing every department. This comprises:

[*name members or say where they could be identified*]

It is the responsibility of the risk committee members to:

- monitor developments in their practice area(s);
- maintain lists of risks associated with the work types of the department and ensure that these are brought to the attention of members of the department;
- maintain lists of work that the department will and will not accept;
- stipulate, [*in conjunction with the head of department if this individual is not one and the same*], arrangements that will need to be made if work is accepted which is judged to be high risk.

It is the responsibility of [everyone in the practice/all fee-earners] to report without delay anything that could give rise to a claim for compensation, however minimal and whatever its merit. If a client threatens legal action against the firm, again all personnel are obliged to report this without delay, even if they do not believe the threat. You must not try to deal with the situation yourself – still less ignore the problem and hope that it will go away. It should also go without saying that you should not make any statement that could be construed as an admission of fault, nor are you entitled to offer compensation, including a discount on any bill that has been issued. Any failure by the firm to meet the requirements of its insurers could lead to penalties against it. Failure to report any such 'circumstances' without delay could therefore potentially be treated as a disciplinary offence.

There may be occasions when you are not sure whether you should deal with a problem as a potential claim or a complaint. The approach of the practice is that this doesn't matter, as long as you do report it.

6.8 Reporting risk

The level of risk presented by every file needs to be considered by the fee-earner. Risk is an issue before, during and after action is taken in every matter. It is quite clear that the proactive management of risk issues will reduce the incidence of claims and complaints in most firms.

Before an individual acts an initial risk assessment must be made as part of the file opening procedures. This is noted on the file opening form (see appendix 8C). All fee-earners must tick to show whether the matter is 'ordinary' or 'high' risk. It should not be left to secretaries to make this judgement if they are assisting in the administrative steps of opening the file. The accounts department will not allocate a client/matter number until a duly completed file opening form has been received, which will include a response to this section.

A matter should be judged to be 'high' risk if:

- there is a novel or unusual aspect of law involved;
- a foreign jurisdiction may be involved (e.g. probate where the deceased held property abroad);
- the value of a potential claim is unusually high [*consider advising on the maximum claim that the firm is covered for*];
- the client has transferred this matter to the firm in circumstances where they were dissatisfied with the advice or service provided by their previous advisers.

In conditional fee matters a specific costs risks assessment should be conducted under procedures established in the litigation department.

The [head of department/departmental risk representative] must have all high-risk assessments brought to their attention when the file is opened. They can then review whether the firm should accept these instructions and, if so, what precautionary steps in relation to responsibility, supervision and review should be imposed.

During a matter it has to be accepted that a risk profile could change at any time. This might involve greater risk to the firm or the client – for example, third parties become involved in litigation, thereby increasing the risks on costs, or the firm receives unfavourable advice from counsel. A change of circumstances so far as the client is concerned will need to be raised with the client: if there is any suggestion that the firm could be at risk from the changed circumstances, especially if the accuracy or appropriateness advice to date could now be questioned, a risk notice must be completed (see appendix 6D) and forwarded to the [risk partner/departmental risk committee member] without delay.

Any adverse costs orders made against the firm must be promptly reported to the client and to the appropriate [head of department/departmental risk committee member].

After a matter is finished there needs to be a concluding risk assessment. This is noted on the [file closing sheet/file closure section of the file summary sheet]. If it is considered that the firm should have done better for a client and that they could fairly complain about the service provided or make a claim the fee-earner must complete a risk notice and forward it to the appropriate [head of department/departmental risk committee member, with a copy to the risk partner]. On receipt of such a notice a view will have to be taken as to whether the firm is required under the terms of its indemnity insurance contract to make a report.

In summary, if you have a concern before, during or after any matter, share it with your colleagues and make sure that it is reported if there could be a complaint or a claim.

APPENDIX 6A

SAMPLE ORGANISATIONAL CHART

The Partnership

Management Committee
(Managing partner and two elected partners)

Departments:	Private Client/ Conveyancing	Family	Litigation	Commercial	Crime
Partners:	Jack Parker John Morley	Karen Dobson Sally Tomalonis	Mohammed Aziz Emma King	John Royle	Bill Horsfield
Assistants:	Geoff Wingate Duncan Wilson legal executive	Marcus Hall	Janet Glass	Martin Evans	Pam Jones
Trainees:	There are two trainee solicitors who are not assigned to any particular department for financial analysis
Secretaries:	3	2	3	2	1

In addition there are two office juniors; Geraldine Lee, chief cashier; two other members of the accounts department; two receptionists; and one general office supervisor.

Total personnel: 8 partners, 6 assistant fee-earners, 2 trainees, 11 secretaries, 8 administrators (35 in all)

APPENDIX 6B

CONSIDERATION OF DEVOLVED POWERS

Client:	Matter number:

Devolved power under consideration

Power exercised? Yes/No

Date and particulars of decision

Reasons for decisions

Reference to LSC guidelines

Comments

Signed _____   Signed _____
Matter Handler_____   Supervisor _____
Date _____   Date _____

APPENDIX 6C

FILE REVIEW FORM

File name: Department:	Matter number: Fee-earner handling:			
File opening: Procedures followed MID label attached Identity checked Note of instructions Instructions confirmed Costs information Conflicts considered Appropriate risk assessment	Yes	No	N/A	Comments
State of file: Appropriately filed Key dates noted on file and in back-up system Summary sheet completed All related files identified Separate papers/items identified				
Progress of matter: Case plan apparent Case plan updated Progress fully noted Costs updated Client informed of progress				
Counsel and experts: Client consulted Approved if used Properly briefed Advice considered Unsatisfactory advice noted				
Other observations				
Short-term corrective action By when? Confirmed	**Long-term corrective action**			
Corrective action taken _____ _____ (Matter handler) (Date)	**Corrective action verified** _____ _____ (Reviewer) (Date)			

APPENDIX 6D

RISK NOTICE

File	Client matter number:	Fee-earner handling:
Stage of matter (please summarise)		
Nature of risk now arising		
Action already taken		
Action that you consider is now needed		

Signed .... Matter handler   Date ....

Received .... Risk partner   Date ....

7 Client care

Introduction

Much has been made in recent years of the importance of client care for the profession as a whole. The area also clearly translates into an important issue for every individual practice. In an increasingly consumerist environment poor standards of service will not be tolerated. With clients increasingly likely to change advisers in response to poor experience and reputation, maintaining high standards of client care needs to be a priority. Client care should address the effective management of clients' expectations.

The section of the Lexcel standard dealing with client care concentrates on the systems that are contained in the professional regulations – Practice Rule 15 in particular. First introduced in 1991 the rule was extensively reviewed in 1999 with the publication in that year of the Solicitors' Costs Information and Client Care Code. There have since been minor amendments to the original wording of the code to reflect the developing law on cost recovery in litigation matters. All the provisions in the code are mandatory for solicitors in private practice while section 2(c) provides that employed solicitors should 'have regard' to the provisions on costs information.

The section starts with the need for a policy commitment to client care. It is good practice not simply to leave this as text in an office manual but to try to make it a reality within the firm. The policy statement could be framed and displayed in the reception area and on staff noticeboards. Likewise it should appear on the firm's website, if it has one, or in any brochure or client literature.

It could be argued, of course, that client care is a theme of most of this publication. The end objective of all management policies, systems and procedures could be seen to be to improve the efficiency of the firm and thereby to enhance client services. It follows that one of the ways to test whether a project to introduce the Lexcel standard to the practice has been successful is to measure any subsequent improvement to client satisfaction.

7.1 Policy on client care

[*Name of firm*] is committed to providing a quality service to all clients. The firm's services should be recognised as being expert, accurate and appropriate. The firm strives to ensure that its advice is cost effective and communicated in a manner that is appropriate for each client. The firm is also committed to providing a truly professional service: it seeks to act with integrity and strict confidentiality in all its dealings with clients.

All personnel should at all times consider the need to perform to the 'four Cs' of competence, confidentiality, commitment and courtesy.

Competence

The firm will accept instructions only where it can meet its commitment to the provision of an expert and professional service to clients. Where instructions would be beyond the expertise or the capabilities of the firm they will be declined. All heads of department maintain lists of work that the firm will and will not undertake; in any cases of doubt as to the ability of the firm to act appropriately for the client, the appropriate head of department should be consulted.

Confidentiality

All solicitors are bound by the Law Society's rules which require confidentiality in all dealings with clients. This means that nobody may reveal to any outsider the nature of instructions provided or advice given to any client, other than in the pursuit of the client's instructions or in accordance with legal duties to do so, as under money laundering legislation. In most circumstances it will also be inappropriate to reveal that the firm is in receipt of instructions from any named client. This is particularly the case in litigation, especially crime or divorce. If you are aware that friends or other people that you know are instructing the firm it may be tempting to reveal this information to others; do not do so. If you are ever in doubt as to whether you should reveal whether the firm acts for a given client, or give out his, her or its address, check with a partner. Breaches of confidentiality could cause considerable problems for the firm and will be treated by the partners as a serious disciplinary offence (see also section 8.16).

Commitment

Clients seek legal advice for a variety of reasons, but many approach the firm when they are vulnerable and in turmoil, whether in their personal lives or their business activities. All clients are entitled to expect a real commitment from the firm in handling their instructions, and for the firm to attach appropriate priority to their requirements. A professional service does not involve becoming emotional, however, and this should be borne in mind in wording correspondence. If it is necessary to make a threat it should be clear that the threat is one that the firm's client makes and not the firm itself.

Courtesy

All clients are entitled to be dealt with in a respectful and courteous manner. This will have many implications, from not keeping clients waiting in the reception area without explanation, to showing them the way to and from meeting rooms, to returning telephone calls and e-mails as a priority and generally taking an interest in them and their problems. The firm should show a genuine concern for its clients by doing its best to help them.

7.2 Dress and demeanour

It is important that the firm should project at all times a sense of professionalism in its dealings with clients. First impressions gained by clients do matter. Everybody should dress in a manner which is appropriate for a professional practice, and in particular avoid [*specify, e.g. jeans, tops with prominent logos, etc.*]. Please also try to conduct yourself in a way that will reassure clients. This can be achieved by appropriate behaviour around the office and a smile or a 'good morning' or 'good afternoon' to those clients you encounter in the office. Please try to be as helpful as possible to all clients of the firm – not just those that you happen to be dealing with.

7.3 Client confidentiality

The firm is under a duty to keep all client dealings properly confidential. It can easily fall foul of this important duty by thoughtless conversations and quick meetings in the reception area. Please keep any discussions of client business in the reception area to a minimum and, wherever possible, take clients into a meeting room when they come in to sign a document or bring papers in. What should be a short and undetailed visit can easily change if the client asks questions and they should be entitled to do so out of the earshot of other clients or visitors.

Would all staff also please keep personal conversations in the reception area to a minimum. The impression gained by clients overhearing conversations in the reception area can be quite negative.

(See also section 8.16 on the duty of confidentiality more generally.)

7.4 Fee-earner responsibilities

The firm is more likely to project an organised and professional image if fee-earners will take responsibility to:

- advise reception of all appointments;
- make a reservation as soon as possible when meeting rooms are required;
- book car parking spaces with reception;
- ensure that clients are not kept waiting;
- ensure that clients are shown hospitality and are provided with appropriate refreshments, coffee, tea, biscuits, etc.;
- are shown to and from any room used for a client appointment;
- inform their secretary (if any) of their whereabouts in the building;
- ensure that reception and their secretary (if any) are informed if they leave the premises other than at lunchtime, telling them when they are leaving the firm's office(s) and their expected time of return.

7.5 Receptionists' responsibilities

The reception area is our 'shop window' and is critical to the first impression that visitors will gain of the firm. The receptionists should take responsibility to ensure that:

- the reception area is clean and tidy;
- newspapers and magazines are up to date and are neatly arranged;
- the firm's publicity material is made available to clients and is kept in presentable condition, and that floral displays are fresh.

If there is a delay of over 10 minutes the receptionist should endeavour to:

- keep clients informed of the reasons;
- provide clients with suitable refreshments, coffee, tea, biscuits, etc.;

- offer an apology and explanation after 20 minutes' delay and suggest a different appointment time, or organise the fee-earner's secretary to do so.

(See also sections 4.1 and 4.2 in relation to the reception area generally.)

7.6 Confirmation of instructions

The general rule is that at or near the outset of every matter the client should receive confirmation of:

- the name and status of the person acting, along with details of the principal partner responsible for the overall supervision of the matter (see *Pilbrow* v. *Peerless de Rougemont* [1999] 3 All ER 355 on the importance as a matter of law of confirming such details);
- specific advice on the costs implications of the instructions received and the advice provided;
- the general terms of business under which the firm acts.

This is achieved by use of the general client care letter (appendix 7A) and the firm's standard terms and conditions (appendix 7B). The client care letter can be tailored to the particular instructions received within the departmental precedents. Although its precise wording is not mandatory in all cases any material variations must be approved by a partner and must still comply with the professional requirements of the Solicitors' Costs Information and Client Care Code. This is most likely to apply where the client is a close friend or a relation to the adviser, but care is needed before any major variation of terms is agreed. The friend or relation becomes a normal client in all other regards and may be just as likely to complain or make a claim in the event of a problem with the services received. The view of the partners is therefore that variations from the approved precedents should be very much the exception rather than the rule.

The code recognises that the full information is not always appropriate (see section 2b of the code). Where the firm has established a settled pattern of dealings with regular clients formal terms should be established which can be referred to on all new matters opened for that client. Agreed terms are reviewed annually by the client partner, with special reference to any variation of fee levels. Since most such clients are commercial clients, the head of the commercial department maintains the formal agreements with regular clients which can be understood to apply unless the contrary is agreed. The list of such clients and the letters setting out agreed terms can be consulted on [*provide computer system reference*].

The other situation where a normal client care letter might not be sent out is where professional considerations would make it inappropriate. Such cases will be exceptional, but could include:

- the client is illiterate or has learning difficulties;
- in certain instances of mental health work where the client might be distressed to receive such correspondence;

- in some cases of domestic violence where a letter that is intercepted could aggravate any problems;
- the deathbed will.

In any such instances a full note must appear on the file setting out the reasons why a client care letter has not been sent out and detailing any alternative action which has been taken.

It is important that the client receives, in addition to client care information, confirmation of their instructions and the action that will be taken on their behalf: see section 8.7.

> The appendices contain various approaches to the issue of Practice Rule 15 compliance. The standard letter at 7A is a client care letter and would generally need supplementing with some specific terms and conditions, as in relation to payment of invoices. The terms and conditions at 7B are a much more thorough approach and deal with many more eventualities. There is no need under Law Society requirements to set out the full complaints procedure when confirming instructions, but there is a need to have a written complaints procedure. It is an issue for every firm to determine its approach to compliance. There are developments to suggest that the firm that has not established terms of business may be unable to recover any costs, so the adoption of a coherent approach is increasingly important, regardless of whether the firm is seeking to achieve Lexcel accreditation.

7.7 Complaints handling

> Section 7 of the code requires all solicitors in private practice to operate an effective complaints handling system. The problem of backlogs of cases at the Office for the Supervision of Solicitors, and the resulting political concern about the regulation of legal services, have been well documented. If all firms could approach client complaints with true resolve to address the client's difficulty and to learn from the experience to lessen the risks of repetition in the future, the profession as a whole would save substantial sums of expenditure and improve its public profile.
>
> It has been said that[1]

'evidence shows that a satisfied client tells 5 friends and a dissatisfied one tells up to 23'

> Different research quotes different figures, but there does seem to be clear agreement in all the available data that there is a disproportionate relationship between good service, which is what the client expects, and poor service which will be much more remarkable.
>
> Ironically an improved complaints handling system may well result in a substantial increase of complaints received by the firm. Research into the handling of complaints conducted by the University of Bristol in 1998 found considerable evidence of a 'tokenist' approach to complaints handling.[2]

'Our findings show that firms may establish sophisticated and elaborate in-house complaint handling procedures on paper, most commonly recorded in the firm's office manual. The motivation for so doing was not a recognition of a shift in complaint handling culture but was in response to ... quality mark providers'

---

[1] *Keeping Clients – A client care guide for solicitors.* (1997). Office for the Supervision of Solicitors. Author Patrick Stevens, Editor Martin Mears, page 28.

[2] 'An investigation into in-house complaint handling by solicitors'. (1998). Christensen, Day and Worthington, page 155.

Such findings were in line with earlier research of the Law Society's Research and Policy Planning Unit that, notwithstanding Practice Rule 15, 89% of complainants surveyed had no recollection of their solicitors explaining their in-house procedure to them.[3]

If a firm enters the arena of complaints handling with real determination to uncover the problems encountered by clients and thereby to encourage feedback an increase in complaints reported to the firm is likely. This is recognised within the area of quality management where the adage is that 'if you've had no complaints, you're not asking the right questions'. What matters is, therefore, not so much how many complaints are received, but how well they are processed and, if possible, resolved. The approach of the OSS for some time has been to refer to the firm any complaint received directly into that office. It will not generally investigate a complaint until it can be convinced that the firm has addressed the complaint as it is required to do.

It also has to be recognised that an effective outcome to every complaint received will not always be possible, though it would nonetheless make a worthy goal for the partner or manager with responsibility for complaints handling. It is clear that the firm will increase its percentage of complaints dealt with to the client's satisfaction if it can recognise that, more often than not, the client simply wants to be reassured that his or her concerns are being taken seriously and addressed, and, so far as the firm's insurers permit, an apology. (The OSS has found that this is used as a common excuse for not adopting a complaints policy. The reality is that most insurers will have no difficulty in distinguishing an expression of regret that the client is disappointed with the service and a full-blown admission of fault. Those of a prudent disposition should check with their insurers, but nobody should use this as an excuse to avoid implementing an effective complaints system.)

As the current guide to complaints handling from the OSS asserts:[4]

'if you must have the last word, say sorry'.

Many firms continue to work on the premise that the full complaints handling procedure has to be contained in initial client care correspondence to the client. This is not the case, though it has in the past been the approach of the legal aid authorities – more obviously so in the earlier LAFQAS standard than the current SQM.[5] To confront the client with a formal complaint procedure at the outset would be inappropriate. The code simply requires that clients be told at the outset whom to contact about any problem with the service provided, and that a written complaints procedure should be in place and should be 'made available on request'. The early client care correspondence might well refer to this, although many firms prefer to avoid the word 'complaint' fully at the outset and there is no reason why the word should not be avoided altogether.

The Lexcel standard makes the requirement that firms should define what they mean by a complaint. The significance of this is that a wide definition of a complaint which appeared in earlier legal aid standards (see LAFQAS V1.2 Guidance Notes):

'a complaint should be defined as any expression of client dissatisfaction, however it is expressed'

---

[3] 'Complaints against solicitors: the complainants' view'. (1996). Research and Policy Planning Unit: Study 19. Jenkins and Lewis.

[4] *Handling Complaints Effectively*. Office for the Supervision of Solicitors, page 12.

[5] In LAFQAS (fourth edition 2000) see P1.1.8 at page 55 where firms were required to inform the client 'to whom, and how, complaints should be made': the requirement in SQM is less specific but potentially contradictory. Section G1.1 provides that clients should 'have information about what to do if they have a problem with the service provided' and section F1.2(a) provides that unless there are exceptional circumstances the client should receive written confirmation as to how they should 'raise any problem concerning the service provided'. The notes to G1.1 (page 123 in the April 2002 version) provide, however, that 'wherever a file has been opened you must provide details of how and to whom they should complain, in writing, at the outset of the case.' It then adds to the confusion by providing that 'if you meet requirements F1.2(a) no further action is required here'. The best advice for firms providing publicly funded services is probably therefore to check the preference of their account manager.

brought with it a considerable onus in relation to in-house complaints reporting. Section 7:3:c of the Lexcel standard requires that firms should record and report centrally all complaints received from clients. An alternative, which would have the advantage of making the management of complaints handling more workable, is to filter out the problems that can be easily resolved. This narrower definition of a complaint has been adopted in the alternative model procedure which follows. Firms should be wary of introducing unfair hurdles as to what can be accepted as a complaint: a requirement that all complaints must be in writing will be seen as inappropriate. There are compelling reasons why clients should not be made to put complaints in writing as a precondition of having them addressed.[6]

The complaints procedure which follows at Appendix 7C is based on that recommended by the OSS and as found in the publication *Handling Complaints Effectively*. Thanks are due to the OSS, and to Mike Frith in particular, for permission to use it. For alternative procedures see **www.lawsociety.org.uk**.

The terms and conditions are reproduced by kind permission of Tony Girling to whom thanks are also due. If adopting any of these precedents please consider them carefully for their appropriateness for your firm and your clients; also please monitor changes to law and procedure, especially on the issue of costs recovery. Please also see the disclaimer of liability in the introduction for all precedents contained in this guide publication.

None of us likes to be the subject of a complaint, but if the firm is truly committed to providing a quality service to clients it needs to pick up on client dissatisfaction when it does arise and address it as best it can. The firm therefore operates a complaints handling process that seeks to ensure that it:

- knows about client dissatisfaction if and when it does arise;
- takes all reasonable steps to ensure that the dissatisfaction is addressed and resolved wherever possible;
- reassures all clients who do complain that the firm will address their concerns without delay and that it takes all complaints seriously;
- learns from experience to lessen the risk of complaints in the future.

A complaint is any expression of client dissatisfaction however it is expressed (wide) or any expression of client dissatisfaction which the fee-earner is unable immediately to resolve (narrow). [*See notes above on implications of a wide or narrow definition of complaints*]

Some degree of common sense is needed in the application of the complaints handling procedure. If a client says 'you solicitors charge a lot for what you do' it would not usually be sufficient to amount to a complaint. If, however, the client claims that a quote or agreed costs ceiling has been exceeded without notice to them it almost certainly will be. If, on checking the file, the fee-earner is able to advise the client that a letter that they had overlooked had been written to warn that the costs would be greater than previously discussed, the problem would probably have been dealt with and there would be no need to report the complaint as such. (Although, if a complaint should be seen as **any** expression of client dissatisfaction it would, strictly speaking, be necessary to report even though the problem had been resolved.) In all cases, however, it is necessary to take a view on how the client is reacting to the particular circumstances. The firm's overriding objective is to address client dissatisfaction.

---

[6] See *A Solicitor's Guide to Complaints Avoidance and Handling*. Emis Professional Publishing. M Frith, pages 59–60.

Internal reporting

If it is necessary to report a complaint please complete the complaints report form at appendix 7D and forward it to [managing partner/senior partner/head of department/other]. Client complaints will usually involve no risk of loss to the firm or the client, but if there is any chance that the complaint could amount to circumstances that should be reported to our insurers you must stray on the side of safety by reporting it as such.

Complaints referred by the OSS

It is possible that a client may complain direct to the OSS without first following the procedures given in the previous paragraphs. In such circumstances the OSS will immediately refer the complaint to [*name*] who is the appointed liaison partner with the OSS. The normal complaints procedures will then be followed.

Complaints review

It is the responsibility of the [client care partner/managing partner/senior partner] to review all complaints records in [*month*] of each year to enable him/her to report to the firm on any trends. This will form part of an annual management review which is considered by the partners and reported to all staff. It is essential that all personnel learn from their experience and address any underlying problems. In this way the firm can use its complaints data to help to prevent future difficulties.

Making complaints

There may be occasions when a complaint may be made by the firm, either against another solicitor through the OSS or through other procedures. The agreement of the [managing partner/head of department/a partner] is needed before doing so in order that the professional and commercial standing of the firm can first receive proper consideration.

7.8 Client surveys

The Lexcel standard now contains a requirement that firms should review, at least annually, whether the firm's commitment to client service is being met in the perception of clients. This could be achieved in various ways. In most firms a simple client satisfaction survey, as appears in appendix 7F, will be appropriate. Many domestic conveyancing departments use such forms as a matter of course. An alternative, which may be more appropriate with referrers of work or more significant commercial clients, could be a face-to-face meeting. In firms that decide to compile a register of standing terms (see appendix 7B) a client satisfaction survey questionnaire could be filled in at or before the annual review meeting which is envisaged by that process.

Many firms have also found that their staff – especially the support or administrative staff – can provide valuable insight to where they feel that the firm could improve: see the form at appendix 7G.

An occasional survey is conducted on client satisfaction. All heads of department can decide when this should be conducted at any time of year, but most will conduct a survey in [*months*] to provide information for the firm's annual review in [*month*]. The survey is conducted by use of the client survey form at (appendix 7F) and in interviews with key clients and referrers.

The partners are aware that asking questions of clients increases expectations and the results of the survey will be published internally, together with any decisions and recommendations, in order that everyone can assist in any improvements that are called for.

APPENDIX 7A

CLIENT CARE LETTER – GENERAL FORMAT

Dear

[Description of matter]

Thank you for instructing me in relation to this matter.

I confirm that [*outline advice given, proposed course of action, limitations to the service that can be provided, if any, and appropriateness of legal services given the circumstances of the matter*].

Costs

There are some important matters that I would like to confirm at this early stage, particularly in relation to costs. Our charges in this matter will be based on the time we expend on your behalf, as outlined in the accompanying terms and conditions leaflet. There may also be expenditure we incur directly on your behalf (disbursements). Value added tax, at the current rate, has also to be added to our bills. At this stage I would not envisage any particular items that would need to be brought to your attention but I will do so if and when they do arise. Please read through the enclosed terms and conditions and contact me if you would like clarification of any of its contents.

I am sure that you will appreciate some guidance on the likely overall costs. It is impossible to predict the costs accurately at this stage as there are so many variable factors in the progress of a matter such as this, but I would assess the eventual figure is likely to be in the region of £[*amount*] [or between £[*amount*] and £[*amount*]]. [*Change this paragraph if providing a fixed quote or estimate*] The approximate breakdown of this figure will be [*fees/VAT/disbursements*].

[In cases that go to court the usual rule would be that, in all cases involving more than minor sums, the successful party gets a contribution towards their costs. Since there is a prospect of going to court in this matter please take into account that if you succeed the contribution to your costs that the court is likely to make is unlikely to be as much as some two-thirds of my costs and that if you are unsuccessful a contribution towards the other side's costs will probably be ordered in addition to this firm's costs] [*Conditional fee arrangements would need further details*]

In order to meet any initial expenditure you have agreed to provide £[*amount*] on account of costs and I look forward to receiving this from you. [*This must always be discussed with the client first*]

Client care

We strive to provide a quality service to all our clients. In the event of any concern about the services provided or the process that you are involved in, please do not hesitate to contact me.

I shall be the person with responsibility for your matter. I am a [partner/associate/assistant solicitor/legal executive/senior manager/junior manager/para-legal/trainee solicitor]. I shall be assisted by [*name*]. [My work is under the direct supervision of [*name*]]. We have arrangements to ensure continuity of cover in the event of my being absent from the office. Please note that my secretary is [*name*] who will generally have access to the file in relation to your matter and who will usually be able to answer any query that might arise.

[*Set out here any preferences that you have in relation to how you work with clients – e.g. 'By and large you are more likely to be able to contact me by telephone if you wait until after* [*time*], *or 'When we meet to discuss your matter you are likely to be offered an afternoon appointment since I am often in court in the morning, etc.*]

In common with most banks and professional advisers we are required by law to conduct identification checks on clients even where they are known personally to us or have had dealings with us in the past. You will be asked to bring in papers to prove your identity and address which we will need to copy and keep on file. We hope that this will not inconvenience you.

Quality standards

The firm [is working towards/is registered under] the Lexcel quality standard of the Law Society. As a result of this we are or may become subject to periodic checks by outside assessors. This could mean that your file is selected for checking, in which case we would need your consent for inspection to occur. All inspections are, of course, conducted in confidence. If you prefer to withhold consent, work on your file will not be affected in any way. Since very few of our clients do object to this I propose to assume that we do have your consent unless you notify us to the contrary. We will also assume, unless you indicate otherwise, that consent on this occasion will extend to all future matters which we conduct on your behalf. Please do not hesitate to contact me if I can explain this further or if you would like me to mark your file as not to be inspected. If you would prefer to withhold consent please put a line through this section in the copy letter for return to me.

[Action by yourself

May I finally confirm the steps which I need you to take or the documentation which I will require to process matters on your behalf]

I look forward to being of assistance to you.

Yours sincerely,

Note: this method of confirming client care issues would require additional terms of business on such issues as payment of invoices, rights to interest, storage and retrieval charges, etc.

APPENDIX 7B

TERMS AND CONDITIONS

These terms are produced by kind permission of Tony Girling and form an alternative to the client care letter above. This is a general draft and will need to be considered from time to time as new issues arise. The difficult area of costs recovery is too fast-changing to provide advice on in this publication, Precedents terms of business with some variations for departments can be obtained direct from Tony Girling Training Limited, Penbourne, Mill View Court, Barham, Canterbury, Kent CT4 6PF at modest cost.

The letter accompanying the terms of business must deal with the costs estimate (or other supplemental costs information, such as any agreed costs ceiling), cost benefit and likely timescale requirements of Rule 15. These do not lend themselves to standard terminology for inclusion in the Terms and Conditions.

[*Name of firm*] TERMS AND CONDITIONS OF BUSINESS

Our aim

We aim to offer our clients quality legal advice with a personal service at a fair cost. As a start, we hope it is helpful to you to set out in this statement the basis on which we will provide our professional services.

Our commitment to you

We will:

- REPRESENT your interests and keep your business confidential.
- EXPLAIN to you the legal work which may be required and the prospects of a successful outcome.
- MAKE SURE that you understand the likely degree of financial risk which you will be taking on.
- ADVISE YOU if legal aid might be available to you.
- KEEP YOU regularly informed of progress or, if there is none, when you are next likely to hear from us.
- TRY to avoid using technical legal language when writing to you – tell us when we fail in this aim!
- DEAL with your queries promptly, for example, we will always try to return your telephone calls on the same day.
- ADVISE you on tax matters, but only if specifically requested to do so.

Our hours of business

- The normal hours of opening at our offices are between 9.00am and 5.00pm on weekdays. Messages can be left on the answerphone outside those hours and appointments can be arranged at other times when this is essential.

People responsible for your work

- The [*specify*] responsible for dealing with your work will be [*name*]. The [*specify*] assistant/secretary who may be able to deal with your queries and who will be pleased to take any message for you is [*name*]. We will try to avoid changing the people who handle

your work but if this cannot be avoided, we will tell you promptly of any change and why it may be necessary.
- The partner of this firm with final responsibility for work done in this department is [*name*].

Charges and expenses

- Our charges will be calculated mainly by reference to the time actually spent by the solicitors and other staff in respect of any work which they do on your behalf. This will include meetings with you and perhaps others, reading and working on papers, correspondence, including e-mails, preparation of any detailed costs calculations, and time spent travelling away from the office when this is necessary. From time to time we may arrange for some of this work to be carried out by persons not directly employed by this firm. You will be charged at rates not greater than those set out below.
- Routine letters are charged as 6 minute units of time and we charge for the time spent on making and taking telephone calls in 6 minute units and considering incoming letters at units of 3 minutes per page.
- The current hourly rates are set out below. We will add VAT to these at the rate that applies when the work is done. At present, VAT is 17.5%.

	£
Partners and Consultants	000
Solicitors	000
Fellows of Inst. of Legal Executives, Senior Executives	000
Executives	000
Trainee Solicitors	000
Junior Executives	000

- These hourly rates have to be reviewed periodically to reflect increases in overhead costs and inflation. Normally the rates are reviewed with effect from 1 January each year. If a review is carried out before this matter has been concluded, we will inform you of any variation in the rate before it takes effect.
- In addition to the time spent, we may take into account a number of factors including any need to carry out work outside our normal office hours, the complexity of the issues, the speed at which action has to be taken, any particularly specialist expertise which the case may demand. In particular, in property transactions, in the administration of estates and in matters involving a substantial financial value or benefit to a client, a charge reflecting, for example, the price of the property, the size of the estate, or the value of the financial benefit may be considered. It is not always possible to indicate how these aspects may arise but on present information we would expect them to be sufficiently taken into account in the rates which we have quoted. Where a charge reflecting any value element is to be added we will explain this to you.
- Solicitors have to pay out various other expenses on behalf of clients ranging from Land or Probate Registry fees, to court fees, experts' fees, and so on. We have no obligation to make such payments unless you have provided us with the funds for that purpose. VAT is payable on certain expenses. We refer to such payments generally as 'disbursements'.
- If, for any reason, this matter does not proceed to completion, we will be entitled to charge you for work done and expenses incurred.

Payment arrangements

- Property transactions. We will normally send you our bill following the exchange of contracts and payment is required on a purchase prior to completion; and at completion;

on a sale. If sufficient funds are available on completion, and we have sent you a bill, we will deduct our charges and expenses from the funds.
- Administration of estates. We will normally submit an interim bill at regular stages during the administration, starting with the obtaining of a Grant. The final account will be prepared when the Estate Accounts are ready for approval.
- Other cases or transactions. It is normal practice to ask clients to pay sums of money from time to time on account of the charges and expenses which are expected in the following weeks or months. We find that this helps clients in budgeting for costs as well as keeping them informed of the legal expenses which are being incurred. If such requests are not met with prompt payment, delay in the progress of a case may result. In the unlikely event of any bill or request for payment not being met, this firm must reserve the right to stop acting for you further.
- Payment is due to us within 28 days of our sending you a bill. Interest will be charged on a daily basis at 4% over [*name of bank*] base rate from time to time from the date of the bill in cases where payment is not made within 28 days of delivery by us of the bill.

Other parties' charges and expenses

- In some cases and transactions a client may be entitled to payment of costs by some other person. It is important that you understand that in such circumstances, the other person may not be required to pay all the charges and expenses which you incur with us. You have to pay our charges and expenses in the first place and any amounts which can be recovered will be a contribution towards them. If the other party is in receipt of legal aid no costs are likely to be recovered.
- If you are successful and a court orders another party to pay some or all of your charges and expenses, interest can be claimed on them from the other party from the date of the court order. We will account to you for such interest to the extent that you have paid our charges or expenses on account, but we are entitled to the rest of that interest.
- You will also be responsible for paying our charges and expenses of seeking to recover any costs that the court orders the other party to pay to you.
- A client who is unsuccessful in a court case may be ordered to pay the other party's legal charges and expenses. That money would be payable in addition to our charges and expenses. Arrangements can be made to take out insurance to cover liability for such legal expenses. Please discuss this with us if you are interested in this possibility.

Interest payment

- Any money received on your behalf will be held in our Client Account. Subject to certain minimum amounts and periods of time set out in the Solicitors' Accounts Rules 1998, interest will be calculated and paid to you at the rate from time to time payable on [*name of bank*] Designated Client Accounts. The period for which interest will be paid will normally run from the date(s) on which funds are received by us until the date(s) of issue of any cheque(s) from our Client Account.
- Where a client obtains borrowing from a lender in a property transaction, we will ask the lender to arrange that the loan cheque is received by us a minimum of four working days prior to the completion date. If the money can be telegraphed, we will request that we receive it the day before completion. This will enable us to ensure that the necessary funds are available in time for completion. Such clients need to be aware that the lender may charge interest from the date of issue of their loan cheque or the telegraphing of the payment.

Storage of papers and documents

- After completing the work, we are entitled to keep all your papers and documents while there is money owing to us for our charges and expenses. In addition, we will keep your file of papers for you in storage for not less than one year. After that, storage is on the clear understanding that we have the right to destroy it after such period as we consider reasonable or to make a charge for storage if we ask you to collect your papers and you fail to do so. We will not of course destroy any documents such as Wills, Deeds, and other securities, which you ask us to hold in safe custody. No charge will be made to you for such storage unless prior notice in writing is given to you of a charge to be made from a future date which may be specified in that notice.
- If we retrieve papers or documents from storage in relation to continuing or new instructions to act in connection with your affairs, we will not normally charge for such retrieval. However, we may make a charge based on time spent for producing stored papers or documents to you or another at your request. We may also charge for reading, correspondence or other work necessary to comply with your instructions.

Termination

- You may terminate your instructions to us in writing at any time but we will be entitled to keep all your papers and documents while there is money owing to us for our charges and expenses. If at any stage you do not wish us to continue doing work and/or incurring charges and expenses on your behalf, you must tell us this clearly in writing.
- If we decide to stop acting for you, for example if you do not pay an interim bill or comply with the request for a payment on account, we will tell you the reason and give you notice in writing.
- Under the Consumer Protection (Distance Selling) Regulations 2000, for some non-business instructions, you may have the right to withdraw, without charge, within seven working days of the date on which you asked us to act for you. However, if we start work with your consent within that period, you lose that right to withdraw. Your acceptance of these Terms and Conditions of Business will amount to such a consent. If you seek to withdraw instructions, you should give notice by telephone, e-mail or letter to the person named in these Terms of Business as being responsible for your work. The Regulations require us to inform you that the work involved is likely to take more than 30 days.

Limited companies

- When accepting instructions to act on behalf of a limited company, we may require a Director and/or controlling shareholder to sign a form of personal guarantee in respect of the charges and expenses of this firm. If such a request is refused, we will be entitled to stop acting and to require immediate payment of our charges on an hourly basis and expenses as set out earlier.

Tax advice

- Any work that we do for you may involve tax implications or necessitate the consideration of tax planning strategies. We may not be qualified to advise you on the tax implications of a transaction that you instruct us to carry out, or the likelihood of them arising. If you have any concerns in this respect, please raise them with us immediately. If we can undertake the research necessary to resolve the issue, we will do so and advise you accordingly. If we cannot, we may be able to identify a source of assistance for you.

Identity and disclosure requirements

- We are entitled to refuse to act for you if you fail to supply appropriate proof of identity for yourself or for any principal whom you may represent.
- Solicitors are not allowed to disclose information about a client's affairs without the client's authority. By signing this Terms and Conditions of Business and returning it to us you authorise us to disclose to the other parties in the transaction and, if applicable, to all other parties in the chain of transactions and their agents and advisers, all information which we have in relation to your involvement in the transaction including any related sale or mortgage and other financial arrangements and wishes as to dates for exchange and completion. You may withdraw this authority at any time but if you do so you should appreciate that we will inform the other party or parties and their agents or advisers that this authority has been withdrawn.
- We will not be liable for any loss, damage or delay arising out of the firm's compliance with any statutory or regulatory requirement.

Communication between you and us

- Our aim is to offer all our clients an efficient and effective service at all times. We are proud that we hold the accreditation [Lexcel/Investor in People/other] and our clients and our staff are of first importance to us. We hope that you will be pleased with the work we do for you. However, should there be any aspect of our service with which you are unhappy, please raise your concern in the first place with [*insert fee-earner name*]. If you still have queries or concerns, please contact our client services manager, [*name*] at [*address*]. [*Name*] is the client care partner to whom any final difficulty can be reported.
- We will aim to communicate with you by such a method as you may request. We may need to virus check disks or e-mail. Unless you withdraw consent, we will communicate with you and others when appropriate by e-mail or fax but we cannot be responsible for the security of correspondence and documents sent by e-mail or fax.
- The Data Protection Act requires us to advise you that your particulars are held on our database. We may, from time to time, use these details to send you information which we think might be of interest to you.

Terms and conditions of business

- Unless otherwise agreed, and subject to the application of then current hourly rates, these Terms and Conditions of Business shall apply to any future instructions given by you to this firm.
- Although your continuing instructions in this matter will amount to an acceptance of these Terms and Conditions of Business, it may not be possible for us to start work on your behalf until one copy of them has been returned to us for us to keep on our file.

I confirm I have read and understood, and I accept, these Terms and Conditions of Business.

Signed ....

Date .... Ref: ....

APPENDIX 7C

SAMPLE COMPLAINTS PROCEDURES

A Model complaints procedure for partnerships

Our complaints policy

We are committed to providing a high-quality legal service to all our clients. When something goes wrong we need you to tell us about it. This will help us to improve our standards.

Our complaints procedure

If you have a complaint, please contact [*name*], our client care partner. [*In multi-office firms*]

You can contact him/her at: [*address*]. [*In large departmentalised practices*] [*name*] will pass your complaint to [*name of head of department*], the partner in charge of the department involved in your complaint. If we have to change any of the timescales set out below we will let you know and explain why.

What will happen next?

1. We will send you a letter acknowledging your complaint and asking you to confirm or explain any details. If it seems appropriate we will suggest a meeting at this stage. We will also let you know the name of the person who will be dealing with your complaint.
*2. We will then record your complaint in our central register and open a file for your complaint. We will also investigate your complaint by examining the relevant file.
3. If appropriate we will then invite you to meet [*name*] to discuss and hopefully resolve your complaint. We would hope to be in a position to meet with you in this way no longer than 14 days after first receiving your complaint. If you would prefer not to meet, or if we cannot arrange this within an agreeable timescale, [*name*] will write fully to you setting out his/her views on the situation and any redress that we would feel to be appropriate.
*4. Within two days of any meeting we will write to you to confirm what took place and any suggestions that we have agreed with you. In appropriate cases we could offer an apology, a reduction of any bill or a repayment in relation to any payment received.
*5. At this stage, if you are still not satisfied, please let us know. We will then arrange to review our decision. We would generally aim to do this within 10 days. This will happen in one of the following ways.

    - [*Name*] will review his/her own decision.
    - We will arrange for someone in the firm who has not been involved in your complaint to review it.
    - [*Name of senior partner*] will review your complaint within 10 days.
    - We will ask our local Law Society or another local firm of solicitors to review your complaint. We will let you know how long this process will take.
    - We will invite you to agree to independent mediation. We will let you know how long this process will take.

6. We will let you know the result of the review within five days of the end of the review. At this time we will write to you confirming our final position on your complaint and explaining our reasons. We will also give you the name and address of the Office for the Supervision of Solicitors. If you are still not satisfied, you can contact them about your complaint. We very much hope that this will not be necessary.

[* *Delete any terms not considered to be appropriate*]

B   Model complaints procedure for sole practitioners

My complaints policy

I am committed to providing a high-quality legal service to all my clients. When something goes wrong I need you to tell me about it. This will help me to maintain and improve my standards.

My complaints procedure

If you have a complaint, please contact me with the details. If I have to change any of the timescales set out below I will let you know.

What will happen next?

1. I will send you a letter acknowledging your complaint and asking you to confirm or explain the details. I may suggest that we meet to clarify any details.
2. I will then record your complaint in my central register and open a file for your complaint and investigate your complaint. This may involve one or more of the following steps.

   - If I acted for you, I will consider your complaint again. I will then send you my detailed reply or invite you to a meeting to discuss the matter.
   - If someone else acted for you, I will ask them to give me their reply to your complaint. I will then examine their reply and the information in your complaint file. I may also speak to the person who acted for you.
   - I may ask another independent local solicitor to investigate your complaint and report to me.
   - I will then write inviting you to meet me and discuss and hopefully resolve your complaint.

3. At this stage I would welcome the opportunity to meet with you. I would aim to be in a position to be able to meet with you within 14 days of first receiving your complaint. If you would prefer not to meet, or if we cannot arrange this within an agreeable timescale, I will write fully to you setting out my views on the situation and any redress.
4. Within two days of the meeting I will write to you to confirm what took place and any solutions I have agreed with you. In appropriate cases I could offer an apology, a reduction of any bill or a repayment in relation to any payment received.
5. At this stage, if you are still not satisfied, please contact me again. I will then arrange to review my decision within the next 10 days. This may happen in one of the following ways.

   - I will review the decision myself.
   - I will arrange for someone who is not connected with the complaint to review my decision.
   - I will ask my local Law Society or another local firm of solicitors to review your complaint. This may take longer than 10 days in which case I will let you know how long this process will take.
   - I will invite you to agree to an independent mediation. This again may take longer than 10 days and I will do my best to let you know how long this will take.

   [*Any of the above options that are not available will need to be deleted*]

6. I will let you know the result of the review within five days of the end of the review. At this time I will write to you confirming my final position on your complaint and explaining my reasons. I will also give you the name and address of the Office for the Supervision of Solicitors. If you are still not satisfied, you can contact them about your complaint, but I very much hope that this will not be necessary.

APPENDIX 7D

CLIENT COMPLAINT REPORT FORM

Client:	Private paying/ Public funding:
Client partner, if any:	Description of matter:
Matter number:	Could a claim be made for any losses?

Details of complaint:

Action already taken:

Action proposed, including possible redress:

Client care partner notes:

Matter resolved   Date

APPENDIX 7E

CLIENT COMPLAINTS REGISTER

Model Central Complaints Register

The OSS recommends that the central complaints record should include the following:

- a complaint reference number;
- the date of the complaint;
- the name of the client;
- the name of the member of staff involved;
- a general description of the complaint;
- the date of any internal meeting and the names of those present;
- the date the file was examined;
- the date of any meeting with the client;
- an indication of whether the complaint is justified in the views of the firm;
- the reasons for the complaint;
- details of any suggestions to resolve the complaint and redress that might be offered;
- the dates of any letters confirming details or suggestions;
- the date of any review and the result of the review;
- the date of the final letter;
- the date the file was closed; and
- any action to be taken internally as a result of the complaint.

Complaint number:_____   Client name: _____

Matter/File number: _____   Fee-earner handling:_____

Description of complaint	Client meeting date, if any	Internal meeting, if any, and who is present	Action taken	Matter resolved? If so – date If not – future action?

APPENDIX 7F

CLIENT SURVEY FORM

Your name: Department:			*(completed by firm)*	
1. How would you rate our reception area and the greeting you received if and when you visited our offices? If poor or fair, how do you think we could improve this aspect of our practice?	Poor	Fair	Good	Excellent
2. How would you rate the personal manner of the adviser who you had most dealings with? If poor or fair, how do you think (s)he could have improved their service to you?				
3. How would you assess the communication, be it by letter or e-mail, that you received? If poor or fair, how could we have improved this for you?				

	Poor	Fair	Good	Excellent
4. How would you rate your understanding and the commitment to the action that was taken on your behalf? If poor or fair, how could this have been improved for you?				
5. In general terms, how would you assess our service for you? If you have any suggestions for how we could improve things that have not been dealt with above, please comment here.				

Would you be likely to recommend this firm to others? Yes ……. No ……. Undecided …….

Thank you for your time and trouble in completing this form. Please return it in the stamped addressed envelope provided.

APPENDIX 7G

STAFF SURVEY FORM

1. If and when you were last aware of a client who was unhappy with the service provided, what was the cause of the problem?

2. What steps do you think should be taken for the firm to improve its service to clients?

3. Would you always recommend the firm to friends and relatives?

   If not, why not?

4. Please add here any suggestions not covered above which could be helpful.

Thank you for your time and trouble. Please return this form to [*name*] by no later than [*date*].

Your name: ....(optional) Your department: .... Date: ....

8 Case and file management

Introduction

The final section of the Lexcel standard deals with what most firms will find the most important change to be achieved – the way that client files are managed. The section deals with the 'life of a file' – from first enquiry to eventual archiving. The procedures set out below follow that model.

Firms will need to decide if they will have one comprehensive set of procedures for all departments. The alternatives are to have different procedures for each department or to have a short appendix for the various work type areas highlighting the particular application of the general procedures in that specialisation following a general draft. This latter format generally seems to make the procedures sufficiently specific without undue repetition of standard procedures and is envisaged in this chapter. An outline example for the conveyancing department is provided at the end of this chapter (appendix 8A).

Firms embarking on a Lexcel or Risk Management project would be well advised to expect difficulties from this section in particular. A limited number of people will control most general areas of management, but in the realms of case and file management it will be necessary to get everyone involved in fee-earning to change the way that they conduct their daily work. In many cases old habits will die hard. The best advice is to avoid standardisation for its own sake and be clear on why every procedure is needed and what benefit the practice expects to achieve from it. In this area in particular, partners and senior managers must be prepared to lead by example.

I PRELIMINARY ISSUES

8.1 Client enquiries

Client enquiries about possible services are received:

- by telephone to the office;
- by telephone directly to an individual known to the client, potential client or referrer;
- by letter, fax or e-mail;
- by callers to the office.

It is essential that all enquiries as to whether the firm could or would be willing to act should be dealt with as quickly, efficiently and courteously as possible. Even if declining to act on this occasion, the firm has the opportunity to make a favourable impression for the next.

The firm does not operate strict response times but would expect to deal with all enquiries within 24 hours, even if simply a 'holding' response. [*Some firms prefer to set target times, in which case they should be set out here*]

It has become standard practice for potential clients in conveyancing to request estimates and this is dealt with in accordance with the specific conveyancing procedures (see appendix 8A).

For procedures on general telephone enquiries and callers into the reception area see sections 4.2–4.3 above.

8.2 File opening

Fee-earners or their secretaries are responsible for opening client matter files. The matter opening form shown at appendix 8C is to be used and should be completed by the fee-earner as part of taking initial instructions. The following outline guidance is given on the main information to be recorded. Other information recorded is self-evident.

Matter opening form

The form comprises two parts. Part One records basic client information such as name, address, telephone details, etc. which are likely to remain constant and will be included in the client database. This information will also be used to support the firm's case management systems. Part Two records information specific to the particular matter and will clearly vary matter by matter.

Client/Matter number

The accounting system allocates sequentially a unique client number to each new client, comprising the first three letters of the surname/company name followed by a sequential number, e.g. John Wilson – WIL4521 and this is to be used for all matters for the client. Automatically, a sequential matter number is then added, e.g. 1, 2, 3, to form the client/matter number WIL4521.1, WIL4521.2 and so on. By this numbering system, all matters for a client can easily be identified and co-ordinated. Care must be taken to use any existing client number and not open a second client number.

Branch office

The branch office number is to be recorded, e.g. [Nottingham – 1 and Derby – 2]. This will enable financial information at branch level to be obtained.

Department

The firm and branch offices are divided under six specialist departments and the department number is to be recorded. Financial information at departmental level can be obtained.

Crime	Department 1
Matrimonial	Department 2
Civil litigation and PI	Department 3
Property	Department 4
Company commercial	Department 5
Wills, Probate and Tax	Department 6

Work type

The firm's work areas have been further sub-divided under a number of specific work types [*include list as appendix if firm has done so*]. By this means, financial information specific to a work type is derived. It is the responsibility of the fee-earner to allocate the correct work type.

Fee-earner/Supervising partner

Record the initials of the fee-earner and the supervising partner.

LSC or CDS matters

Record the additional information required if a matter is legally aided.

Conflict check

Record that a conflict check has been carried out [*see appendix 8C*].

Risk assessment

Record that a risk assessment has been carried out [*see appendix 8C*].

Money laundering identity checks

[*See section 1.8 and appendices 1A and 1B. Firms may prefer to deal with identity checking here*]

Labels will be produced for placing on the actual matter file.

With the exception of the client matter number, all of the client or matter details can be amended and it is the responsibility of the controlling fee-earner to ensure that changes when required are made promptly. For example, change of name or address, change of work type or change of fee-earner. Please liaise with the accounts department if help is needed.

8.3 Acceptance of instructions

There is no 'cab-rank' principle for solicitors in private practice, so decisions will need to be made on whether the firm should accept the particular instructions in question. In this regard solicitors should bear in mind the principles in chapter 12 of the *Guide to the Professional Conduct of Solicitors* and have particular regard to situations where:

- the instructions would involve illegality or a breach of the rules of professional conduct (12.02);
- the client could not be represented with 'competence or diligence' (12.03);

- the client is thought to be acting under duress or undue influence (12.04);
- the client has already retained another firm of solicitors to act and they are still doing so (12.07).

The main rule in 12.01 is that 'a solicitor is generally free to decide whether or not to accept instructions from any particular client'. The one major exception is that the decision not to accept instructions could not be based on grounds that would offend the anti-discrimination policy.

The firm is not obliged to act in all cases. Greater consideration will need to be given to enquiries from new clients as opposed to new matters from existing clients. The firm may not decline to act on grounds that would offend its policies on anti-discrimination (see sections 1.6 and 1.7). It could decline to act, however, on the following grounds:

- the enquiry is for a work area that the firm does not undertake or wishes to restrict;
- the firm lacks the expertise or the resources to represent that client effectively, or the instructions would put at risk current commitments;
- the client has a track record of not paying the firm's bills or has threatened or assaulted personnel within the firm;
- the client is engaged in business activities that the firm would not wish to be associated with;
- there is, or could be, a conflict of interest – professional or commercial (see section 8.6);
- the client refuses to undergo identity checks as required by the anti-money laundering procedures, or the Council of Mortgage Lenders *Lenders' Handbook* in the case of conveyancing.

In all such cases the client should be given such explanation as is appropriate in the circumstances.

8.4 Authorisation

The signature of a partner on a matter opening form is evidence that the firm is satisfied that the work can and should be undertaken by the practice and will not jeopardise the profile or reputation of the practice. Wherever there is doubt on the part of any fee-earner as to whether instructions should be accepted the situation must be referred to the appropriate work area/departmental supervisor or, in the event of their absence from the office, the next most appropriate authority.

For details of initial risk assessments on file opening see section 6.8.

8.5 Miscellaneous files

New matters often emerge from current matters and it is not always apparent when an issue is first raised as to whether a distinct new matter will develop. Fee-earners must be aware of the need not to run separate matters under the same file and must be prepared to open a new file, perhaps transferring any papers to a colleague, as soon as it becomes clear that the issue is something other than a minor incidental issue related to the matter in hand.

Similarly, general files for commercial clients must not be used as a means of bypassing the normal file opening procedures. It is acceptable, however, for commercial fee-earners in particular to run 'miscellaneous' files for a particular client where a composite bill will eventually be raised or for miscellaneous enquiries from different clients where a record of the conversation or communication is needed but it is not appropriate to open specific files.

8.6 Conflicts of interest

Conflicts of interest can be a significant problem for many firms and should be seen as a risk factor given the possible non-recovery of fees, claims and professional proceedings that could ensue if practices act improperly (see *Guide to the Professional Conduct of Solicitors*, 8th edition, chapter 15). Practices will need to review how great the risk of conflicts of interest are for them.

Any procedures that are particular to an area of work will need to be highlighted. It may well be that more strenuous checks are needed in some areas of the practice than others. If the practice embraces conveyancing work it might set out its approach to the circumstances where seller and purchaser can both be represented, if at all.

There will need to be a record of conflicts having been considered. This could be achieved by requiring fee-earners to tick the file opening form to show that it has been considered. In the circumstances (which will be rare in most areas of most practices) that there is a possible issue an attendance note would need to be added to state what steps the practice has taken to consider the issue.

Although the standard envisages that professional conflicts of interest should be the subject of these provisions, commercial firms in particular may wish to extend their procedures to embrace commercial conflicts: i.e. the situations where the firm would not wish to act for fear of being conflicted out of other work in the future.

Much has been made in recent years of so-called 'Chinese walls', where internal barriers are erected to safeguard the client's interests. Although the House of Lords decision in *Bolkiah* v. *KPMG* (1999) 2 AC 222 does envisage circumstances where these could be permissible, the better view is that they may be an expedient to safeguard client confidentiality but do not counter a professional conflict of interest. The available decisions suggest that firms should proceed with very considerable care if they do decide to set up this form of safeguard.

Conflict of interest must be considered at the earliest opportunity before accepting instructions and then throughout the matter as it progresses. The evidence that this has been considered is a tick by the fee-earner instructed in the conflict of interest box on the matter opening form. Any further deliberations must be the subject of an attendance note on file outlining the considerations and action taken.

It is the fee-earner's responsibility to check for conflicts of interest and to monitor the risk of conflicts arising after the matter has commenced. The accounts department will check in all matters whether a conflict of interest appears to exist by checking the name of any opponent against the computer database of existing clients. It is important that all possible variations of names and identities are supplied. The accounts department will bring any concerns to the attention of the fee-earner, whose responsibility it is to take the issue up with his/her head of department.

Common-sense checking for conflicts should never be disregarded. A fee-earner having a concern that will not necessarily be highlighted by an accounts department check should consider an e-mail around the firm to see if any colleague knows of any reason why the practice should not act. It should be stressed that for the firm to act where it should not do so could be seen as a professional offence and lead to disciplinary proceedings; the firm is also open to a claim for compensation or lost fees and the risk of at least one alienated client.

Where a conflict is found or believed to exist any doubts as to the propriety of accepting instructions should be considered by the head of department, if possible or, if not, another partner. If it is felt that instructions should be declined the client should be informed of this as soon as possible and they should be offered such explanation and recommendation as in all the circumstances is professionally appropriate.

Fee-earners must be alert to the risk that a conflict may develop after a matter has started and must bring any such concerns to the head of department as soon as possible.

So-called Chinese walls arrangements will not be sanctioned by the firm to permit different fee-earners to act where a conflict of interest does or could exist between two clients. The firm may only act for seller and purchaser in conveyancing matters with the express, written consent of the head of department.

II TAKING INSTRUCTIONS AND EARLY ACTION

8.7 Taking instructions

> It is curious how often the file does not record the client's full instructions. Vital information can easily be missed if the fee-earner neglects to do this and simply acts on his/her memory of the first meeting or telephone instructions.

It is essential that all fee-earning personnel act upon the client's full, considered instructions. Instructions may be received by letter, telephone or at a meeting. If they are received other than at a meeting they should be acknowledged promptly, having regard to the sensitivity of the matter and its urgency to the client and legal process. Particular attention must be given to circumstances where instructions are received by one fee-earner and passed to another for attention.

Any instructions taken by telephone must be confirmed to the client in writing. Where this is done contemporaneously with the call the copy letter/e-mail on file could function as an attendance note of the conversation. Even then the file should contain an attendance note giving details of the time and duration of the call.

Any particular methods of taking instructions, as through the use of checklists, are noted in the additional departmental procedures and precedents.

It is important that instructions receive critical analysis on receipt. If there are inconsistencies or errors, or if carrying out the instructions would involve illegality by the client or the firm, unprofessional conduct by the firm, or potentially lead to undesired results for the client, any such problem must be raised with the client as soon as possible and must be resolved before the instructions can be acted upon, though it may be possible to undertake some work in the interim.

At the outset of the matter the fee-earner will establish the following:

- as full an understanding of the background facts as possible;
- the client's objectives and desired results;
- what the fee-earner will do;
- whether the fee-earner is the appropriate person to deal with the matter or whether it should be referred to a colleague;
- whether the client is an existing or new client;
- method of payment;
- whether the intended action would be merited on a cost benefit analysis and whether, in public funding cases, the guidance in the funding code would be satisfied.

In all litigation matters particular care is needed with possible sources of funding that the client might overlook to inform us of. The evidence that we have raised this with the client is a copy of the checklist appearing at appendix 8B which must be used on [*all files within the litigation department*]. All of the above should be confirmed to the client, usually in writing.

8.8 Terms of business

The terms of business under which the firm will act must be confirmed to the client. See section 7.6.

8.9 Consent to inspection

> At a Lexcel assessment (or an audit under ISO 9000) the view taken by the Law Society is that an inspection of the file by the assessor could amount to a breach of the duty to keep client dealings confidential, as explained in chapter 16 of the *Guide to the Professional Conduct of Solicitors*. The client's consent to the opening of their file to an assessor will be needed. This is explained in the *Guide*, but it may be useful to have a procedure in the manual setting out why and how consent should be obtained.

As a general principle, the client's consent to inspection of files is necessary at any assessment for Lexcel. You should note that the firm will obtain a confidentiality undertaking from the assessor but in pursuance of Law Society guidelines the firm asks for the client's consent by use of the standard wording on the point in its client care letter (see appendix 7A).

Where the client has indicated that they do not consent to inspection this should be clearly marked on the file and any information that would enable the assessor to know what the firm is doing for that client (e.g. matter printouts) must not be disclosed.

Where the client has not refused consent the firm is entitled under Law Society guidelines to assume that consent has been obtained. In such circumstances, however, if the fee-earner feels that matters have developed in such a way that the client would not now approve of disclosure, or if the firm feels that it would not be appropriate because of particularly sensitive aspects of the file, the firm may decline to submit the file to inspection.

8.10 Welfare benefits

The provisions in relation to welfare benefits advice for those firms that practise in legal aid work were scaled down in the SQM from the previous provisions in LAFQAS (see SQM 14, appendix 3, Changes to Requirements from LAFQAS). The requirements for training on welfare benefits and for further sessions with all 'caseworkers' were removed, but it may still be necessary for individual caseworkers to be trained in welfare benefits if it is appropriate to their work.

The welfare benefits representative is [*name*]. (S)he attends update training as necessary and ensures that all issues appropriate to the work of the fee-earners in publicly funded work are brought to their attention.

8.11 Key dates

With missed time limits remaining one of the principal causes of claims against solicitors, the importance of this procedure will be readily apparent. The requirement is that the key date should be noted on the file, but also 'backed up' in some system that will be available in the event of the fee-earner's absence or illness. There is no approved list of what will amount to a key date in all areas of work, but the obvious examples include:

- striking out;
- appeals;
- limitation dates;
- time limits for reviews, renewals, surrenders, and termination of leases;
- time limits in probate matters;
- dates by which options to purchase and rights of pre-emption must be exercised;
- dates by which share offers must be taken up.

Some firms have overlooked the need to have effective procedures to ensure that key dates are checked and signed off. Having the record in itself is fairly pointless – it must be used as a true check against what can be very costly errors. The recommendations in relation to amendments of dates are inspired by guidance from the Solicitors Indemnity Fund (SIF) in their self-assessment questionnaire and are borne of experience in avoidable litigation.

We are required to maintain a back-up system for all key dates. Key dates should be regarded as 'any date, the missing of which could give rise to a cause of action in negligence'. The list of key dates is to be found in each set of departmental precedents (see appendix 8A).

It is the responsibility of all fee-earners to notify the administrative secretary in each department of any back-up dates and to ensure that an entry is made to the departmental central diary. The entry for any expiry of time periods such as limitation periods must be two-fold:

- the date in question (e.g. the last day for issue of proceedings);
- the date sufficiently in advance of the actual key date to enable appropriate action to be taken. This is a specific fee-earner responsibility ('countdown' dates). It is recognised that some dates do not require countdown dates, but others (e.g. limitation periods) may require several warnings.

It is the responsibility of the administrative secretary to notify the fee-earner responsible for any matter listed of an entry. This is done on a weekly basis. In the absence of the administrative secretary the head of department will ensure that someone deputises for him/her. The notice is to be treated by the fee-earner as incoming post and must be replied to. During the absence of any fee-earner the notice therefore passes to another fee-earner supervising that colleague's activities in his/her absence and must always be actioned.

On occasions the fee-earner may wish to amend a key date after it has been entered into the back-up key date reminder system, the procedure for so doing being that:

- the existing entry must be clearly crossed out and initialled and the update or correction must be clearly shown;
- if approval was obtained for the change, this should also be marked and the partner approving the change identified by his or her initials;
- in no circumstances should any amendment be made by correction fluid.

8.12 Case planning

> Every matter should have a clear strategy. This will need to be established at the outset and then kept under review. The case plan will need to take into account all the circumstances of the matter, but the client's objectives in particular.

As a matter of principle every matter should have a clear strategy apparent from the file. This 'case plan' should show that thought has been given to how each client's needs will be acted upon. It is recognised that it will often be difficult to finalise this in detail at the outset of a case or transaction because it may be impossible to assess the likely response of any other parties. It is essential, however, that clients are presented with a strategy for meeting their instructions as soon as possible with an explanation of how and why this might need to be varied.

In most cases a case plan will simply be either a letter to the client or a separate memorandum on file. If the case plan is by memorandum steps must be taken to ensure that the client is made aware of it and their agreement is obtained. In other cases a more detailed case plan will be required. It is a matter of professional judgement for the partner or fee-earner in charge of the matter to determine whether a first letter or detailed case plan is required. The following matters must be considered and dealt with:

- written description of matter and person(s) dealing;
- responsibility and supervision;
- frequency of team meetings, if any;
- agreed objectives of legal action;
- main steps to be taken by firm and client;
- frequency of file review if different from the normal frequency;
- billing frequency and procedures.

A 'separate case plan' is a requirement in any public funding matter where the matter is a multi-party action, e.g. 10 certificates or more have been granted; the matter is subject to High Court jurisdiction; or the firm's costs, including disbursements and VAT, are likely to exceed £25,000.

III FILE MAINTENANCE

8.13 File maintenance

> Ensuring proper standards of file maintenance across the firm may well be one of the most obvious benefits of a Lexcel and/or risk management programme. It is recommended that each work type area or department consider its own rules of how files should be maintained. There are obvious efficiency gains in improving the state of files generally, especially when covering for colleagues on holiday or sick leave.

It is the responsibility of the fee-earner handling the matter to ensure that the file is well maintained and, in particular:

- notes all conversations and communications of any substance with the client or otherwise on the matter;
- is kept up to date with regular and careful filing;
- is kept tidy, with the progress readily apparent to any colleague who might need to check the position on the matter (as on holiday cover);
- is maintained in accordance with any departmental guidelines appearing in the appropriate departmental appendix (see appendix 8A).

Well-maintained files reduce wasted time and effort for all and are likely to enable the firm to portray a more professional and organised image to clients and others.

8.14 File summary sheets

> Section 8.9(d) of Lexcel requires that 'the status of the matter and the action taken' should be capable of being checked by other members of the practice. In most matters the use of a file summary sheet is a good way to achieve this, but this may be too simplistic in very lengthy litigation or commercial files. A summary sheet in itself is not essential, but the firm may wish to stipulate that if they are in use they must be completed.

It is mandatory that a file summary sheet is used on all matter files and is kept up to date at all times by the fee-earners handling that matter. This ensures that the state of the matter will be readily apparent to anyone else checking the file.

8.15 Attendance notes

Attendance notes are vital to provide a record of advice given, instructions received, or decisions made about which there may be a dispute. Attendance notes are also the primary evidence of time expended on a matter and are therefore vital for billing, notwithstanding the computerised time records.

Secretaries are frequently in direct contact with clients and others concerned with professional work, especially when a fee-earner is not available. It is therefore equally important that secretaries should record written attendance notes on all issues that progress a client matter. All attendance notes must be filed on the correspondence clip to date order as soon as possible. Handwritten notes must be intelligible to the writer and others.

8.16 Traceability and confidentiality

All papers, documents and items in relation to client work must be traceable within the office through their being filed or stored on the matter file at all times. The location of all items and papers which are not kept within the file must be clearly recorded on that file. Items of evidence which are in the possession of the firm, or other physical items which the firm is required to retain in pursuance of instructions, must be labelled with the appropriate matter number and the client's name.

Deeds and files are to be stored and tracked [*specify procedure*].

Consideration should always be given to copying items of particular sensitivity where their loss could cause particular difficulty for the firm or the client.

Proper care must be taken of files taken from the office. If taking files home the fee-earner is required to leave a note on his or her desk or in his or her diary of which files have been taken. This is to minimise the time that can be wasted by looking for files that are not in the office. Please take particular care about files in cars: when paying for petrol please lock your car if files are in it and in no circumstances should you leave files in a car overnight. Please also ensure that any work done on a client file on train journeys does remain confidential. Do not leave your files out of your briefcase while visiting the buffet or the toilets. In this respect please also consider who might overhear your telephone calls on mobile phones in trains or in public places.

IV PROGRESSING MATTERS

8.17 Maintaining progress

All matters must be progressed in an appropriate manner, having regard to the importance of the matter to the client, any instructions that they have provided on desired or necessary timescale and the constraints of the process concerned. In particular, fee-earners will:

- provide regular and reasonable information to clients on progress or reasons for the lack of it and any change of adviser or supervisor;
- respond to any telephone calls or communication from clients promptly;
- reply in a professional manner to solicitors acting for the opponent or other parties;
- check all matters regularly for progress (see section 6.4).

8.18 Case plan and costs updates

Any changes to the case plan should be made in a full and appropriate manner, such as a letter documenting the agreed amendments and agreed with the client. Any development which would cause the fee-earner to doubt the costs information already provided should be reported to the client without delay. (See in general rule 6 of the Solicitors' Costs Information and Client Care Code. The rule requires costs summaries to clients at least every six months 'unless otherwise agreed' and written information to the client 'as soon as it appears that a costs estimate or agreed upper limit may or will be exceeded' (6c).)

The costs position should be reviewed and reported to the client at least every six months by way of a costs update unless they have agreed otherwise, as where the work is being done to a fixed quote. It is important to revise any estimates as soon as it appears that they will or may be exceeded.

8.19 Undertakings

Poorly worded or ill-advised undertakings have caused substantial losses for firms and their insurers. A failure to observe an undertaking is a professional offence and it is well worth checking the obligations on undertakings in the *Guide to the Professional Conduct of Solicitors* at chapter 18. Many solicitors are not aware that undertakings given outside the course of practice can, in appropriate circumstances, be binding on them (see 18.01(b)).

The main provisions in an office procedure for undertakings should be to:

- require partner or senior manager consent to the giving of non-routine undertakings;
- set out clear procedures on who may give routine undertakings (as most obviously to exchange contracts or discharge mortgages in conveyancing);
- provide for the effective discharge of undertakings;
- make it clear that the firm will not be liable for personal undertakings arising outside the scope of the work of the practice.

Some firms find a central register of undertakings helpful. These are sometimes a relic of earlier Legal Aid Board requirements where various auditors tended to insist on them, but they are not essential under SQM (see E1.2(d) and the accompanying guidance which states that the procedures 'may or may not include a central record') and so could be discarded if the firm prefers.

Undertakings are an important consideration for the firm. The *Guide to the Professional Conduct of Solicitors* defines an undertaking as 'any unequivocal declaration of intention addressed to someone who reasonably places reliance on it'. The following points should be noted:

- there is no rule that the undertaking has to be written, though it may be difficult to prove an oral undertaking;
- the undertaking is binding on the firm if given by 'a solicitor or a member of a solicitor's staff';
- an undertaking is binding even if it is to do with something outside the solicitor's control;
- ambiguous undertakings are generally construed in favour of the recipient;
- solicitors who fail to honour an undertaking could be seen to be guilty of professional misconduct.

The first rule is not to offer undertakings unless necessary. The second rule is that all undertakings require partner consent or approval. The exceptions to this rule are set out in the departmental appendices (see appendix 8A) and include:

- the giving of routine conveyancing undertakings;
- undertakings that are offered to court by non-partners.

In all cases, whether partner consent is required or not, great care must be taken to ensure that the firm will be able to honour any undertaking given. It is vital that the firm limits undertakings to those for which it is competent. For example, the firm may not give an undertaking to repay a loan if this depends upon a third party paying the monies to it. Do not give open undertakings; make each one for a specific amount and as detailed as possible. Furthermore, the wording of undertakings needs to take into account that the firm will only do what is within its power: do not offer undertakings that the client will do a stated action.

Non-routine undertakings are noted by use of an Undertaking sticker which must be placed on the outside front cover of the file and initialled by the partner giving or approving it. On the discharge of the undertaking the person doing so must initial to show that it has been discharged. No file may be archived until any undertaking has clearly been discharged. [In addition, a central register of undertakings is maintained by [*name*]. *If so, state arrangements and responsibility*]

An undertaking by e-mail should not be accepted.

8.20 Experts and counsel

> Where outsiders are involved in the services delivered to clients it makes sense that they should be subject to controls to make sure that they support the firm's commitment to deliver quality services. Many firms will take the view that the most useful list is the 'non-approved' list of experts and counsel that should not be instructed in future. The combined effects of data protection rights and defamation are such that firms should be very careful about such lists – the 'C' list in the procedure that follows.
>
> In larger firms it will be best to entrust the task of maintaining lists to the departments. In smaller practices one firmwide list should be quite acceptable.

It is the responsibility of all departments to keep up to date the list of approved counsel and other professional contacts.

The list identifies experts and counsel as follows:

- A: approved without reservation;
- B: approved with reservation;
- C: not approved for use by the department.

Those experts who have provided an effective service to the firm in the past may be entered onto the 'A' list. When a new expert is first instructed steps must be taken to verify their suitability, as by checking professional status or receiving a reliable recommendation. If the services prove to be satisfactory the fee-earner contracting the services may recommend that they be entered onto either the 'A' or 'B' list as appears appropriate. Any caveat should also be recorded. Experts and others providing unsatisfactory service may be entered onto the 'C' list. All recommendations for entry to or removal from the list should be made by submitting a form (see appendix 8E) to the departmental supervisor.

The performance of those approved in the register will be constantly monitored. If an approved expert fails to meet the required standards, details are to be recorded on the matter file and a recommendation to transfer to the 'C' list could be considered.

Where appropriate, clients should be consulted on both the decision to involve experts and the selection of them. In the unlikely event of a client choosing an expert appearing on that department's 'C' list the reservations of the firm should be mentioned, but the client has the right to override the firm's reservations, subject to normal professional standards on the propriety of all actions taken for clients. In all cases a client may require that a particular medical examiner not be used on grounds of previous personal experience.

Experts will receive instructions through letter, brief, telephone conversation or at a meeting. Where instructions are provided orally they must be confirmed subsequently in writing. In all cases a note of instructions or a copy of them must appear on the matter file.

On receipt of advice from any counsel or expert the fee-earner receiving it must consider its suitability and value. If (s)he considers it inappropriate (s)he should refer it back to the adviser with a detailed request for the improvement which is felt to be necessary to bring it into line with the firm's expectations. If the standard of advice remains unsuitable, consideration should be given to the non-payment of the fee and to recommending that the individual be considered for inclusion on the 'C' list. The failure of a barrister or expert to meet the firm's standards must be noted on the matter file and the central record.

In public funding matters it is necessary to make a file note as to why an expert or barrister has been instructed if they do not at that time appear on the approved list.

Counsel's fees are met at the end of the case either in full or the net amount if they have already received part payment on account from the LSC office. As and when experts' fees notes are received they are met and settled if before the end of the case unless a deferred payment arrangement is in place. In private paying matters, counsels' fees should be discharged on receipt of a fee note. In public funding matters, experts' fees which are incurred through the duration of the case are applied for to the LSC and are paid when received.

V MATTER CLOSING

8.21 File closing

As soon as a client matter has been fully completed, the controlling fee-earner is to close the file so that it can be archived. The form at [*appendix 8D*] is to be used.

The fee-earner must ensure that all ledger balances have been reduced to nil otherwise the matter cannot be archived on the accounting system. The fee-earner is also to assess and record the year for the eventual destruction of the file. Advice on retention periods is given in *The Guide to the Professional Conduct of Solicitors*.

The file is then to be passed to the archive clerk [*name*] who will archive the file on the accounting system and store the file in [*location*]. The process will allocate the file a sequential storage number which will be recorded in the client matter details for future reference. The archiving process prevents any further postings from being made to the client or time ledgers and shows the matter as being closed, but all detailed entries including the matter details will be retained permanently in the accounting database and can be printed out if required later.

8.22 Final review

Before a file is archived there must be a final review of it in writing to see whether the client's objectives were met and, if not, why not. There should be a final report to the client which will usually accompany any final invoice or receipt against monies held on the client's behalf. The final review sheet questions on the file summary sheet must be initialled in order that the file can be archived – the archiving clerk has been instructed to return any files where this has not been done. Likewise, files that have obviously not been 'thinned' will be returned to the fee-earner concerned.

Clients may need advice on storage of documents and files and of review dates that they should note. If it is felt inappropriate for any reasons not to provide a final report to the client (e.g. the firm is acting for a minor) this must be explained in a file note which details what alternative steps, if any, have been taken.

On the need for a concluding risk assessment see section 6.8.

Formal after-care does not feature as a major element of the firm's work, but such arrangements as do exist are dealt with in departmental instructions (for example, wills reviews and company secretarial work).

8.23 Archiving

[State here arrangements for file storage, including who has responsibility and where the files are stored. If outsourced it may be appropriate to state retrieval charges and delivery times]

> Former editions of the *Law Society Office Manual* would suggest destroy dates, but this is now a much more sensitive issue. In *The Guide to the Professional Conduct of Solicitors* it is provided in annex 12A (1999, page 254) that 'the Society cannot specify how long individual files should be retained', but it does state that the general rule is six years. Other factors for firms to consider are the wishes of their indemnity insurers on this point, if any, and the possible criminal liability for not storing records as required by the Money Laundering Regulations 2003.

APPENDIX 8A

FORMAT OF DEPARTMENTAL APPENDIX

(CONVEYANCING)

1. The range of work undertaken by the department
2. Generic risks of conveyancing work
3. Conflicts in conveyancing work: if and when the firm would act for both parties and Practice Rule 6 compliance
4. List of key dates in conveyancing work
5. Departmental arrangements for noting key dates
6. Procedures for alerting fee-earners of key dates and responses required
7. Undertakings: authority of fee-earners to provide 'routine' undertakings and instructions to be followed: Law Society formula for exchange, etc.
8. Rules on how files must be maintained: e.g. colour coding of files, what goes where on files, use of summary sheets
9. Issues particular to work type: e.g. handling and noting requests for quotes, including monitoring success rates
10. Any after-care provisions – work done after the matter is completed (unlikely)
11. Arrangements for departmental meetings
12. Any special departmental file review arrangements

APPENDIX 8B

COSTS AND FUNDING CHECKLIST

	Method of funding	Yes/No
1.	Could this client qualify for public funding?	
2.	Does the client have household or business protection insurance ('before the event' insurance)?	
3.	Could this matter be conducted under a CFA (conditional fee agreement): if so has this been discussed with the client and explained to them?	
4.	Does the matter involve goods or services that could be covered by credit card insurance?	
5.	Is the client a member of a trade union? If so, could cover be available?	
6.	Has consideration been given to the availability and suitability of 'after the event' insurance?	
7.	Are contingency arrangements appropriate in this case?	

I confirm that:

1. The above funding options have been discussed with me.
2. I know of no possible source of funding that I have not mentioned.
3. I wish [*firm's name*] to act for me on the basis set out in their letter to me confirming instructions.

Signed .... Client name ....

Matter number .... Date ....

APPENDIX 8C

FILE OPENING FORM

Private client name Previous names	Surname: _____ First names: _____ (if relevant): _____

Company name: _____
Trading name: _____
Contact name: _____
Status: _____
Address: _____
_____

Telephone numbers:	Home: _____ Work: _____ Fax: _____ E-mail: _____ Home: _____ Mobile: _____

Special circumstances (e.g. notify sending fax): _____

Matter description: Enter work code_____	State names of any other connected parties for conflicts check
I consider this matter to be: high risk/ordinary risk	Unusual circumstances – instructions
Identity checks already conducted? State date on system if so: (If not ML1 must accompany this form)	
I agree to this matter being opened _____ (initials) _____ Date	*Or* I do not agree to this matter being opened _____ (initials) _____ Date

APPENDIX 8D

FILE SUMMARY SHEET – GENERAL
(could be adapted for particular work types)

(to be placed on file when opened and kept up to date)

Client:	Matter no:	Client partner (if any):
Useful contacts Addresses and phone numbers	Instructions 1. Note of instructions on file? 2. Funding code in public funding? 3. Cost benefit discussed with client? 4. Does this work involve high risk for the firm? 5. Evidence of identity? In all cases note below any concerns:	Y/N Y/N Y/N Y/N Y/N
Conflict of interest?	Full instructions taken from client? Y/N Regular client? If so identify terms which apply: _____ If not, show date of client care letter: _____ Version of terms and conditions sent: _____ Other reason client care letter not sent: _____	
Special instructions from client	Tick if no consent to audit inspection _____	
Departmental checklist	File review Date_____ Corrective action? If yes, confirm taken Date_____ Corrective action? If yes, confirm taken	Final review (must be completed before archiving) Objectives met? (if not report to supervisor on form _____) Future review date: _____ Nil balances: _____ File thinned: _____ Client advised storage: _____ Further action notified: _____ Papers/items returned to client: _____ Destroy date: _____

APPENDIX 8E

EXPERTS/COUNSEL RECOMMENDATION FORM

To: _____ (Dept supervisor) From: _____ Date: _____

I recommend that the following expert/barrister should be

    added to the fully approved list   ('A' list) _____

    added to the provisional list   ('B' list) _____

    added to the non-approved list   ('C' list) _____

Details of Expert/Barrister

Name:

Address:

Phone: Fax: E-mail:

If recommending inclusion as approved service, details of qualifications/recommendation received, etc.

I have used this expert barrister on matter no. _____ and my experience was:

(consider oral report if negative experience)

If recommending the use of this expert/barrister. I would add the caveat that (if any):

Signed:	Agreed/Not agreed
	_____ _____
	Departmental supervisor Date

Index

Accident book 59
Accounting *see* Financial management
Age discrimination 5
Appointments
  confirmation 44
  notification to receptionist 45
  procedure 44
Appraisal
  appraisers 76
  attributes, guidance on completion 119
  competency based appraisal form 114–16
  competency based interview paperwork 99–100
  completion timetable 76–7
  confidentiality 74–5
  documentation 76
  fee-earners 109–10
  follow-up action 77
  forms 103–18
  generally 73–5
  job descriptions 69
  objectives 73, 77
  partners 74, 103, 104–5
  pre-appraisal questionnaires 106–8
  procedures 75–6
  responsibility 76
  staff appraisal forms 111–18
Attendance notes 168–9

Bills
  billing guides 41
  credit control 38–40
  delay in issue 37
  draft bills 41
  issue of 37
  time recording 41–2
Burglar alarm system 61
Business continuity 64–5
Business plan
  development and maintenance 25–8
  disseminating the plan 28
  documenting services 28–30
  financial aspects 26, 28
  format 28
  generally 25
  objectives 25, 27
  review 26, 32

  SMART criteria 27
  SWOT analysis 26
  see also Marketing plan; Services plan
Business reply service 49
Business structure, review of 2

Case and file management
  acceptance of instructions 161–2
  after-care 173
  archiving 172, 173
  attendance notes 168–9
  authorisation 162
  case plan 167, 169
  client enquiries 159–60
  closing file 172–3
  confidentiality 169
  confirmation of instructions 138–9, 164, 165
  conflict of interest 163–4
  consent to inspection 165
  costs and funding checklist 175
  costs updates 169–70
  counsel, use of 171–2
  countdown dates 166
  departmental appendix format 174
  experts, use of 171–2
  file closing 129, 172–3
  file inspection 165
  file maintenance 168–9
  file opening procedures 129, 160–1, 176
  file reviews 125, 126–7, 133, 173
  file summary sheet 168, 177
  final review 173
  generally 159
  inspection of files 165
  instructions 138–9, 161–2, 164–5
  key dates 166–7
  limitation periods 166
  miscellaneous files 162–3
  progressing matters 169–72
  storage 169, 173
  taking instructions 164–5
  terms of business 138, 165
  time limits 166
  traceability 169
  undertakings 170–1
  welfare benefits advice 166

Cash
cash flow 34
petty cash 36–7
receipts for 35
receipts of 15, 35
CCTV cameras 18–19
Central heating, safety of 59
Cheques
amendments to 37
delay in issue 37
hand-written 36
issue of 37
payment out of client monies 36
printing 36
receipts for 35
receipts from third parties 37
receipts of 15, 35, 37
requisitions 35–6
Client care
appointment procedure 44
attendance notes 168–9
client surveys 142–3, 155–6
commitment 136
communication 3
competence 135–6
complaints handling 139–42
confidentiality 136, 137
confirmation of instructions 138–9
consumer expectations 3
courtesy 136
dress and demeanour 136
enquiries 159–60
fee-earners 137
generally 135
letter 138, 144–5
policy 135–6
reception 137–8
review 143
staff survey form 157
surveys 142–3, 155–6, 157
terms and conditions 138, 146–50, 165
welfare benefits advice 166
Client ledger balances report 37–8
Commitment 136
Communication 3
Company search 17
Competence 135–6
Complaints handling 139–42
client complaint report form 153
client complaints register 154
complaints referred by OSS 142
complaints review 142
internal reporting 142
making complaints 142
sample complaints procedures 151–2
Computer system *see* Information technology
Confidentiality
acting for buyer and lender 15
appraisals 74–5
client care 136, 137
file management 169
reception and 137
Confirmation of instructions 138–9, 164, 165
Conflict of interest 163–4
Continuing professional development (CPD) 77, 78
Contracts of employment 73
format 93–7
Control of Substances Hazardous to Health (COSHH) 60
Costs
checklist 175
costs bill 37
updates 169–70
Counsel
recommendation form 178
use of 171–2
Countdown dates 166
Courier service 49
Courtesy 136
Credit control 38–40
debt management report 40

Data protection
CCTV cameras 18–19
codes of practice 17–18
generally 17
interview assessment form 98
principles 17
security of data 18
subject access requests 18
Debts
credit control 38–40
debt management report 40
reservation 40
write-offs 36–7, 40–1
Demeanour 136
Disability discrimination 5, 8
Disciplinary procedures 9
Discrimination
barristers 6
clients 6
direct 8
disciplinary procedures 9
grievance procedures 9
harassment 9

indirect 8
legislation 5, 8
maternity policy 9
model code 6–9
partners 7
personnel 7–9
positive action 8
promotion 8
recruitment 8
service provision 5–7
victimisation 8
Document Exchange (DX) system 48–9
Dress 136

E-conveyancing 43, 55
E-litigation 43, 55
E-mail
attachments 53, 54
deletion 53
generally 50, 51
incoming messages 52
legal issues 51
monitoring 52
notices 52
outgoing messages 53
protocol 51
retention periods 53
security 51
sending and receiving 51
undertakings by 171
virus protection 53–4
Electrical equipment 61
Electronic delivery of legal services 55
Experts
recommendation form 178
use of 171–2
Eye tests 59, 61

Facsimile (fax) 47
Fee-earners
appraisal 109–10
job description 84
File management *see* Case and file management
Financial management
bills *see* Bills
cash *see* Cash
cheques *see* Cheques
client ledger balances report 37–8
computer system 33–4
credit control 38–40
draft bills 41
generally 33
income and expenditure budgets 34

ledger queries 38
management reports 34
money laundering *see* Money laundering
payment out of client monies 36
petty cash 36–7
repairs and decoration 43
reservation of debts 40
responsibility for 33
third parties, receipts from 37
time recording 41–2
transfers 36
write-offs 36, 40–1
Fire
alarms 62
extinguishers 63
immediate action 62
instructions 61–3, 66
protection in strong-room 63
wardens 63
First aid 59

Grievance procedures
discrimination 9

Harassment 9
Health and safety
accident book 59
central heating 59
circulating information 58
COSHH 60
electrical equipment 61
external advice 57
eye tests 59, 61
fire *see* Fire
first aid 59
generally 19, 55–6
legislative background 56–7
no-smoking policy 60
personal security 61
personnel, role of 57
risk assessments 57–8
security 61
teleworkers 60
VDUs 59, 60, 61
Health and Safety Manager 19

Incentive schemes 68
Income and expenditure budgets 34
Induction 73
training form 102
Information technology
accounting system 33–4
computer system 33–4
e-conveyancing 43, 55

e-litigation 43, 55
e-mail *see* E-mail
electronic delivery of legal services 55
generally 43, 49–50
health and safety 59, 61
Internet *see* Internet
management of IT system 50–1
security 18
service maintenance contracts 63–4
time recording 33, 41–2
VDUs 59, 60, 61
virus protection 53–4
Instructions
acceptance of 161–2
confirmation of 138–9, 164, 165
taking 164–5
Insurance
business continuity 64–5
indemnity 127, 130
Internet
library searches 65
monitoring use 52
use 50, 54–5
Interview rooms 45
Interviews
assessment form 98
competency based interview paperwork 99–100
feedback 71
recruitment 71, 72

Job descriptions 68–9
appraisals 69
fee-earner 84
legal cashier 89
legal secretary 87
office junior 90
para-legal 86
partner 81, 82–3, 85
receptionist 88
recruitment 70
trainee solicitor 91

Legal Aid, welfare benefits advice 166
Legal cashier, job description 89
Legal secretaries *see* Secretaries
Legal status of firm 1–2
Library 65
Limitation periods 166

Mail
business reply service 49
class 49

courier service 49
Document Exchange (DX) system 48–9
incoming 47–8, 125
morning post 48
opening 47, 48
outgoing 48–9
second post 48
unidentifiable 48
Management reports 34
Marketing plan 30–1
communicating the plan 31
documentation 31
generally 25
marketing methods 30–1
review 32
see also Business plan
Maternity policy 9
Misconduct claims 14
Mobile phones 47
Money laundering
cash receipts 15
company search 17
consent for transactions 14
danger signs 12–13
form ML1 11, 20, 21
form ML2 13, 22
form ML3 23
generally 9
identity checks 10–12, 16, 20, 161
legal professional privilege 9
Money Laundering Reporting Officer 9–10, 11, 13, 14, 17
professional misconduct claims 14
receipts from third parties 37
record-keeping 14–15
reporting to MLRO 13, 23
reports 9–10
suspicious transactions 12
tipping-off 9, 13, 14
training and guidance 10
verifying signatures 16
Mortgage fraud
acting for buyer and lender 15–16
indicators 16–17
prevention 15–17
reporting and acting upon suspicions 17

No-smoking policy 60
Non-discrimination *see* Discrimination

Office
equipment 63–4
facilities 63–4

security 61
tidiness 43
Office junior 48
    job description 90
Office for the Supervision of Solicitors
    complaints referred by 142
Organisational chart 131

Panic button 61
Para-legal, job description 86
Parking 44
Partners
    appraisal 74, 103, 104–5
    job description 81, 82–3, 85
Pension provision 68
Performance appraisal *see* Appraisal
Person specification 92
Personal security 61
Personnel plan 67–8
    development 68
    outline 80
    resourcing 67
    welfare and entitlements 68
Petty cash 36–7
Photocopying 63
Planning *see* Business plan; Marketing plan;
    Personnel plan; Services plan
Positive action 8
Post *see* Mail
Premises
    interview rooms 45
    parking 44
    repair and decoration 43
    security 61
    tidiness 43, 137
Professional misconduct claims 14
Promotion 8
Publicly funded work 29, 39, 166

Quality
    accreditation 2
    commitment to 2–3, 4
    consumer expectations 3
Quality assistant 4
Quality assurance system
    changes to 4
    generally 3
    process of review 4
    responsibility for maintenance 3–4
    suggestions box 4
Quality manager 18, 19
Quality partner 4, 18

Race discrimination 8
Reception area 43, 137
    panic button 61
Receptionist
    appointment procedure 44, 45
    client care 137–8
    confidentiality 137
    job description 88
Recruitment
    assessing needs 67, 68
    discrimination 8
    identification of vacancies 69–70
    interview assessment form 98
    interviews 71
    job confirmation 72
    job descriptions 70
    person specification 92
    pre-joining communication 72
    pre-selection/appointment information 71
    selection methods 70
    support staff 72
Reference library 65
References, request for 71, 72, 101
Religious discrimination 5
Risk
    assessments 57–8
    avoidance 123
    file opening procedures 129
    health and safety 57–8
    management 123, 127–8
    notice 134
    reporting 129–30

Secretaries
    attendance notes 168
    computer system 34
    job description 87
Security
    burglar alarm system 61
    CCTV cameras 18–19
    computer system 18
    data, of 18
    e-mail 51
    offices 61
    panic button 61
    personal property 61
    personal security 61
    premises 61
    property 61
Service maintenance contracts 63–4
Services plan 28–30
    documentation 29–30
    internal provision 30

publicly funded work 29
review 32
service delivery methods 29
see also Business plan
Sex discrimination 8
SMART
business plan 27
performance objectives 74
Smoking 60
Staff appraisal form 117–18
Storage
advice to clients on 173
e-mails 53
files 169, 173
fire protection in strong-room 63
retention periods 53, 172
Strong-room, fire protection in 63
Structure of firm, review of 2
Suggestions box 4
Supervision
devolved powers 126, 132
file reviews 125, 126–7
generally 123–4
incoming mail 47–8, 125
maintaining progress 125–6
systems 125
work allocation 125
Switchboard 45
SWOT analysis 26

Telephone
answering 45
appointment procedure 44
conveyancing quotation 44
direct lines 46
diverting calls 46
generally 45
group pick-up systems 46
individual's extensions 45–6

instructions 164
mobile phones 47
personal calls 46
switchboard 45
voice mail 46
Teleworkers 60
Terms and conditions of business 138, 146–50, 165
Tidiness 43, 137
Time limits 166
Time recording
billing guides 41
computer system 33–4
non-chargeable time 42
time postings 41–2
Trainee solicitor, job description 91
Training 77–9
assessing needs 68, 78
continuing professional development (CPD) 77, 78
evaluation form 78, 121
external courses 78, 121
induction training 73, 102
money laundering prevention 10
post-course review 122
request form 120
welfare benefits 166
Transfers of monies 36

Undertakings 170–1

VDUs, health and safety 59, 60, 61
Victimisation 8
Voice mail 46

Welfare benefits advice 166
Work allocation 125
Write-offs 36, 40–1